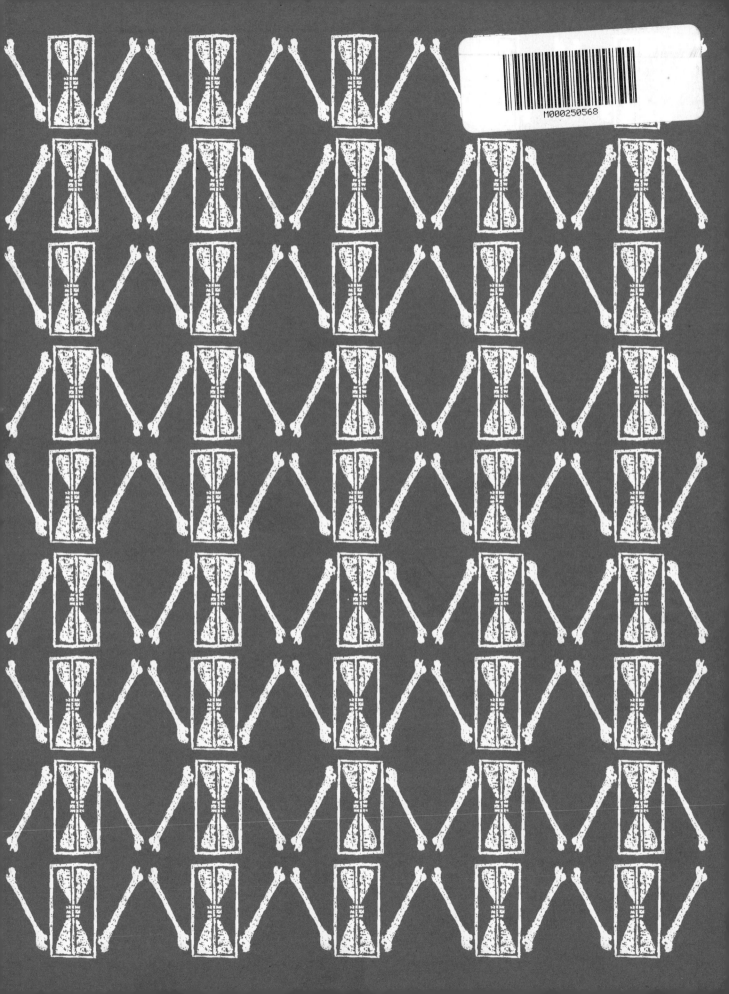

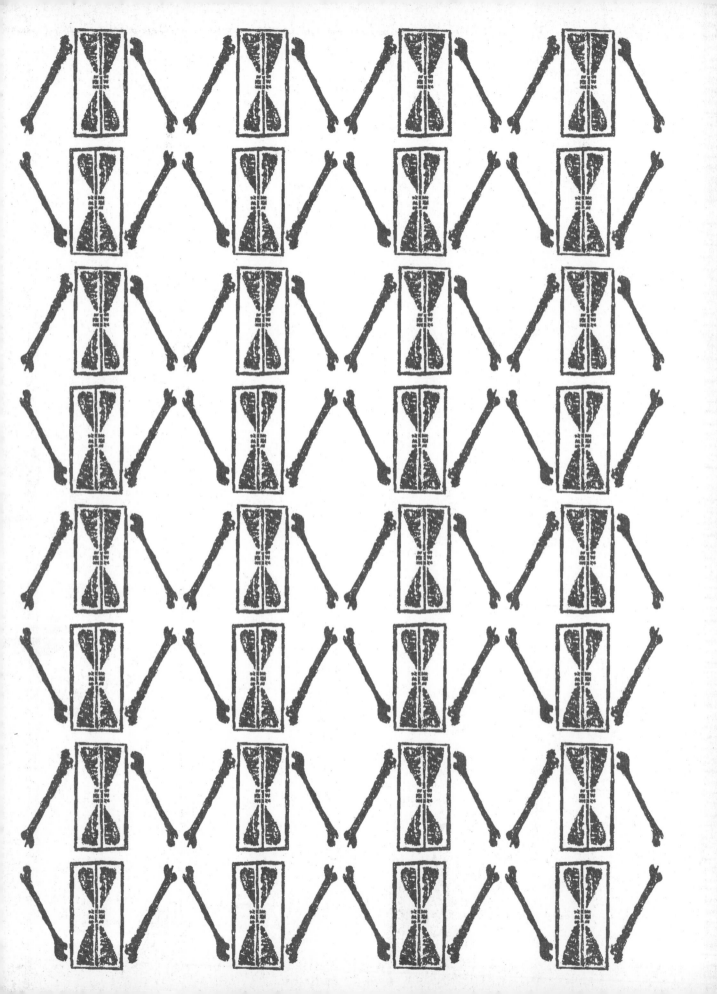

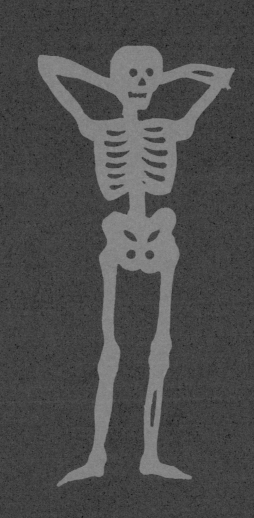

EDITED BY
JOANNA
EBENSTEIN

FOREWORD BY
WILL SELF

# DEATH

## a
## graveside
## companion

Thames & Hudson

# contents

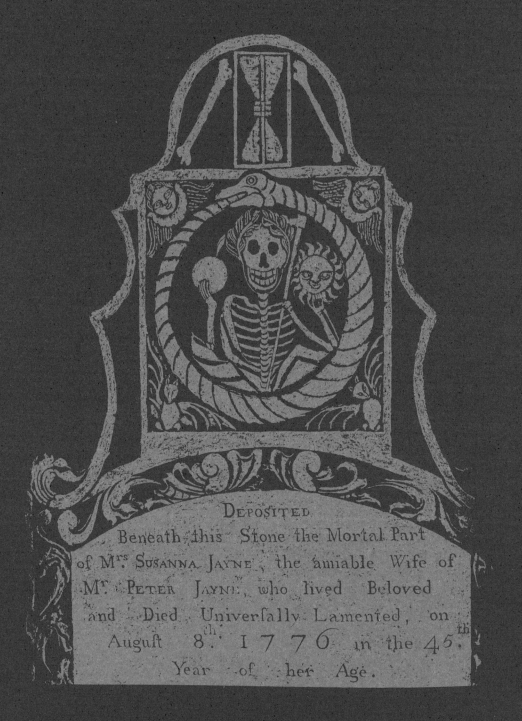

DEPOSITED
Beneath this Stone the Mortal Part
of Mrs. SUSANNA JAYNE, the amiable Wife of
Mr. PETER JAYNE, who lived Beloved
and Died Universally Lamented, on
August 8th. 1776 in the 45th.
Year of her Age.

# foreword

A terrifying paradox, surely, is the sheer vitality we find in the representations of death illustrating this volume – a paradox only trumped by the vivaciousness with which the various essayists treat every aspect of human mortality and its depiction. My first published short story was called *The North London Book of the Dead* (1991), and it was a eulogy – of sorts – for my mother, who'd died three years earlier. In the tale, the unnamed narrator re-encounters his deceased mother some months after she died, ensconced in the dull – some might say moribund – suburb of Crouch End. She explains to him that death, far from being a final surcease, is merely a form of downward mobility: the dead being compelled by a nameless bureaucracy to move to more and more somnolent districts, before reaching that terminal state known as 'the country'.

The wish fulfilment Freud detected in all creative endeavours is plainly evident here: I loved my mother – and she'd died prematurely. Hers was the first dead body I'd seen, and I was amazed by the way death instantly made her over: ironing out the suffering creases, relaxing the knotted features, and rendering her skin an implausible ivory. I can't have spent more than a few minutes with her corpse – but I sat with my father's for hours: he died in the night, and I maintained the vigil until the undertakers arrived in the morning. My mother had appeared calm – my father's face was twisted in a horrible rictus. I've often wondered in the intervening years if it's this alone which explains why his imago has remained present to me – while my mother's has faded to near oblivion.

I expect most older people reading this will have had similarly singular experiences: ours is a culture that medicalizes death, rendering the process aseptic to the point of invisibility. It's tantamount to a cherished value for us to live out our lives in the sunny uplands – sometimes glancing, but never staring for too long at the shadows that adumbrate this bright scene. Our fascination with the apparent morbidity of other cultures and eras has an anthropological cast; it's understandable that the Toraja people of Sulawesi in Indonesia should keep their loved ones' corpses at home for years, because they're surrounded by death anyway. But us? Why, we're progressing rapidly towards immortality – aren't we?

Well, no – the headline in the satirical US magazine *The Onion* says it all: 'World Death Rate Holds Steady at 100%'. But although the certainty of death should encourage us to take it with the (profoundly jocose) seriousness it deserves, still we recoil into outright denial – or Gothic affectation. It's perhaps only when we enter the Dantean dark wood of middle age that we apprehend the truth: death is – quite simply – bigger than life. You were born out of death – and will collapse back into its entropic embrace. The future is yet to be born, the past is ashes – and the present expires even as we cradle it to our wanting breast. Lives are beads of quicksilver, trapping us in their mirroring surface tension, so that for the most part we can see the world lightly. But the truth is that death – not love – is all around.

WILL SELF, LONDON

# introduction

In this book, on page 252, readers will find a curious image in which a jauntily posed, carved ivory skeleton rests his weary skull on his bony hand; the other hand lays on the handle of a downward-facing scythe. At his feet are piled symbols of what constituted worldly glory in the 17th century: a knight's helmet, flags, a bishop's mitre, a sceptre and an ecclesiastical staff. This ivory statue is a memento mori, an object or artwork created to remind viewers that they, too, will die. Memento mori date back at least to ancient Rome, where their message was akin to our modern idea of carpe diem – eat, drink and be merry, for tomorrow you will die. This piece, however, was created in a Christian context, to urge the viewer to live a pious life in order to avoid divine punishment.

Bizarre to the modern eye, such images – along with the hundreds of others that fill this book – were once commonplace. Taken together, they constitute an alternative art

## timeline of death

**6000** BCE
The Chinchorro fishing communities of Peru are the first civilization known to preserve their dead.

**2686–2181** BCE
The ancient Egyptians begin building pyramids and mummifying their dead.

**1550** BCE
Gold death masks are made at Mycenae, in ancient Greece.

history, a collection of artefacts that illustrate humankind's attempts – metaphysical, mythological, scientific and popular – to imagine, respond to or find meaning in the mystery of death.

Today, many people consider it distasteful, or even morbid, to contemplate death and its representation. But, as is clear from this book, this was not always the case. How can we have changed so greatly over the past 150 years that these images seem strange to us today? What can we learn about both the past and the present by looking at them? And what can they tell us about humanity's changing relationship with death?

These are the questions that led me to found Morbid Anatomy in 2007. The project began as a blog, which I intended as a research tool for an exhibition about medical museums and their artefacts. Over the years, it developed an audience and expanded to include The Morbid Anatomy Library, which made my collection of books, art and artefacts available to the public; The 'Morbid Anatomy Presents' series of lectures, classes, field trips and exhibitions in London, New York, Amsterdam and Mexico; a series of publications and films; and, finally, the now closed Morbid Anatomy Museum in Brooklyn, New York. One of the main goals of Morbid Anatomy was to demonstrate that modern attitudes towards death are the exception rather than the rule. From my studies and travels, I discovered that just about every other era and culture used meaningful practices to make sense of this great mystery. The idea of an interest in death being distasteful appears to be unique to urban Western culture in our particular time.

How, I wondered, could one not be interested in death? Death is the great mystery of human life. You and I – barring some medical miracle – will die. Despite various

**1200** BCE
Mesoamerican cultures develop belief systems that include blood-letting and human sacrifice.

**79** CE
Mount Vesuvius erupts in southern Italy, burying Pompeii, Herculaneum and other small towns in volcanic debris.

**2nd century**
Greek anatomist and physician Galen of Pergamum performs public dissections of animals in Rome.

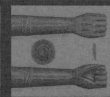

**4th century**
Belief in the power of saintly relics, including body parts, spreads through the Christian world.

**5th–15th century**
In Britain, death is dramatized in medieval mystery plays.

**600**
Kali, a Hindu goddess of death, first appears in Hindu tradition.

scientific and medical advancements, we are no closer to knowing what death means or what its purpose is. Foreknowledge of our own death is a defining characteristic of humanity; the ancient Greeks reserved the word mortal – meaning 'subject to death' – for humans alone. Some people even believe that it is foreknowledge of our own death that drives all human culture, from religion and philosophy to mythology and art.

The very possibility of denying death is a luxury unique to our own time and place. For many in the Western world, perhaps for the first time in history, death has become distant and exotic; it tends to happen offstage, behind closed doors and, we are led to expect, at the end of a long full life. Violent death in armed conflict has largely disappeared from view, save through the distancing medium of television and print media. We no longer butcher our own meat, but purchase it in packaging that disguises its source. And mourning the dead, once highly visible and ritualized, has dropped out of sight, its accepted duration reduced from years to months or even weeks.

Today, most people die in a hospital and are then whisked off to a funeral home. In earlier times, the ideal death occurred at home surrounded by loved ones, after which the body was laid out in the home parlour for friends and family to view. In America, when this ritual moved from the private home to the funeral home, the home parlour, at the behest of *The Ladies Home Journal*, was renamed the 'living room' while the funeral home became the 'funeral parlour'.

Around the time that death became less apparent in daily life in the West, it also disappeared from our traditional systems of creating meaning – religion, ritual and mythology. In the 21st century, many people think of themselves as rational, post-religious

**14th century**
Outbreaks of the Black Death sweep through Europe and the Mediterranean, killing an estimated 25 million people.

**1424–25**
A mural of the Dance of Death, the earliest known visual representation of the concept, is painted on the walls of the Cimetière des Innocents in Paris.

**16th–17th century**
The vanitas genre of painting flourishes, especially in the Netherlands.

**1519**
The Spanish Conquest of the Aztec Empire ends the practice of human sacrifice in Mesoamerica.

**1521**
Hans Holbein the Younger paints *The Body of the Dead Christ in the Tomb*.

**1523–25**
Holbein creates the drawings for his forty-one woodcuts known as the *Dance of Death*.

beings. But death continues to elude our rational minds. Death and the dead body still have meaning, but precisely what they mean is unclear. Death has moved from the domain of mythology or religion to that of science, and science provides little comfort.

For most of human history, people's understanding of the world they lived in was shaped by the religion or mythology of their culture. The oldest known traditions involved the figure of the shaman, whose job was – and continues to be in some tribal communities – to mediate the mysteries of human life and to heal the body and the soul by arbitrating between the world of humans and those of the gods and spirits. In early religions – and still, in places such as Mexico where indigenous ideas have been maintained – ideas of life and death tended to be cyclical, based on what was observable in the natural world: fertility and dormancy, summer and winter, death and rebirth, the waxing and waning of the moon.

Gods and goddesses presided over life and death, as well as the journey from the land of the living to that of the dead. Sometimes one over-arching figure oversaw both life and death, thereby illuminating an essential paradox: that life is defined by its ephemeral nature, and death is an essential part of the cycle of life. Eventually, the arbitration of life and death became the domain of larger centralized religions, such as Judaism, Hinduism, Buddhism, Christianity and Islam. In Buddhism and Hinduism, life and death are seen as cyclical, with multiple reincarnations. Nothing is permanent, and the ultimate goal is to end the cycle of life, death and rebirth, along with its unavoidable suffering. To be incarnated as a human is an opportunity to become enlightened and thus terminate this cycle.

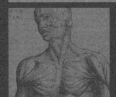

**1543**
Flemish anatomist Andreas Vesalius publishes *De humani corporis fabrica* (On the Fabric of the Human Body), a book that revolutionized the study of human anatomy.

**1596**
Caravaggio paints his first *Medusa*.

**c. 1660s**
Dutch anatomist Frederik Ruysch discovers a new method of embalming dead bodies, which preserves the vividness of life.

**Late 17th century**
Italian sculptor Gaetano Zumbo and French surgeon Guillaume Desnoues create the first anatomical wax model.

**1751**
Thomas Gray's 'Elegy Written in a Country Churchyard', a meditation on death, is published.

**1752**
The British parliament passes the Murder Act, which allows the dissection of convicted murderers.

Early Judaism professed that, after death, all souls went to a sketchily defined 'Sheol', which has much in common with Hades in Greek mythology. Later, some Jews came to believe in heaven, hell and final judgment. In Islamic belief, death was always a part of the cosmic order and, when you die, God will oversee a final judgment that leads to either heaven or hell.

The vast majority of the images in *Death: A Graveside Companion* were created as part of the Christian tradition. In Christianity – and in Judaism, too – Adam and Eve were created as immortal. It was their sin in the Garden of Eden – the eating of the forbidden fruit from the Tree of the Knowledge of Good and Evil – that introduced death to humankind. In Christianity, the antidote to the curse of death is Jesus Christ: an incarnated manifestation of God, paradoxically, both fully God and fully man. He ultimately offered up his body on the cross in order to absolve the sins of humanity, especially the original sin of Adam and Eve. His resurrection became the model for his followers, who, it was believed, would be reborn into eternal life on Judgment Day, when the world ends and God judges all.

The corporeal human body has an unusual importance in the Christian world view. Because Adam and Eve were created in God's image, to know the body of man becomes, in a very real sense, a way to know the mind of God. Also, Christ's role as simultaneously man and God transforms his body into part of a divine mystery. And, finally, on Judgment Day, it is believed that one's body will rise from the grave and be reunited with its soul. This leads to a sacralization of the body evidenced in the highly naturalistic yet metaphysically charged images of Christ on the cross; it is also manifested

**1762**
French professor of anatomy Honoré Fragonard creates the first of his écorché (flayed) figures.

**1763–64**
Dr Giuseppe Salerno commissions the anatomical studies known as the 'anatomical machines', now in the Sansevero Chapel, Naples.

**1775**
La Specola, the world's largest collection of anatomical waxworks, opens in Florence.

**1789**
The guillotine is invented in revolutionary France. During the Reign of Terror (September 1793–July 1794), more than 15,000 enemies of the revolution are guillotined.

**1790s**
Seance-based entertainments known as *fantasmagorie* become all the rage in Europe.

**1832**
The British Parliament passes the Anatomy Act, permitting the dissection of donated human bodies.

in the Catholic cult of the saints, in which the bodily remains of saints and martyrs, prized for their miraculous powers, are preserved and displayed.

For many centuries, the Christian world view dominated Western civilization. The past few centuries, however, saw the rise of a competing world view – that of science and scientific medicine. Scientists have become our main mediators between the realms of life and death, and between humankind and the invisible world. A biological world of germs, blood cells and viruses, only visible through microscopes, has replaced the invisible world of Gods and spirits. The torch has been passed from the shaman to the priest to the doctor/scientist in the goal of prolonging life, vanquishing disease and making sense of death.

In our own time, estranged as we are from nature and its visible cycles of life and death, as well as belief systems that give it meaning, death has become the enemy, the antithesis of all we hold dear: light, pleasure and life. The contemplation of death is no longer seen as a tool for living a better life; it is instead a problem to be solved. The fact that we have not managed to figure it out is a sort of embarrassment, marking a failure in our progressive march towards an earthly utopia. Perhaps it is this embarrassment that ends a frank dignified discourse around death. Yet this silence serves to make it more powerful in our imagination. As death becomes more exotic and outside our daily experience, it also becomes increasingly terrifying. Our interest in death does not disappear, nor will it ever; instead, like other unacknowledged or suppressed psychological material, it goes underground to emerge in different, less conscious, shadowy forms, expressed in the unpoliced realms of popular culture.

**1838**
Edgar Allan Poe's 'Ligeia', the first short story about the death of a beautiful woman, is published.

**1849**
In Rochester, New York, teenagers Kate and Margaret Fox become the accidental founders of spiritualism when they claim to communicate with the dead using coded rapping.

**1851**
Pre-Raphaelite painter Sir John Everett Millais completes his painting of the drowning Ophelia from Shakespeare's *Hamlet*.

**1858**
*Gray's Anatomy*, an anatomical text book still in use today, is published.

**1860s**
William Mumler becomes the first 'spirit photographer'.

**1861**
Queen Victoria begins forty years of mourning after the death of her husband Prince Albert.

In his book *The Death and Resurrection Show* (1985), anthropologist Rogan P. Taylor traces the history of popular entertainments back to shamanistic performances that were both healing and entertaining. He points out that the Church ultimately lost its battle against secular entertainments, which it viewed as 'rivals for the same mystery: transformation magic'. It is Taylor's belief that our need for entertainment 'has risen in response to our new sickness – our loss of soul to science'. Or, in the words of Marcel Marceau (quoted in *The Death and Resurrection Show*), 'When the man in the street forgets his dream the theatre becomes a myth and a dispenser of signs.'

*Death: A Graveside Companion* can be seen as a treasury of images – ranging from fine art to scientific illustration to pop culture ephemera – related to humanity's attempts to imagine and understand death. It is a huge topic, spanning the history of humanity, and this book does not seek to be encyclopaedic. The majority of the images are from the collection of Richard Harris, who, since 2001, has accumulated more than 3,000 artefacts related to death and mortality; other pictures were drawn from ten years of reportage on the Morbid Anatomy blog. All the images are organized into seven thematic chapters, and each of these contains essays by thinkers, artists, collectors, curators and scholars – outré and orthodox – who have participated in the Morbid Anatomy community as presenters, collaborators, tour guides, teachers, and colleagues of various sorts.

Chapter one, 'The Art of Dying', examines the moment of passage from life to death – when life ends and a human being becomes a corpse – and the amorphous boundaries in between. It includes the allure of the beautiful corpse, the martyrdoms of Catholic

**1871**
Spiritualist artist Georgiana Houghton exhibits her automatic paintings at the New British Gallery on London's Bond Street.

**1884**
The London Spiritualist Alliance, now the College of Psychic Studies, is founded, supported by Arthur Conan Doyle.

**1890s**
The Cabaret du Néant, one of several death-themed places of entertainment, operates in Paris.

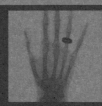

**1895**
A chance discovery of X-rays by German physicist Wilhelm Conrad Röntgen leads to the ability to see inside the human body.

**1897**
In Rome, Father Victor Jouet begins collecting the artefacts that form the basis of the Museum of the Holy Souls in Purgatory in the Church of the Sacred Heart of Suffering.

**1897–1962**
In the Pigalle district of Paris, tales of murder and horror thrill audiences at the Théâtre du Grand Guignol.

saints and the debates about the boundaries between life and death generated by the introduction of the guillotine in revolutionary France.

The next chapter, 'Examining the Dead', contemplates the human cadaver and explores its uses. It not only traces the ways in which the nascent science of anatomy incorporated metaphorical, metaphysical and memento mori meanings into its own representations, but also examines the preservation of the human body.

The third chapter, 'Memorializing the Dead', investigates the material culture of remembrance and mourning. It touches on mummification in ancient Egypt, in which the body was preserved so that it could be reunited with the soul. In addition, it looks at rituals related to honouring dead ancestors, such as Mexico's Día de Muertos, or Day of the Dead.

'The Personification of Death' explores the tradition of anthropomorphized death, in which Death is often portrayed as a skeleton trampling bodies underfoot, as in the Triumph of Death, or leading people of every class and station to the grave, as in the Dance of Death, or Danse Macabre. In artworks, Death is sometimes shown seducing – often quite graphically – a beautiful young woman residing at the seemingly paradoxical intersection of Eros and Thanatos – sex and death.

The fifth chapter, 'Symbolizing Death', considers the role of the skull and skeleton in the traditions of both memento mori and vanitas (still life paintings symbolizing the fleetingness of beauty and earthly pleasures). Many of these works date from the Baroque period, in which anatomically accurate representations of the skeleton came to be the most popular way of representing death.

**1898**
A decree of the Holy Office of the Roman Catholic Church condemns spiritualistic practices.

**1907**
A new attraction at Coney Island, New York, 'Night and Morning; or a Journey through Heaven and Hell' – based on the earlier attraction 'Darkness and Dawn' – invites visitors to 'experience their own death'.

**1913**
Mexican artist José Guadalupe Posada produces the etching *La Calavera Catrina* (Dapper Skeleton), a satirical comment on Mexican society.

**1914–18**
Some 14 million people are killed during World War I.

**1920**
Austrian psychoanalyst Sigmund Freud publishes *Beyond the Pleasure Principle*, asserting that human existence is governed by two opposing principles: the life drive (Eros) and the death drive (Thanatos).

**1939–45**
More than 60 million people are killed in World War II, including some 6 million victims of the holocaust.

The penultimate chapter, 'Death as Amusement', examines popular entertainments and arts that reveal a counter-intuitive delight in death, horror, violence and pain. Taken together, they illustrate philosopher Edmund Burke's adage from his essay of 1756 on the Sublime: 'When danger or pain press too nearly, they are incapable of giving any delight, and are simply terrible; but at certain distances, and with certain modifications, they may be, and they are, delightful.'

Finally, 'The Dead After Life' explores our relationship with those who have passed, and our imaginings of the liminal spaces dividing the living and the dead.

Once, not so very long ago, the contemplation of death was regarded as an important element of a good and considered life; today, death is seen as our antithesis, and its contemplation is deemed morbid. It is my hope that this book might act as a gesture towards redeeming death, to invite it back into our world in some small way. By contemplating these images, and by engaging with the many ways in which our ancestors imagined a death that was not antithetical to beauty, we might rediscover what they knew so well: the seemingly paradoxical notion that it is precisely by keeping death close at hand and coming to terms with its inevitability that we are able to lead full rich lives.

JOANNA EBENSTEIN, NEW YORK

**1961**
Suicide is legalized in the United Kingdom.

**1977**
Hamida Djandoubi is the last person to be executed in Western Europe; he is guillotined at Baumettes prison, Marseille, France.

**1995**
The first Body Worlds exhibition, displaying posed human bodies preserved by plastination, opens in Tokyo.

**2007**
British artist Damien Hirst unveils a platinum skull covered in more than 8,000 diamonds.

**2014**
An exhibition of paintings by Victorian spiritualist artist Ethel Le Rossignol is held at the Courtauld Institute in London.

**2016**
Capsula Mundi launches its capsules. The project creates biodegradable egg-shaped coffins that convert the body into nutrients for a tree growing above.

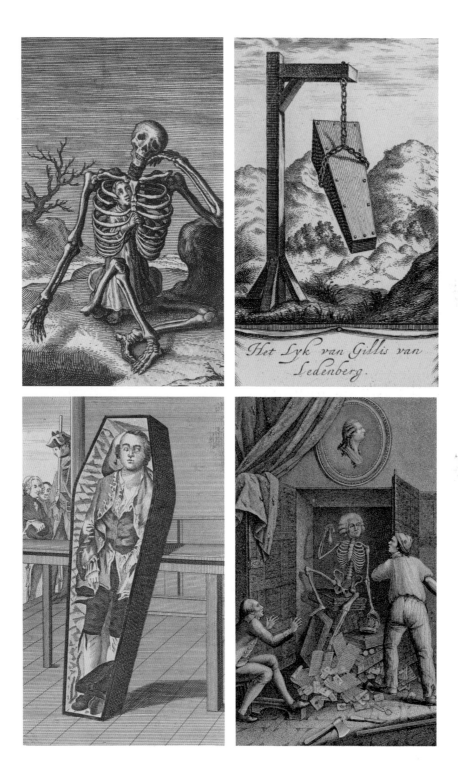

**Skeletons in the closet**
Clockwise from top left: from Herman Hugo's *Pious desires emblem, elegies and emotions*, 1624; the coffin of Gilles van Ledenberg was posthumously hung from the gallows in May 1619; the ghost of Comte de Mirabeau, a leader in the French Revolution, emerges from a hiding place in Louis XVI's Tuileries Palace; Lord Laurence Earl Ferrers, hanged for the murder of his steward.

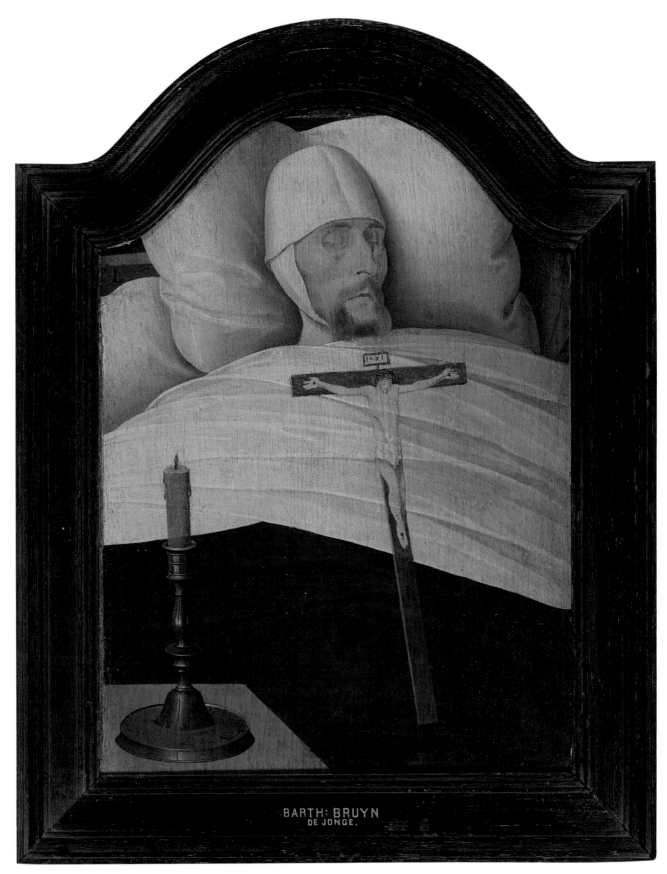

**Last portrait**
German artist Barthel Bruyn the Younger painted *Man on His Deathbed* between 1607 and 1610. Painted portraits of the dead first became popular in the 16th century and they could be prohibitively expensive. In a time before photography, it is likely that such portraits were the only visual record a family would have of a loved one.

18

**Final intimacy**
Painted around the same time as the portrait opposite, Barthel Bruyn the
Younger's *Woman on Her Deathbed* is similarly austere. Her identity is unknown
but the dates of her birth and death are recorded on the frame. By the 19th
century, post-mortem paintings such as this one had largely been supplanted
by the more affordable and accessible medium of photography.

**Hess's Dance of Death**

These hand-coloured lithographic plates by Hieronymus Hess appeared in *La Danse des Morts* (Dance of Death), first published in 1841. The images were copied from 17th-century watercolours documenting a well-known 14th-century Dance of Death fresco on a cemetery wall in Basel, Switzerland, that was destroyed in 1805. The Dance of Death is a genre in which an animated skeleton or corpse representing death leads people from all walks of life on a dance to the grave. Such images serve as a reminder of the inevitability and democratic nature of death. The genre is also part of a larger tradition of memento mori, objects that are intended to remind viewers of their own deaths in order to encourage them to lead a pious life on Earth in preparation for the Final Judgment.

**Vision of hell**
A personification of Death spreads its wings over a writhing mass of the damned in this detail from Jan van Eyck's diptych *The Crucifixion; Last Judgment, c.* 1440–41. The upper section of the painting (not seen here) shows the resurrected emerging from their graves to await the Final Judgment while Christ and a host of angels preside above.

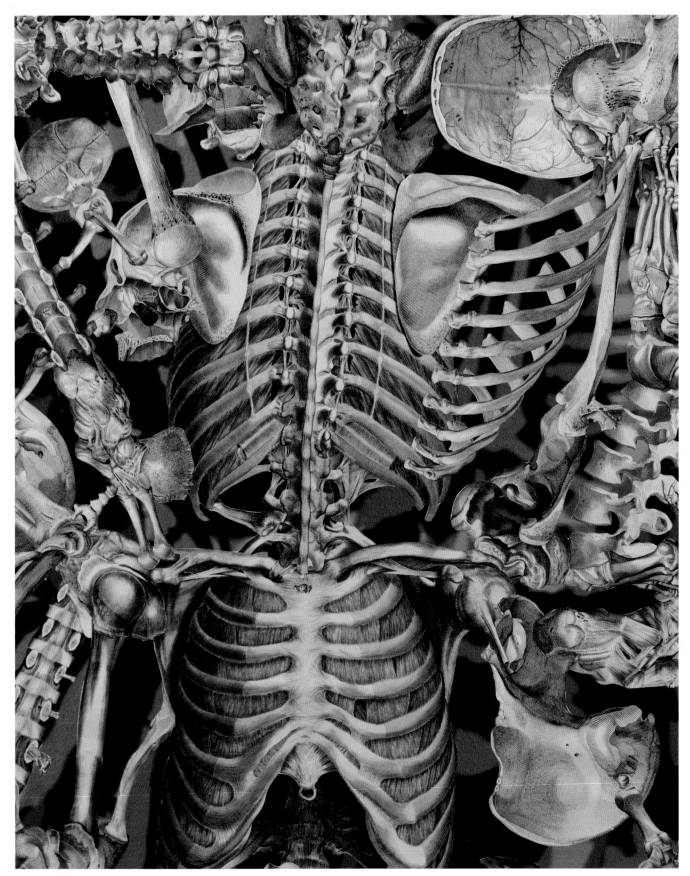

*Monolith* (detail)
Canadian artist Balint Zsako's *Monolith*, 2010, is a 2.7 metre-high (9 foot) paper collage crafted from reproductions of engravings from the great anatomical atlases of Vesalius and Albinus. The monumental structure is flanked by comparatively small cutouts of a nude man and woman, connected to the main composition by the human bones they hold.

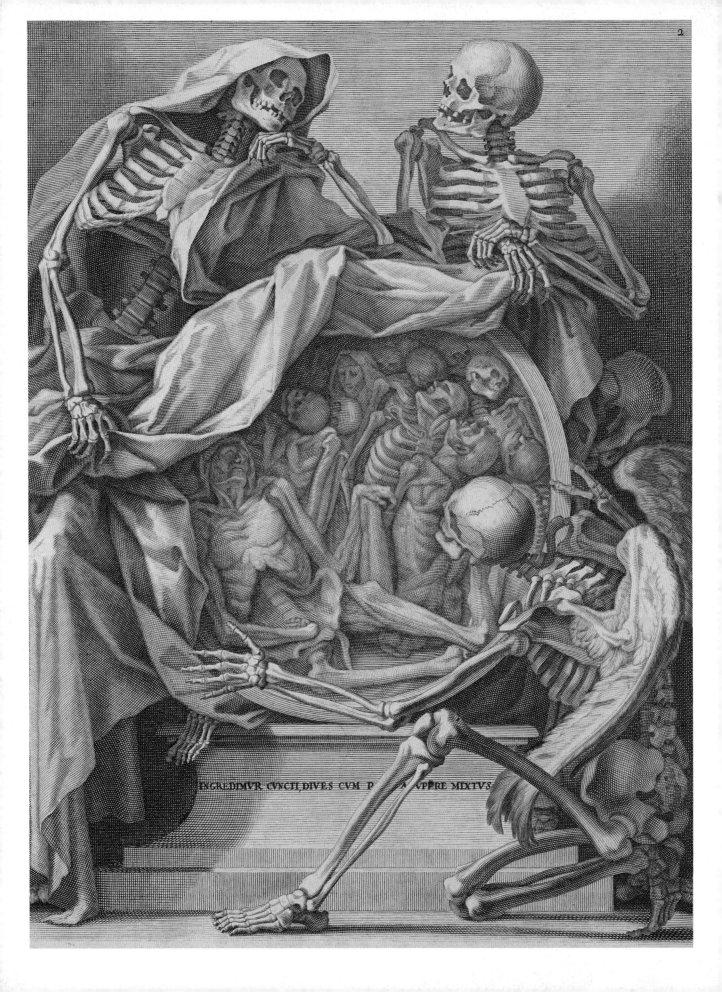

INGREDIMVR CVNCTI DIVES CVM PAVPERE MIXTVS

# the art of DYING

Laetitia Barbier

# medusa and the power of the severed head

E tre *médusé* is a French expression that I find particularly appealing. It derives from Medusa, the reptile-coiffed female monster of Greek mythology who turned to stone anyone who looked at her. The term loosely translates as 'to be dumbfounded' or 'stupefied', but the best definition is perhaps conveyed by Caravaggio's portrait of the gorgon reflected on Perseus's mirror-like shield. Painted on an actual shield for the Grand Duke of Tuscany, the image captures the brief liminal moment in which the freshly beheaded Medusa is still conscious enough to contemplate. As her head flies, the gaping hole of her mouth utters a silent scream and the snakes of her head attack each other. Whether it is caused by the sight of her own image or by the fatal blow of Perseus's sword, Medusa's terror keeps her alive for a split second before her petrification.

Being *médusé* goes far beyond being dumbfounded or stupefied. It seems to be a state of active paralysis, a profound paradox in which the intense confusion of surprise, pain and fear momentarily suspends both life and death. The concept of a living severed head belongs to the realm of myth, but in 18th-century France the power of the severed head gained fresh resonance with the invention of the guillotine, which was viewed briefly as a progressive solution in an ongoing debate on the death penalty. With its 4.2 metre-high (14 foot) wooden frame, eye-shape hole where the neck was placed, and angled blade like an iron fang, the guillotine now lies in the collective subconscious as the most horrendous apparatus of death. Its reputation can be partly attributed to the Reign of Terror that followed the French Revolution, during which more than 15,000 'enemies of the Revolution' were beheaded over the course of nine months.

The guillotine had several forerunners in medieval Europe: the Halifax Gibbet and the Scottish Maiden in Britain, and the Italian Mannaia (cleaver). But these were local exceptions. For centuries, most prisoners condemned to capital punishment would endure far

Page 24
Mirror on life
Skeletons present a roundel, or mirror, full of corpses in an allegory on death in *Anatomia per uso et intelligenza del Disegno*, 1691, an anatomical book written by Bernardino Genga and illustrated by Charles Errard. Genga taught anatomy to artists at the French Academy in Rome.

worse methods of execution. Depending on the social rank of the condemned or on precedence, the sentence – always public – would involve varying degrees of cruelty, including torture and dismemberment.

At the end of the 18th century, Dr Joseph-Ignace Guillotin, an heir of the Enlightenment, sought to get rid of the barbaric methods of the past. In 1789, the physician proposed a reform of capital punishment in front of the French National Assembly and King Louis XVI. He advocated the standardization of decapitation 'by means of a simple mechanism'. The task of designing a prototype was given to Dr Antoine Louis, a French army surgeon who, after examining several decapitation techniques, gave his apparatus its iconic bevelled blade. After testing his invention on cadavers and live sheep, Dr Louis declared the machine ready.

The guillotine was a product of humanism for many reasons. It allowed humankind to distance itself from an act of killing prescribed by law; it normalized the procedure of decapitation in one blow; it transformed the executioner into a passive technician; and, most importantly, it was supposedly painless for the victim because it was swift. Death in the blink of an eye.

A series of unforeseen realities soon caught advocates of the machine off guard, though. The guillotine was perceived instinctively as detestable by the public, who did not appreciate the egalitarian principles behind its invention, while the satirical press quickly anthropomorphized it as the biblical Moloch, thirsty for victims. Yet the real transgression of the guillotine was not so much the gallons of blood sent pouring over the scaffold, but the fact that the speed of the blade obliterated the transition between life and death. The guillotine's efficiency trivialized the instant of death, cancelling any intermediary state and the possibility of spiritual redemption that suffering was believed to offer. It also became impossible for the crowd to feel an empathic connection with the condemned, or for the authorities to justify that such spectacle had moral virtues that could prevent criminality.

Soon the story of Charlotte Corday, executed for murdering Jacobin leader Jean-Paul Marat, spread across Paris. After Marat's murderess went through the fatal machine, a zealous executioner took her head out of the basket and, holding it by the hair for the audience to admire, slapped her face twice. There was a collective gasp as some in the crowd noticed, to their horror, Corday's skin blush. The executioner was punished for his scandalous behaviour, but questions were on everyone's lips: was Corday's head conscious enough to understand the affront, and did she blush out of indignation?

A faction of physicians believed so. Led by German anatomist Samuel Thomas Soemmerring, they began to question the ability of the guillotine to suppress life instantaneously. In an essay written for the Parisian newspaper *Le Moniteur Universel* in 1795, Soemmerring invoked his scientific knowledge, based on experiments of his own and other doctors' accounts, to postulate that one's vital force lingers for a short time – between a few seconds and a few minutes – after decapitation, invigorated by the shock of the blade on the nerves in the neck. He claimed that the beheaded victim, still sensitive, was overwhelmed by mental torture and the traumatic realization of being between life and death – the same paradoxical state in which Caravaggio represented Medusa.

Soemmerring's article sparked a complex debate not only among medics but also throughout the nation, where everyone had heard stories of post-decapitation afterlives. While physicians poked the lacerated medullas of freshly guillotined heads, searching for a reaction, some executioners related stories of being bitten while reaching for a severed head. Others described the accusative stare of heads looking up from the bottom of the basket, or reported hearing whispers, howls and insults. Suddenly the guillotine was perceived as the stuff of nightmares – a restless death factory, producing the dead and the undead. It is said that even Guillotin, its first advocate, gave his closest friends poison so that they could commit suicide if they were ever condemned to lie on 'La Veuve' (the widow).

The controversy of the living heads and the machine that generated them inspired numerous French artists and authors, from Alexandre Dumas to Victor Hugo, and no doubt a couple of Grand Guignol horror shows. Even after the abolition of the death penalty in France in 1981, the guillotine continued to fascinate scientists. In 2011, Dutch neuroscientist Clementina M. Van Rijn of Radboud University in the Netherlands tested brain activity in rats, some conscious and others sedated, as they were beheaded by 'a guillotine with a sharp blade'. The encephalogram used to measure activity in the brain quietened completely three to four seconds after 'the wave of death'. Dr Van Rijn concluded that decapitation was 'not an inhumane method for euthanizing small animals' but reported an aesthetical disadvantage on her part: 'performing and observing this technique is displeasing.'

Could it be the guilt of the 'displeased' – the legislators, technicians and scientists intent on quantifying the 'humanity' in a method of execution – that keeps the severed heads alive. And behind that, is it humankind's eternal challenge to rationalize death itself?

# poe and the pathological sublime

*I Could Not Love Except Where Death/
Was Mingling His With Beauty's Breath*

EDGAR ALLAN POE,
'ROMANCE' (TEXT C), *POEMS* (1831)

The death of a beautiful woman is 'unquestionably the most poetical topic in the world,' decreed Edgar Allan Poe (1809–49) in his essay 'The Philosophy of Composition' (1846) – an innocent sentiment in its day, but one destined to live in infamy in those quarters where ideology keeps aesthetics on a choke chain.[1] Feminist critic Beth Ann Bassein, for example, believes Poe's work should be 'exorcized' from contemporary culture on the grounds that, by forging a symbolic link between women and 'the most passive state occurring, that of death,' Poe damaged the 'self-image and aspirations of generations of vulnerable readers.'[2] The irony, of course, is that the deathless women of Poe's short stories, if not his poems, are anything but passive. Sisters under the skin of Sylvia Plath's fearsome Lady Lazarus, who eats 'men like air', they transfix their male devotees with Medusan gazes and overshadow them with their brilliance.[3]

In Poe's 'Morella' (1835), the unnamed husband recalls that Morella's 'powers of mind were gigantic'; in their shared study of 'mystical writings', her vast erudition consigns him to the status of her pupil.[4] Ligeia, in the story of the same name, is an occultist whose learning is 'immense', a polymath whose mastery of 'mortal, physical and mathematical science' outstrips that of any man: 'I was sufficiently aware of her infinite supremacy to resign myself, with a child-like confidence,' Poe's narrator recounts, 'to her guidance through the chaotic world of metaphysical investigation at which I was most busily occupied....'[5] Even the sickly Madeline Usher in 'The Fall of the House of Usher' (1839) is tough as nails, refusing to take to her bed despite the ravages of a wasting disease. In Poe's world, not even burial can keep a good woman down: when Madeline's brother Roderick inters her alive, she bursts out of her coffin to stalk him through their decrepit mansion, a horror-movie reckoning that crescendos in Roderick's death from sheer terror.

Morella and her kin are queens of the night whose forays into forbidden knowledge take them where no man has gone before. Poe's male narrators are their devotees, in thrall to their hermetic wisdom and their command of the dark arts. Feminist writer Camille Paglia sees Poe as an exponent of 'Decadent Late Romanticism', whose cult of morbid beauty, keen sense of the Dionysian wildness of nature, and loss of faith in reason and science constitute a backlash against the Enlightenment tradition.[6] As such, Poe 'demands overt male subjection to female power,' she argues in *Sexual Personae* (1990). 'Like Shelley and Mill, [he] dreams of male eclipse by a Muse-like female mind.'[7] Of course, Poe's women also partake in what the feminist theorist Barbara Creed calls the 'monstrous feminine' – Freud's worst nightmares about 'castrating' women and the horrors of the female genitalia, given Gothic shape.

By contrast, the women in Poe's poetry – the 'saintly souls' and 'queenliest dead' of 'To Helen' (1831), 'Lenore' (1831), 'Eulalie' (1845), 'The Raven' (1845), 'Ulalume' (1847), 'For Annie' (1849) and, most famously, 'Annabel Lee' (1849) – are dream lovers, more Platonic ideal than corruptible flesh. They are objects of philosophical contemplation, their ethereality diametrically opposed to the corporeality of Madeline Usher in her gore-spattered shroud or to the undead Ligeia rising from her deathbed, wreathed in 'huge masses of long and disheveled hair…*blacker than the raven wings of midnight*.'[8] We see Poe's poetic muses through the scrim of his Gothic Romanticism but also through the Sublime, a term used by the 18th-century philosopher Edmund Burke for the mixture of rapture and terror that we experience in the face of nature's awful grandeur. We make sense of them, too, in light of the 19th-century cult of mourning, with its worship of 'the beautiful death' (from consumption), and, closer to home, the women in Poe's luckless death-haunted life.

Annabel Lee, 'the rare and radiant maiden whom the angels name Lenore' ('The Raven'), and all the other dead women who inspire melancholy raptures in Poe's poems are apparitions from his past. They are variations on a Romantic archetype, to be sure, but are charged with the psychic voltage of Poe's very real trauma. He lost almost every woman he ever loved, from his mother, carried off by tuberculosis when he was two years old, to his stepmother, Frances Allan, cut down by the same disease, and his wife Virginia, who succumbed to consumption. (The death of Poe's wife drove him half-mad with despair. 'He did not seem to care,' an acquaintance remembered, 'after she was gone, whether he lived an hour, a day, a week or a year; she was his all.'[9])

To Poe, women were, in a sense, always already dead: frail, consumptive creatures, fated to be snatched away by the Red Death of tuberculosis. At the same time, their association with death and their constant presence in the 'haunted palace' of his memory – dead yet undying – made them liminal beings, trespassers across the border between this life and the next. Ligeia returns from the underworld to hijack the body of her widower's dying wife; Morella dies in childbirth but is reborn from her own womb, reincarnated in a daughter who is her mirror image; Madeline Usher rises, Lazarus-like, from the tomb. Some, such as the lost Lenore in 'The Raven', are so sharply etched in the narrator's memory that they seem present – like table-rappers at a seance, tapping at the chamber door or brushing past unseen – their presence betrayed by 'the silken, sad, uncertain rustling of each purple curtain.'[10]

As Poe biographer James M. Hutchisson notes, children who lose a parent at an early age lack the psychological tools to process that loss in a normal healthy way. As a result, they remain bound, with all the intensity of infantile emotions, to the dead parent.[11] 'The finality of death is denied, as it is in so many of Poe's macabre stories, many of which concern ways of arresting, forestalling, and/or cheating death,' Hutchisson notes in *Poe* (2005). 'The most bizarre of them concern life-in-death: that is, the desire simultaneously to experience the process of dying and still not die.')

Poe was a resurrectionist of the unconscious, exhuming universal terrors as well as his own phobias and obsessions half a century before Sigmund Freud's *The Interpretation of Dreams* (1899). Accused of owing too great a debt to German Romanticism, Poe retorted, 'Terror is not of Germany, but of the soul.'[12] He knew that our darkest fears lurk not in the 'ghoul-haunted woodland of Weir' ('Ulalume') or the ancestral crypt beneath some 'mansion of gloom' ('Fall of the House of Usher') but locked away in the oubliette of the unconscious, scrabbling to be let out.[13] We can read his use of then prevalent ideas about mesmerism (an 18th-century precursor of hypnotism), the transmigration of the soul and the 'science of mind', whose mysteries Ligeia penetrated as Gothic metaphors for psychoanalysis, *avant la lettre*. Likewise, we glimpse premonitions of the Freudian unconscious in the doubles that recur throughout Poe's work – most obviously in his doppelgänger tale 'William Wilson' (1839), but also in the twinship of Roderick Usher and his sister; the dark/light binary of Ligeia, with her 'raven-black' tresses and the 'fair-haired and blue-eyed Lady Rowena'[14]; and the Jekyll-Hyde nature of the narrators of 'The Black Cat' (1843) and 'The Cask of Amontillado' (1846).

Poe's verse and fiction are a psychoanalytic mother lode, revealing, among other things, the profound ambivalence that inflects his use of woman as symbol. In his poetry, we see the worshipful reverence of a child who watched his mother, little more than a child herself at twenty-four, face the terror of oblivion alone and destitute. All the melancholy seraphs and nurturing angels in Poe's poems wear the same face – the face of Jung's imago, the 'subjective and often very much distorted' mental image of a parent, shaped by child-hood memories, that persists into adulthood, where it leads 'a shadowy but nonetheless potent existence in the mind of the patient.'[15] There was a Dickensian pathos to the orphaned Poe's never-ending quest for a surrogate mother, from his early attachment to his chronically ill stepmother to his veneration of Jane Stannard, the kind-hearted mother of a schoolfriend, who died insane a year after they met ('the first, purely ideal love of my soul'), to his depth of feeling for his mother-in-law, Maria Clemm, for whom he wrote a sonnet, tellingly titled 'To My Mother' (1849).[16]

Yet women to Poe were also Death's brides, dangling the promise of motherly love only to abandon him for the blackness of the grave cave. 'Death in Poe's lexicon is rejection,' asserts the critic and novelist Diane Johnson.[17] 'Fragile, frightening, liable to die,' the women in Poe's stories 'are mostly terrible (in their power to disappoint),' she notes, 'and must be destroyed as the narrator destroys his wife in 'The Black Cat' or as Roderick Usher destroys by inaction his sister Madeline.'[18]

Poe was the high priest of a cult of Gothic Romanticism that, like the Wildean Aestheticism that would follow it, worshipped beauty, though in Poe's case it was a morbid beauty. 'I could not love except where Death/Was mingling his with Beauty's breath,' he wrote, when he was just twenty.[19] In the same poem ('Introduction'), he declared himself 'in love with melancholy'.

In 'The Philosophy of Composition', Poe under-scores the psychological nature of his work. 'The contemplation of the beautiful,' he points out, is a means to an end: a psychological effect – 'that intense and pure elevation of soul,' he calls it, using the language of the age before Freud.[20] Nothing supercharges that effect like melancholy ('the most legitimate of all the poetical tones'), and what is more melancholy than death? Returning to his theme, Poe reasons that death is at its most poetical 'when it most closely allies itself to *Beauty*.' (Italics his.) Thus, the death of a beautiful woman 'is, unquestionably, the most poetical topic in the world – and equally is it beyond doubt that the lips best suited for such a topic are those of a bereaved lover.'

Poe was that bereaved lover, and his vision of a euphoric sadness is the Romantic dream of death trans-formed into something beautiful, perhaps even art, and of melancholy as a kind of ecstasy. It is also informed by Romanticism's aestheticization of consumption as an artistic malady caused by an excess of passion, perhaps because refined souls such as John Keats and Elizabeth Barrett Browning died from it, perhaps because sufferers became thinner, paler and thus more 'beautiful' as they declined. (Truth to tell, the dying had a habit of spoiling the effect by coughing up blood.)

The better part of Poe's genius, though, is in his appropriation of Burke's Sublime in the service of something darker, a sort of moral and aesthetic rapture of the deep in which the death of a beauti-ful woman, and her disquieting afterlife, produces the same psychological vertigo as did the natural phenomena – cloud-wreathed peaks, towering thun-derheads, titanic waves – that, for Burke, epitomized the Sublime. Poe is no stranger to the Burkean version: he is always game for a jaw-dropping special effect, whether 'whirlpool of mountainous and foaming ocean' ('MS. Found in a Bottle', 1833) or 'sheer unobstructed precipice of black shining rock, some fifteen or sixteen hundred feet from the world of crags beneath us' ('A Descent into the Maelström', 1841).[21] His brilliance, however, lay in his discovery that the night terrors of the psyche can produce a Sublime all their own; that the maelströms of the mind are more dizzying than anything nature can conjure.

Bruce Goldfarb

# the nutshell studies of unexplained death

The Nutshell Studies of Unexplained Death are a collection of eighteen exquisitely detailed, hand-made dioramas depicting scenes of violent and sudden death. Housed at the Office of the Chief Medical Examiner, in Baltimore, the models have been used for decades to hone the observation skills of homicide detectives.

Created by Frances Glessner Lee (1878–1962) in the 1940s, the dioramas are a small portion of Lee's body of work as a miniaturist, an activity she originally took up as a hobby. In 1913, Lee completed an ambitious project: depicting the ninety members of the Chicago Symphony Orchestra, on a scale of 1/12, as a gift for her mother. She personalized the Viennese bisque figures with facial hair and hairlines that matched those of the real-life musicians they represented. Today, this miniature orchestra is displayed at the Glessner House Museum in Chicago, on a tiered platform nearly 2.5 metres (8 feet) long. The figures wear hand-stitched dress shirts and tuxedos, each with a minuscule carnation on the lapel, and sit behind music stands with a perfectly legible score on tiny sheets of paper.

A year after making the orchestra display, Lee created a miniature of the Flonzaley Quartet, a Swiss string quartet popular in the early 20th century. Built on the same 1/12 scale, the miniature musicians matched the expressions and poses of their real-life counterparts in concert, with an original composition propped on little music stands. The cello, barely more than 7.5 centimetres (3 inches) tall, actually produced sound. Lee presented the miniature ensemble to the musicians after a dinner at the Glessner home. It is now on display in a museum in Switzerland.

The Nutshell Studies, though, are Lee's enduring legacy. They helped revolutionize how detectives investigate homicides. Each hand-crafted diorama cost Lee as much to construct as a real house. Built in her usual 1/12 scale, the models are obsessively detailed, with working light switches, keys that fit into keyholes, and tiny hand-rolled cigarettes containing real tobacco burned and stubbed out in an overflowing ashtray. Most of the dioramas depict disenfranchised and marginalized members of society – alcoholics, prostitutes, a prisoner – people far removed from Lee's own social circles. Poverty and alcoholism are recurring themes, although the affluence apparent in a few dioramas is a recognition by Lee that violence exists in every class. Most of the victims are female, and most of them are at home. All are intricately, vividly rendered, demonstrating deep empathy and an eye for fine detail. Lee went to painstaking lengths to achieve realistic blood splatter patterns, lividity, bruising and discoloration of the skin due to poisoning or decomposition. Aside from the facts of the deaths, Lee wanted viewers of the Nutshells to gain a sense of who the victims were, their lives and socioeconomic condition.

Indeed, all the dioramas were based on real homicides. The facts are true, but details were changed to protect the identities of those involved. 'No model is a replica of any known crime or crime scene,' Lee wrote in a note. 'Everything represented has actually happened but not necessarily in conjunction with the other events shown. The models are all composites.'

Lee was an unlikely protagonist to lead a revolution in the field of police science. Born into an immensely wealthy Chicago family, she was tutored at home in music, art and literature, and learned sewing, needlepoint, knitting and other needlework from her mother. Lee had wanted to go to college, like her brother, and perhaps to train as a nurse. However, 'It just wasn't done,' she said. 'A lady shouldn't know anything about the human body.'

When she was in her forties, Lee was introduced to forensic science by George Burgess Magrath, a pioneering medical examiner in Boston who had been a classmate of Lee's brother at Harvard. Magrath served as Lee's guide into forensic medicine, taking her into the autopsy room, where she learned about postmortem changes, and to crime scenes to observe evidence. She was fifty-three years old when she embarked on her career in police science.

The lessons learned from Magrath and an abiding interest in Sherlock Holmes mysteries led Lee to use $250,000 of her fortune to establish America's first legal medicine training programme at Harvard Medical School in 1931. 'Luckily, I was born with a silver spoon in my mouth,' she once told a reporter. 'It gave me the time and money to follow my hobby of scientific crime investigation.' Harvard's legal medicine programme, which later developed into a full department, trained hundreds of doctors as medical examiners. But this was not enough. As Magrath explained to Lee, by the time a medical examiner arrived at a crime scene, critical evidence had usually been altered. Not knowing any better – at the time, there was no training programme for homicide detectives – police moved bodies, walked through blood and handled weapons and evidence improperly. Seeking to address this deficiency, in 1945 Lee helped establish a seminar in homicide investigation for law enforcement officers. She was sixty-seven years old.

Lee created the Nutshell Studies of Unexplained Death to use as teaching tools in her week-long homicide seminars on the observation of indirect evidence at crime scenes. Participants were taught about bullet wounds, sharp-edged weapons, strangulation and drowning. Police officers studied the stages of decomposition and varieties of poisonings. They also learned how to gather information with their eyes and their mind, without touching or altering anything at the crime scene. It was not intended that the crimes depicted should be solved by such means – viewers lacked autopsy findings and crime scene forensics – but observation was the first step. The Nutshell Studies are still used in the same way during homicide seminars today. Although the dioramas are more than seventy years old, the facts of violent death depicted in the models are timeless.

Lee took great pride in her seminars. At one point during the week, she would host a dinner at Boston's Ritz-Carlton, paying the same fastidious, obsessive attention to the menu and centrepiece flower decorations as she devoted to the Nutshells. The banquets cost her more than $50,000 in today's money. Police officers who attended were expected to act as gentlemen and dress accordingly. For many of them, it was the best dinner they had in their lives.

A group photograph was taken at every seminar, and participants were encouraged to remain in contact with one another and to exchange information. Every attendee was automatically made a member of Harvard Associates in Police Science, an educative organization whose conferences continue today. It was important to Lee that participants received a diploma and a lapel pin, perhaps because she wanted to impress upon the homicide detectives that they were now the best-trained investigators in the nation, an elite group. They were no longer gumshoe cops, but professionals with a duty to use their skills and expertise to convict the guilty, clear the innocent and find the truth in a nutshell.

The annual homicide seminar, now known as the Frances Glessner Lee Seminar in Homicide Investigation, is the longest running and most highly regarded training of its kind. It marked its seventieth anniversary in 2015. Thousands of officers from throughout America and around the world have attended the seminar over the years. They still examine the Nutshell Studies of Unexplained Death.

Much of what the public knows and expects in a homicide investigation, as portrayed in movies and *CSI*-type television dramas, is derived from Lee's efforts in education and training. Through the Harvard Medical School programme and seminars, she elevated homicide investigation into a scientific discipline.

The Nutshell Studies of Unexplained Death remain objects of fascination, the subject of documentaries, books, television shows, photographs, podcasts and countless feature stories. This remarkable and singular collection of artefacts is only a footnote in Lee's mission to modernize homicide investigation. The Nutshells were never meant to be considered, individually or collectively, as works of art. No matter the extravagance, the dioramas were merely the most suitable medium for teaching crime scene investigation.

**Battle for the soul**
Death springs from behind the Tree of the Knowledge of Good and Evil in Hans Rottenhammer's *Adam and Eve*, c. late 16th/early 17th century (top left), while in Ignacio de Ries's *El Árbol de la Vida* (The Tree of Life), 1653 (top right), merrymakers in the branches of the tree are unaware that Death and the devil are battling Christ for the fate of their souls below. The saints plead for the soul of the deceased while Death and the devil lurk nearby in *El Árbol de la Vida* (The Tree of Life), by an unknown artist of the 19th century (bottom left). In *Juicio de un Pecador* (Judgment of a Sinner, bottom right) by an unknown 18th-century artist, the fate of the deceased is already sealed. The sinner is dragged in chains to hell while angels weep for his fate.

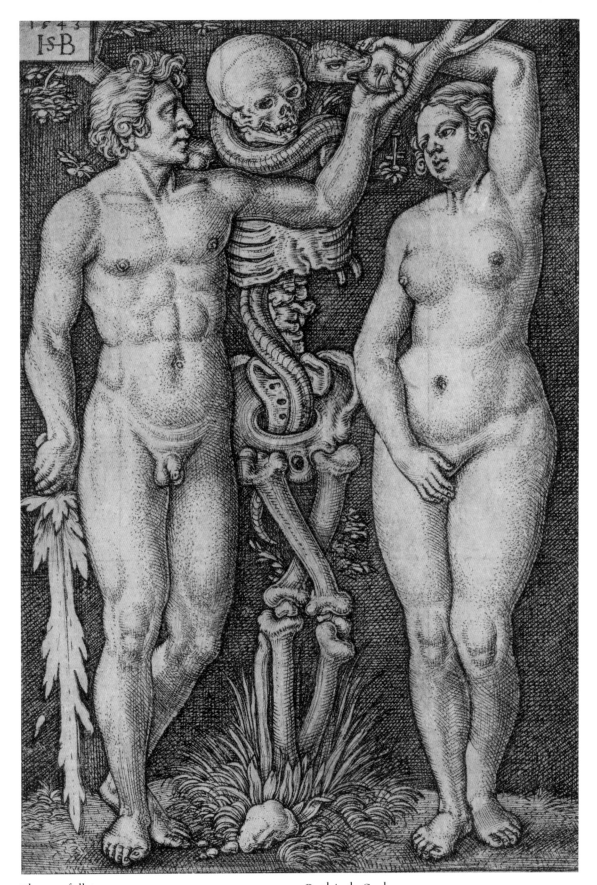

**The root of all sin**
In Hans Sebald Beham's *Adam and Eve*, 1543 (above), the Tree of the Knowledge of Good and Evil takes the form of a skeletonized personification of Death, signifying that it is Adam and Eve's original sin of eating the forbidden fruit from the tree that introduces death to humankind.

**Death in the Garden**
The Garden of Eden in 'Homo ex Humo' (Man from the Ground or 'dust'), from Johann Jakob Scheuchzer's *Physica Sacra*, 1731–35 (opposite), is framed by scientifically accurate foetal skeletons and embryos, perhaps inspired by the work of Scheuchzer's contemporary, the anatomist Frederik Ruysch.

TAB. XXIII.

GENESIS Cap. I. v. 26. 27.

I Buch Mosis Cap. I. v. 26. 27.

Homo ex Humo.

Erschaffung und Zeugung des Menschen.

The noble martyr
*Landscape with the Legend of St Christopher*, early 16th century, by Jan Mandijn, portrays the legend of St Christopher, as described in the *Golden Legend*, a 13th-century hagiography by Jacobus de Voragine. St Christopher (Christ-bearer) carries the baby Jesus across a river. The head with the cleaver symbolizes the saint's martyrdom by beheading; the monsters represent the seven deadly sins that tempt humankind.

## Graphic depictions of beheadings

Biblical and mythological beheadings were popular themes for Renaissance artists. Caravaggio's *Medusa*, c. 1597 (centre), captures the moment Perseus decapitates the Gorgon. A year later, Caravaggio painted *Judith Beheading Holofernes*, 1598 (top), illustrating the biblical story of the widow Judith decapitating a general of the tyrannical Nebuchadnezzar. Another popular Bible story was that of Salome, who demanded the head of John the Baptist as a reward for her 'dance of the seven veils'. *Salome*, c. 1530, by Lucas Cranach the Elder (bottom right), depicts Salome carrying the freshly severed head. The aftermath of a beheading is also captured in *David with the Head of Goliath*, 1606, by Guido Reni (bottom left), in which the shepherd calmly exhibits the giant's head.

**The last public execution in France**
In March 1939 serial killer Eugen Weidmann was sentenced to death after a sensational trial in Versailles. On 17 June 1939 crowds gathered outside the prison Saint-Pierre, Versailles (top left and centre) as Weidmann was led from his cell past the wicker basket that waited to receive his body (bottom left) and placed on the guillotine (bottom right). The rowdy behaviour of the bloodthirsty crowd led French president Albert Lebrun to ban all future public executions, and, until the final death by guillotine in 1977, they were conducted within prison walls. The guillotine fascinated and horrified the French in equal measure. The miniature operational guillotine (centre), from the collection of John Whitenight and Fred LaValley, was carved from animal bone by a French prisoner of war during the Napoleonic Wars (1803–15).

**The sacred and profane**
Salome holds aloft the head of John the Baptist in this pen and ink illustration
by Aubrey Beardsley for the English translation of Oscar Wilde's play *Salomé*,
1893. The story of Salome, who demanded the head of John the Baptist, was
popular with 19th-century artists and writers fascinated by the femme fatale.

Head on a platter
In Beardsley's *The Dancer's Reward*, 1894, another illustration commissioned by Wilde for *Salomé*, the protagonist revels in her bloody prize. An eccentric British artist, Beardsley became famous for his macabre, erotic and fantastic images, but died of tuberculosis at only twenty-five years of age.

**Death by drowning**
The story of Ophelia, who went mad and committed suicide by drowning in Shakespeare's *Hamlet*, was a popular subject for 19th-century artists. The model in Sir John Everett Millais's painting *Ophelia*, 1851–52 (top), was Elizabeth Siddal, a muse to many of the Pre-Raphaelite painters. Plagued with physical and mental illness, Siddal died aged thirty-two.

**Death of a general**
The figure reading from a book in *Napoleon on his Deathbed, One Hour Before his Funeral*, 1843, by Jean-Baptiste Mauzaisse (bottom), is Abbé Ange Paul Vignali, Napoleon's chaplain. Vignali amassed a collection of Napoleonic relics, including his preserved penis, described in an auction catalogue in 1924 as a 'mummified tendon taken from [Napoleon's] body during post-mortem'.

**Death by suicide**
*The Death of Chatterton*, 1856, by Henry Wallis (top), portrays the suicide at the age of seventeen of the 18th-century romantic poet Thomas Chatterton. The poet's Gothic works, depressive nature and early death inspired many writers and artists, including the Pre-Raphaelite Wallis. In Wallis's painting, Chatterton's poems lie scattered on the floor beside a vial of poison.

**Death of a broken heart**
John Atkinson Grimshaw's melancholic *The Lady of Shalott*, 1875 (bottom), was inspired by Alfred Lord Tennyson's poem of the same name: 'A gleaming shape she floated by, Dead-pale between the houses high, Silent into Camelot.' Tennyson based his poem on the Arthurian legend of Elaine of Astolat, who died of unrequited love for King Arthur's companion Sir Lancelot.

**Death and drink**
'Suicide of daughter' (top) is an illustration from George Cruikshank's *The Drunkard's Children*, 1848. The book demonstrates through eight sequential images the fate of a family who succumb to the temptations of gin. It includes scenes of gambling, robbery and death in prison, and culminates in this image of the daughter ending her life in despair.

**Horror of entombment**
The text on the coffin in *The Premature Burial*, 1854, by Antoine Wiertz (bottom) reads *Mort du cholera* (Death by cholera). At the time this painting was made, the fear of being buried alive (taphophobia) was a common concern. Edgar Allan Poe made it the subject of his short story 'The Premature Burial', 1844. There was even a market in 'safety coffins' which incorporated air tubes or bells.

**Death of a step-daughter**
*Study for Young and his Daughter*, c. 1804, by Pierre-Antoine Augustin Vafflard was inspired by Edward Young's autobiographical poem 'The Complaint: or Night Thoughts on Life, Death, and Immortality', 1742–45. Vafflard's painting depicts the midnight journey of Young to find a burial ground that would accept the body of his Protestant step-daughter Elizabeth Temple after her sudden death in Lyon, France. Young's meditative poem met with great success (it was illustrated by William Blake) and was especially popular during the French Revolution. The painting above is an oil on paper study for the final piece, which Vafflard premiered at the Paris Salon Exhibition of 1804.

45

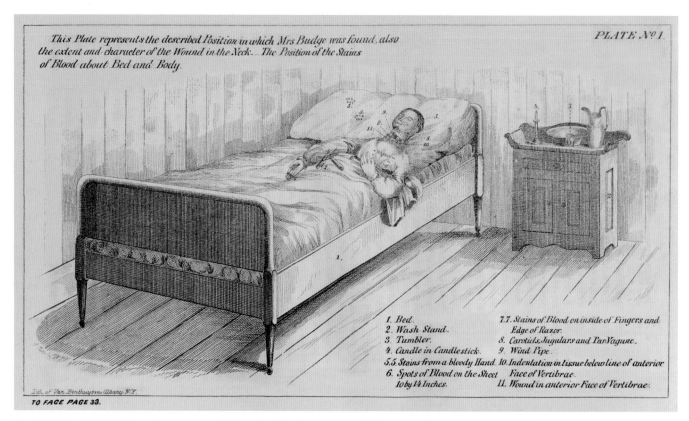

This Plate represents the described Position in which Mrs Budge was found, also the extent and character of the Wound in the Neck. The Position of the Stains of Blood about Bed and Body.

PLATE Nº 1.

1. Bed.
2. Wash Stand.
3. Tumbler.
4. Candle in Candlestick.
5,5. Stains from a bloody Hand.
6. Spots of Blood on the Sheet 10 by 14 Inches.
7,7. Stains of Blood on inside of Fingers and Edge of Razor.
8. Carotids, Jugulars and Par Vagune.
9. Wind Pipe.
10. Indentation in tissue below line of anterior Face of Vertibrae.
11. Wound in anterior Face of Vertibrae.

Lith. of Van Benthuysen, Albany, N.Y.

TO FACE PAGE 33.

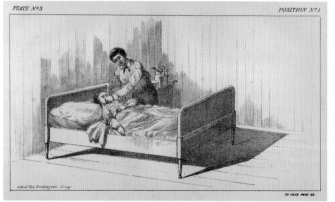

PLATE Nº 3    POSITION Nº 1

Lith. of Van Benthuysen, Albany

TO FACE PAGE 32.

PLATE Nº 4.    POSITION Nº 2.

Lith. of Van Benthuysen, Albany

TO FACE PAGE 83.

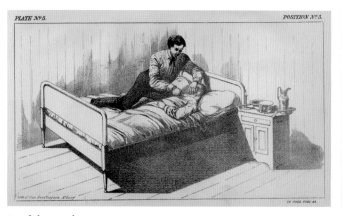

PLATE Nº 5.    POSITION Nº 3.

Lith. of Van Benthuysen, Albany

TO FACE PAGE 83.

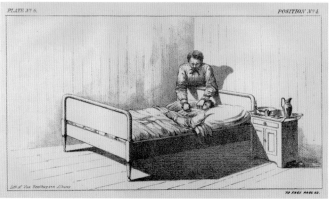

PLATE Nº 6.    POSITION Nº 4.

Lith. of Van Benthuysen, Albany

TO FACE PAGE 83.

**Death by murder**
These illustrations are from a murder pamphlet titled 'A review of the case, the People agt. Rev. Henry Budge, indicted for the murder of his wife, Priscilla Budge, 1862'. Murder pamphlets, in circulation from the 17th century, were precursors to true-crime novels and claimed to present genuine accounts of recent murders uncovered in criminal trials.

**Reading a murder scene**
The Nutshell Studies of Unexplained Death, miniature models of crime scenes, were created by Frances Glessner Lee in the mid-20th century. Lee, a wealthy socialite, was the mother of scientific death investigation. She created more than a dozen of these miniature dioramas, each of which was a composite of a real crime. They are still used to educate murder investigators today.

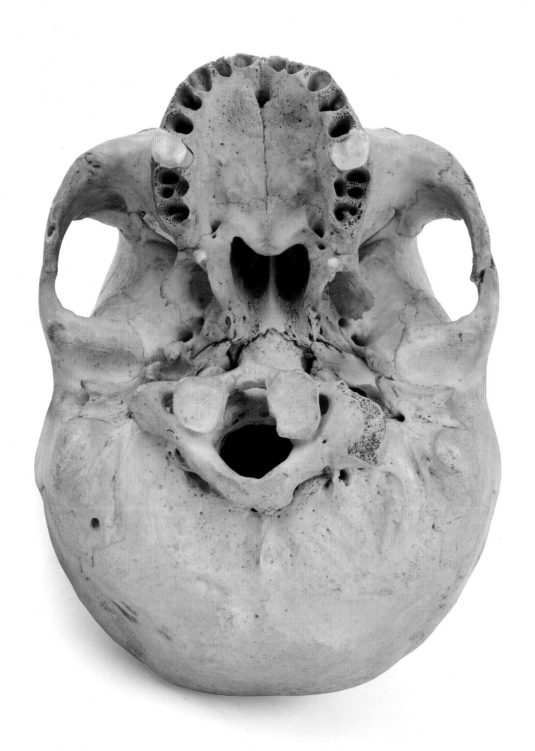

# 11

# examining the
# DEAD

*Excavating the ancient dead*

THE DRAMA OF 18TH-CENTURY ANATOMY

Artful dissection

*Cabinets of curiosities*

ANATOMICAL EXPRESSIONISM

Eviscerated dolls in glass coffins

Michael Sappol

# art, science and the changing conventions of anatomical representation

natomy is our inner reality; anatomy is us. Even if we haven't studied anatomy formally, we carry around an anatomical image of self – a pocket map that divides us into regions and terrains, with internal place names and borders. This anatomical self-image has a history – the history of anatomical representation – a shifting negotiation between anatomists, artists, engravers, patrons, printers and readers. Until the invention of the X-ray, sonograms and MRI technology, the only way to see into ourselves was by dissecting the dead. The dissected cadaver was our mirror.

Early modern anatomists peered into that mirror and made faces. A spirit of play pervaded the anatomy of Belgian physician Andreas Vesalius in 16th-century Italy, and also his predecessors and successors. They earnestly investigated the human structure and functions, and tried to describe and represent the body accurately, but they also sought to amaze, entertain and morally instruct students, colleagues and patrons. They were a feisty bunch, constantly striving to outdo each other with flashier dissections and bigger and more expensive books, filled with more beautiful and artful and witty and outrageous illustrations of cadavers in silly or provocative poses. Anatomists were showmen. When they performed their dissections and delivered their lectures in the pit of the anatomical theatre, their audiences included the local aristocracy, magistrates and clergymen, as well as the general public. Their showmanship carried over to their illustrated publications, and to their museums and specimens.

The anatomical revolution associated with Vesalius certainly produced knowledge about the human body. However, anatomy was a dark science. It acquired its mystique from its wilful transgressions, violations of funerary customs and incursions across the boundary that separates life and death. Anatomists took, often stole, dead bodies and cut into them, and dissection became the preeminent ritual that inducted young men

Page 48
Inca skull, 16th century
Inca skulls are of particular interest to skull collectors, as the Incas engaged in cranial deformation, or 'head flattening'. This was done by binding the heads of children in various ways to encourage an elongated growth pattern.

into the cult of medical knowledge. Medicine became something of a death cult. Yet scientific anatomy was more than just dissection: it took the observation of the body's interior from the dissecting table to the pages of a book (and back again). Visual representation was a key innovation of the new science of anatomy: ancient anatomical treatises consisted of written descriptions of the body. Illustrations were rare. After Vesalius, the authoritative anatomical treatise had to be illustrated, had to have richly detailed and intensively captioned pictures of the dissected body and body parts. Given the complexity of the interior of the body, it could not just be described, it had to be shown.

And what was shown was the dead body. Early modern representations of the anatomical body confronted death head on: the dead mocked the living; the living mocked the dead. The cadaver was an effigy; it served as a reminder of our mortality, our fallibility, our folly – the fragility of human life and civilization. Anatomy cited, parodied or augmented long-established artistic traditions and iconography – memento mori, Danse Macabre, Christian and classical martyrology – as well as newer painting genres such as still life, which often took mortality as one of its tropes. Early modern anatomists made their work their pleasure and their pleasure their work. But it was morbid play, death play.

Vesalius took unprecedented care in getting his anatomy books right. He was a great scholar of the Greek physician Galen, but wrote about the errors of Galen's ways and made sure to depict them in his illustrations. Some of these were represented in a highly developed naturalistic manner; others show nonexistent muscles, to make the point that Galen described anatomical structures that were not there, or show a human skull atop a dog's skull to signify that Galen's knowledge of anatomy was obtained from dissecting dogs and other animals, not people. Yet neither Vesalius nor his artists could conceive of a work governed entirely by austere naturalism. They wanted to entertain their readers and themselves.

During the 17th century, anatomy became even wittier and more theatrical. In this period, forms of theatre, dance and literature emerged that are recognizably modern: the ballet and opera, and all kinds of court entertainments. This was the era of Shakespeare, Montaigne, Molière, Donne and Cervantes. It was a time in which great courts and salons emerged, a time when people vied to outdo each other with manners, repartee and fashion. It was also a time in which people began to develop the concept of individuality and personality, what literary historian Stephen Greenblatt calls 'Renaissance self-fashioning'.

In their dissections and written works, early modern anatomists fashioned themselves. In their book illustrations, they modelled the fashioned self in all its variety. In this cultural milieu, the producers and audience for anatomical representation expected, even demanded, that anatomical illustration represent the human body morally, socially, theologically, theatrically, balletically and literally, as well as scientifically.

And so anatomists and their artists taught the moral and scientific truth of the human body, and they fooled around for no reason other than to have fun. Their illustrations and objects operated in multiple dimensions of meaning and function. The anatomist studied dissected cadavers, and enjoyed manipulating and presenting them; readers and viewers studied dissected cadavers, and enjoyed looking. This convergence of work and play, this multiplicity of function and meaning, was not problematic. The only victim was the anatomical subject, denied funerary honour and conscripted to serve as the raw material from which anatomical knowledge was produced.

Then it all changed. Between 1680 and 1800, the conventions, meanings, audience and uses of anatomical representation shifted. Anatomists began to develop new criteria for what constituted acceptable scientific illustration. Play and the pursuit of truth became incompatible. The cadaver was no longer made to pose and dance. The artist was no longer asked or permitted to embellish the background, to provide fantasy architecture and landscapes for the anatomical figures to frolic in. And the reader was no longer asked to meditate on human mortality. Now scrutiny of the structure of the body, in all its particularity and specificity, took up all of the representational space. Science, anatomists argued, needed to focus. Suddenly, a boundary was drawn around anatomy. Art and science came to be defined in mutually exclusive ways, a separation that, with some important revisions, still has force today.

This is not to say that art and aesthetics were completely expunged from anatomy, only a particular kind of art and aesthetics. The artful representation of anatomical objects continued to be a crucial part of the science of anatomy, and anatomists continued to work with artists and to value high artistry, but only of one type: the art of the real.

The triumph of harsh anatomical realism was not, however, the end of anatomical history. In the late 18th century, another style emerged that achieved even greater dominance: a universalist anatomy featuring composite, idealized and often intensely coloured views of the body. In this genre, bodies and body parts float in air, free of all context, and anatomy is cleansed of its association with death. The process of dissection is expunged; the prosthetics of dissection and the dissecting table are suppressed. Everything except the body is viewed as a distraction.

Because particularity is also regarded as an obstacle to the truth, a specific body always has pathologies and idiosyncrasies that obscure the 'general' principles and characteristics of bodies, organs and systems. Anatomical universalism, the style of *Gray's Anatomy* (1858), was much in vogue in the 19th century. It featured in the most widely used 20th-century anatomies.

In both new styles of realism, iconographic, theatrical and ornamental elements were purged. Science dealt with the real, with the truth of the body and of the physical universe. Art was given everything else: moral truth, history, aesthetics, embellishments, metaphor, myth. Outside of scientific illustration – in academic art, political cartooning, advertising art, horror films and other productions of popular culture – imaginative, humorous and moral representations of the anatomical body continued to be made and viewed.

I began with the assertion that we think of ourselves as anatomical beings, a self-image derived from the work that anatomists and artists have produced collaboratively over the centuries. We all have multiple identities, some loudly proclaimed, others understated or even implicit. Anatomical identity is one of the latter. It is so pervasive, so routine, that we don't tend to notice it. In the year 1700, most people in Europe and North America thought of themselves as an unstable amalgam of meat, spirit, reason and corruption, or as a microcosm of the universe. Only a thin upper crust of learned physicians and gentlemen had ever seen a detailed anatomical illustration or thought of themselves as anatomical entities.

This is obviously no longer the case. Even if we have never been taught anatomy in school, we still see the anatomical body in the doctor's surgery, magazine advertisements and television shows, and see our own bodies represented in X-rays and scans. The subject of anatomical representation and the boundaries between art and science are not purely academic: they have reference to our own experience.

We believe anatomy is our inner reality. Science therefore has a legitimate claim to be the highest authority over that domain. However, the artist also has claims to be the oracle of anatomical truth. Since the advent of Romanticism in the early 19th century, the artist has assumed the role of prophet, a reader of augers and signs.

Such is arguably still the case, even in the era of postmodernism. In traditional academic art, which still has many adherents, anatomy is the technical knowledge out of which the artist crafts insightful representations of the human figure. But modernist and postmodernist anatomy – the art of Paul Thek, Damien Hirst, Marc

Quinn, Carolyn Henne, Lisa Nilsson and many others – is open-ended, conceptual and only partly legible. Instead of insight, the anatomical body is a glyph: we no longer know what to make of it. This resonates because we spend much of our lives sitting in front of computers and television screens, doing almost nothing with our bodies. And we need something strong to feel the connection with embodied life and embodied death. We need an aura of realness, which the anatomical specimens and sculptures of the art world and Philadelphia's Mütter Museum, Body Worlds and other anatomical displays seem to supply.

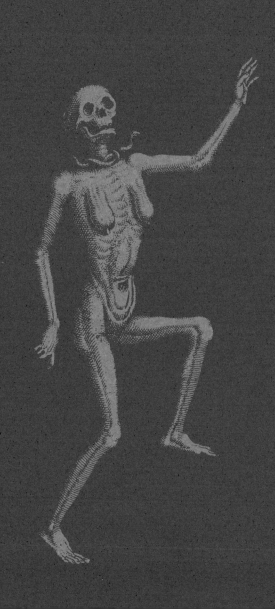

Bert van de Roemer

# anatomy embellished in the cabinet of frederik ruysch

The anatomical preparations of Dutch anatomist and physician Frederik Ruysch (1638–1731) would strike a modern audience as remarkable and perhaps even shocking. Ruysch, who displayed his specimens in his home cabinet, which he opened for visitors and students to view, was famous for his skill at preserving the dead using a method that seemed to retain the flush and vividness of life.

Ruysch was also well known for the imaginative and allegorical presentation of his specimens – the preserved head of a baby resting peacefully on a pillow of human placenta; a poisonous gecko holding a human foetus between its jaws – and combined preparations such as a child's arm delicately holding female genitals, or a child's leg standing on a poisonous scorpion. One version of his cabinet even featured a 'tomb' assembled from human bones and skulls. The tomb's centrepiece was an embalmed foetus with a floral wreath on its head and a bouquet in its hands, surrounded by posed skeletons of adults, children and other foetuses holding memento mori-themed banners. The cabinets also held phials containing baby heads, embellished with caps and collars crafted from lace and damask, which appear to be sleeping rather than dead. Ruysch often used the arms of babies adorned with delicate cuffs as a kind of frame or stage for other preparations.

A number of these pieces can be seen at the Kunstkamera in St Petersburg, which houses more than 900 of Ruysch's creations. Sadly, however, Ruysch's most remarkable preparations did not stand the test of time and are known to us today only though illustrations from the catalogues he published to document his collection. The most famous of these are his tableaux featuring posed foetal skeletons holding memento mori symbols, such as mayflies, a scythe or a corroded piece of bone. These figures reside in landscapes crafted from human kidneys, bladder and gall stones, augmented by blood vessels fashioned into the shapes of trees. The tableaux were accompanied by inscriptions meditating on the transitory nature of human life, such as 'Ah Fate, ah bitter Fate' or 'The first hour that gave me life, took it away'.

It was reasonably easy for Ruysch to get such material. In addition to being a physician, he was an obstetrician, an instructor of midwives, a forensic adviser and a praelector anatomicus. Commissioned by the city government, the praealector conducted anatomical lessons in the anatomical theatre of Amsterdam once or twice a year. These lessons were the only opportunity for anatomists and doctors – as well as the general ticket-buying public – to examine real dissected human bodies.

While still a student in Leiden, and in collaboration with the entomologist Jan Swammerdam, Ruysch perfected a special technique for preserving human organs and body parts. Instead of the dry embalming technique used hitherto, he found a way to inject the vessels with coloured waxes and a secret ingredient; he would then preserve the specimens in phials containing alcohol. Ruysch displayed anatomical preparations in at least five rooms of his home on the Bloemgracht in Amsterdam. He confided to one of his visitors that if he combined all the body parts housed within, they would form more than 200 human bodies. Ruysch's remarkable technique led to a huge improvement in anatomical knowledge, enabling him, and others, to study the structure of the human body in the tiniest detail for as long as necessary.

The remarkable aesthetic qualities of Ruysch's preparations have led some modern scholars to describe his collection as 'bizarre', 'extravagant' or 'baroque'. They also raise the question of whether we should view Ruysch as primarily a scientist or an artist. However, there is hardly any evidence that visitors in the early 18th century would have been troubled by such distinctions. They were certainly amazed by the spectacle that Ruysch's rooms presented, but no one would have questioned his integrity as a scholar or scientist. There were some negative comments made by his contemporaries about his collections, but these usually came from rivals who envied his skills as a prosector. Today, we expect scientific knowledge to be presented in a neutral, transparent and objective way, but in Ruysch's time collectors were expected to present their holdings in an appealing way. And Ruysch knew how to do this like no other.

In order to understand his creations as his contemporaries would have done, we should first remember that the division between art and science, the aesthetic and cognitive, was not as clear cut in Ruysch's time as we expect it to be today. The word 'art' referred to a much broader concept of knowledge that enabled humans to do or make something; it was much more closely related to the modern word 'technique'.

This becomes noticeable when we look at the way Ruysch used the word 'art' (in Dutch, 'konst' or 'kunst') in his writings. He wrote about his anatomical findings extensively, mostly in letters to other scholars. Furthermore, he described his collection meticulously in twelve catalogues; each catalogue – or thesaurus (storehouse), as he called them – described the content of one cupboard. When Ruysch spoke about his 'art', he was usually referring to his new and special method of preparing specimens. He was quite secretive about this, but we now know his technique: first, he would take a small piece of human tissue and press all the fluids out of the veins and vessels. Next, he would dry the vessels by blowing air into them through tiny pipes. Then, using delicate syringes, he would inject a mixture of wax, red pigments and other ingredients into the vessels to give his specimens the uncanny, rosy flush of life that they still have today. Once the wax had coagulated, he would carefully place the preparation in a phial containing alcohol, usually hanging it from the lid with a horsehair.

For Ruysch, it was a small step to elaborate his 'art' by adding delicate fabrics such as damask and lace to make the preparation more beautiful, or to make arresting combinations of disparate objects. It belonged to the same artful process as making fascinating and visually appealing preparations.

In addition to acknowledging the fluid relationship between art and science, and handiwork and knowledge, we should remember that the human body was perceived in a fundamentally different way in Ruysch's time. It was not seen as the autonomous result of evolution, but as a construct: an artifice of divine will and the crowning glory of God's creation. As the product of a creating entity, the body was compared with man-made artefacts. In the writings of Ruysch and the many poems that visitors wrote in praise of his cabinet, the complexity of the design of the human body was often stressed by comparisons to works made by man. For example, Ruysch described a handkerchief into which one of the crying foetuses wept over its short life as 'a very thin membrane, saturated with countless tiny, red-coloured arteries, of which the serpentine course amusingly represents an actual embroidery'. The handkerchief reminded Ruysch of Psalm 139, which describes how God wrought the human body as a piece

of your Omnipotence, purely art, Like embroidery neat entwined...' The visitor referred to the art and omnipotence of God, but this wonder was only made visible through the art of Ruysch.

The embroidery metaphor stresses the intricacy of the human body. The cabinet contained many visual bridges between handwoven fabric and the tissue found within the human body, such as the foetal skeleton holding the handkerchief. Ruysch also created decorative covers for his phials from a variety of luxurious fabrics, along with diligently prepared membranes and skins drawn from the human body. According to Ruysch, these covers functioned on two levels: 'All these covers appear to us very red and elegant, in which the blood vessels, filled with a red kind of wax, are countless; this is not only pleasing to see, but is also useful for one who likes to verify accurately the course of the arteries.' A foetus lying in a tomb wore a nightgown made from the membrane of a sheep 'through which many red filled arteries run, replacing a silk embroidered spread'. In an illustration of one jar, the borderline between bodily tissue and tissue made by man is deliberately blurred. The jar contains a child's arm, with a slice of an infected testicle on the right and a fragment of an ulcerated uterus on the left. The delicate structure of the lace fluently transfers into the human tissue of the uterus.

Ruysch viewed the human body as a godly piece of needlework and even wrongly believed that the whole body, apart from the bones, was constructed from tiny vessels. He believed it was only the inadequacy of the human eye that prevented us from seeing this. For Ruysch and his contemporaries, the aesthetic and scientific qualities of these collections were not seen as divergent. On the contrary, God had created nature beautifully and man could enhance this beauty even more through his arts. They believed that in the first paradisiacal state, nature, including the human body, was harmonious and perfect, and it was the Fall of Man that had wiped out this perfection, bringing painful discomforts such as disease and death. The art of Ruysch tried to dissolve these agonies that disturbed human life.

As a physician, Ruysch tried to cure diseases and prevent people from dying; as an anatomist and prosector, he prevented dead material from further decay and restored and immortalized their life-like qualities. His art enabled him to learn more about the wondrous and textile-like microcosm of the human body, that godly piece of embroidery.

Eleanor Crook

# anatomical expressionism

or an anatomically inclined artist, a cadaver is an underworld to explore, a labyrinthine and layered place beset by ignorance, technique, taboo, revulsion and dissolution. You would not enter without a mortal question that is always fundamentally the same. What is life? As though death could provide the answer.

Many have entered the depths of a body in search of the secrets of life and consciousness to return only with a more fractured understanding of physical structures, organized matter, flows, conduits, cells and networks. Such things can give the illusion of knowledge yet make the secrets of life more impenetrable. Artists who journey into the corpse using their eyes and fingers return changed by the experience, darkened and made tense, captivated by the intricacies and repulsed by the gross matter. The structural complexity makes the mind whirl, while the frustrations of the journey, depending on one's personality, leads to macabre hilarity or pessimism. Contrary to what many people think, artists who enter the body as privileged guests of the medical profession do not affect a professional detachment. The proper stance of the anatomical artist is professional attachment.

I am speaking as an anatomical sculptor, a maker of wax medical models, écorché figures in bronze and wax, effigies with more than a whiff of the tomb. I am one of the tribe that have been initiated into first-hand anatomical study – sculpting and drawing in dissecting rooms and pathology collections, training alongside medical students through my work as a medical artist and modelmaker – and am privileged to be given access to a specialist field in order to illustrate it and make memorials of surgical achievements and rare conditions. With this background, I can always spot

heightened awareness of the cadaver's charge. The sensibility of these sinew-pluckers transcends style and historical period: right there on the surface of the artwork is its imprint, a nervous tension, an exaggerated attention to anatomical fact, an X-ray penetration of the body's surfaces and layers, a feeling that the body is about to fail and fall (cadaver means that which falls). Very often their artworks exude an abysmal, gleeful threat of mortality. To contemplate them is to be reminded that one's own body will fail and that death awaits it, as all others. 'Memento mori,' they seem to say: remember that you must die. I call this sensibility, this style of figuration, Anatomical Expressionism.

One reason for the artist to repeat the doomed search within the body of the dead is to heighten their power of expression. The body hides its secrets with exquisite mechanisms, and its materials are various:

**Bone**, the body's most Gothic part, architectural, delineated, polished, haematopoietic
**Muscle**, where we are Baroque, our curvature and upholstery, our *primum mobile*
**Fat**, our emotional and hormonal store, butter-yellow and globular, changeable and swelling
**Fascia**, iridescent membrane that organizes our sections and encloses us like corsets of shot-silk
**Vessels**, the tubular labyrinth of endless flow, dilation and constriction
**Nerves**, our electric inner thicket, whose count-less connections may not even end within us
**Sinews**, the body's strain and taut vibration, our toughness and fibrous resolve
**Hair**, which outlasts us, minute pipelets of horny extrusions
**Blood**, a juice of cells and antibodies, proteins and platelets

I respect and envy those artists and anatomist-sculptors who have tackled this head-on, missed out the middleman and made their body representations actu-

corpse itself, object of love and loathing. For my part, I use the next best thing available – wax, wood, occasionally wigs and acrylic teeth. Preservers of actual remains are more direct. Not for them the replication and substitution of life-like materials: they reuse the dead and resurrect their parts as animate objects. Here we find the mummifiers, the headshrinkers, the wax injectors, the scrapers of skulls, the bottlers, the tanners, the taxidermists, the preservers of saints, the embalmers – those who with every fibre of their being longed to keep the plump and rosy blush of life in that which fades and shrivels.

Death subjects the body to a giddying, woeful transformation. Deterioration bubbles up and bursts from deep within. Death is a cruel sculptor. Few can look upon its work without horror, and a great deal of human endeavour goes into delaying and concealing the textural and formal distortions. I have long thought that the Catholic belief in bodily resurrection is a colossal and moving act of faith in the teeth of all evidence to the contrary. The body without life rushes to non-being, to combine in the foulest way with every other element and to feed itself promiscuously to vermin. Can we believe this seething stew of juices and glues can reascend to glory, or support consciousness again? What a magnificent act of faith that must be.

Halfway between preservation and replication is the process of casting. First a three-dimensional print of the corpse – freshly dead perhaps, or expertly dissected – is taken in the negative (a hole in the world where the deceased has been), and into the gap is poured a hardening liquid. To paraphrase an advertising slogan of a post-mortem photographer in 19th-century New England, whose memorial work had much in common with that of the *mouleur* (moulder), 'The void is fixed ere the substance fades.' Today, the plastination techniques of Gunther von Hagens and his followers perform the same function, although the petrifying liquid enters the cellular matrix of the body, replacing the water that makes up 70 per cent of the human body.

Cast anatomies and death masks exist in wax, plaster, rubber and terracotta, bringing to mind the filled death voids of the victims of the erupting Mount Vesuvius in ancient times. They are a possessive act, betraying a need to preserve the unpreservable. Occasionally, the making of a permanent memento is an act of judicial punishment and a declaration of ownership by the State: visitors to historic prisons often come across the death masks of inmates or prisoners who were executed. Casts of écorché victims (criminals who were flayed after execution) still instruct art students in muscle anatomy in Britain's Royal Academy Schools. Yet casting alone does not reveal the intricate detail of inner structures. Lungs and livers, for example, appear in negative form in our medical collections. Injected with wax, they are then soaked in acid to destroy the tissue, leaving a tracery of cast wax.

The next step in the illusion is to copy the cast. To present copies of dissections as objects of contemplation or of learning, anatomy must be replicated exactly. Wax has long been the substance of choice. It accepts colour and texture, mimics vessels, fascia (with a little gold dust), sinew and bone, the sheen of skin and, with a varnish (Sandarac resin), the wet flayed surface of myological display. These wax bodies are to be found in half-forgotten medical cabinets all over Europe. They are so expressive because the wax speaks loudly to us. The best wax anatomy fulfils more than a didactic purpose. It teaches us how sorely we may be hurt.

Those artists of any period who seem to have entered the valley of the shadow and returned able to express it in a bearable form present liminal artworks where life and death share an impossible simultaneity. The works of the Austrian Symbolist sculptor Adolfo Wildt or of the early 20th-century Polish prodigy Stanislaw Szukalski, who learned anatomy by dissecting the corpse of his own father, spring to mind as examples of this.

Anatomical Expressionists can be prone to hysterical exaggeration, emotion emerging as neurotic elongation: the bone pressing on awareness, the fingers stretching to what is slipping away. The skull states its presence as though exoskeletal, and the consciousness in swimming eyes is at once here and beyond, adding vivid animation to images of saints. Donatello's gaunt and haunting Mary Magdalen and John the Baptist could hardly be more ambiguously life-like and death-like. Like Proserpina they seem to have eaten the seeds of life and death, like Eurydice they evade our gaze, like Lazarus they are disappointed to return. In the most ghostly apparition of the Renaissance body, Sanmartino's *Veiled Christ* (1753), the veil, a lovingly carved illusion, seems to separate the figure from our world.

The most important body in Christian culture is that of Christ. Images of Christ's corpse doomed to rise and the man doomed to die tend to pall these days, perhaps due to their contradictions, but their power can be felt afresh when conditions are met – verisimilitude, anatomical realism, the simultaneous presence of nervous tension and utter spent force. That a wooden, wax or stone dummy can rekindle our beliefs and hopes seems far-fetched, romantic perhaps, a doomed attempt, but it is one that Anatomical Expressionists have made throughout the ages, knowing that the body is only matter configured to support a life, knowing that the life in our matter can transfer its energy into shaped figures that communicate it to other – future – minds.

Garden of the Fugitives
These plaster casts capture the last moments of people caught in the flow of
volcanic debris that covered the city of Pompeii during the eruption of Mount
Vesuvius in 79 CE. The disaster both annihilated and preserved the Roman
city. Eventually, the bodies decayed, leaving a void in the hardened volcanic
mud; these figures were produced by filling that negative space with plaster.

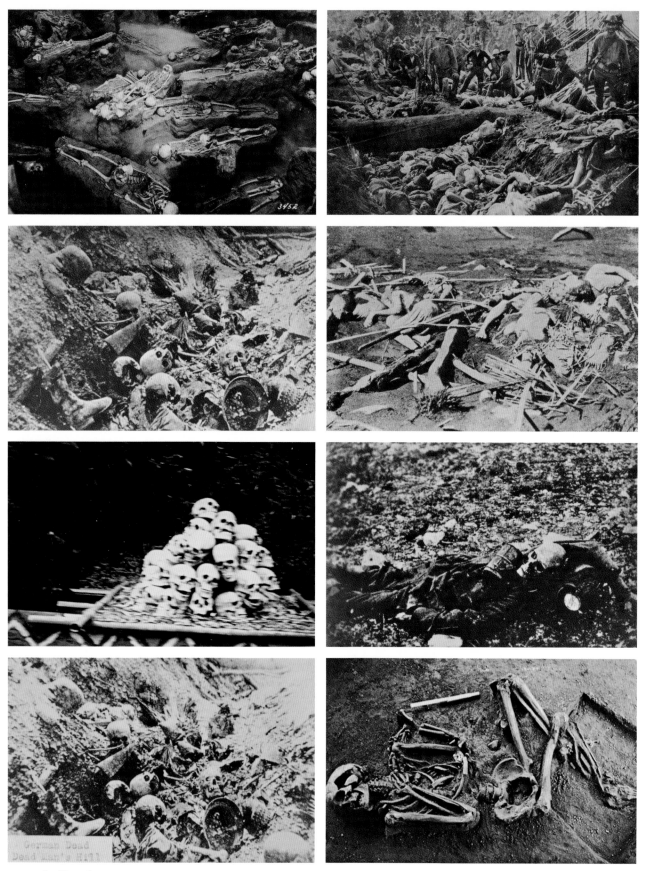

Postcards of burial sites
This collection of 20th-century postcards shows various sites of human remains, from Dickson Mounds Builders Tombs (top left), a Native American burial site dating from 800–1250, in Lewiston, Illinois, to a trench filled with dead bodies after the Battle of Bud Dajo, a US counterinsurgency operation in the Philippines in 1906 (top right).

58

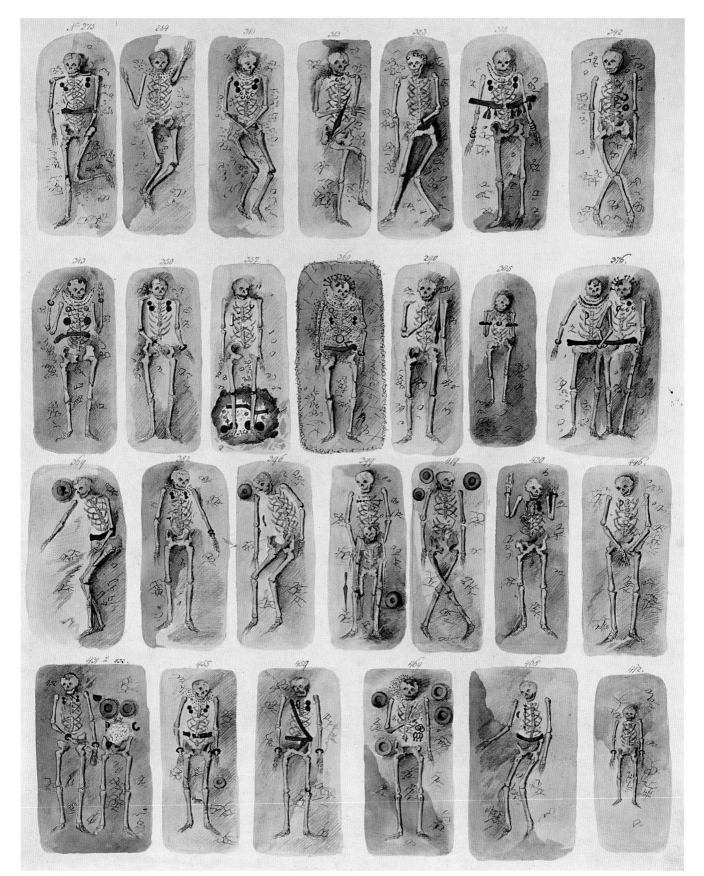

Hallstatt burials
These watercolours depict twenty-seven graves excavated at Hallstatt burial
site near Salzburg, Austria, in 1846. The burials, dating from 800 to 350 BC,
were painted on site by Isidor Engel in 1878. More than 2,000 graves were
found during the excavations, which lasted until 1899. The good condition
of some of the remains was attributed to large deposits of salt in the earth.

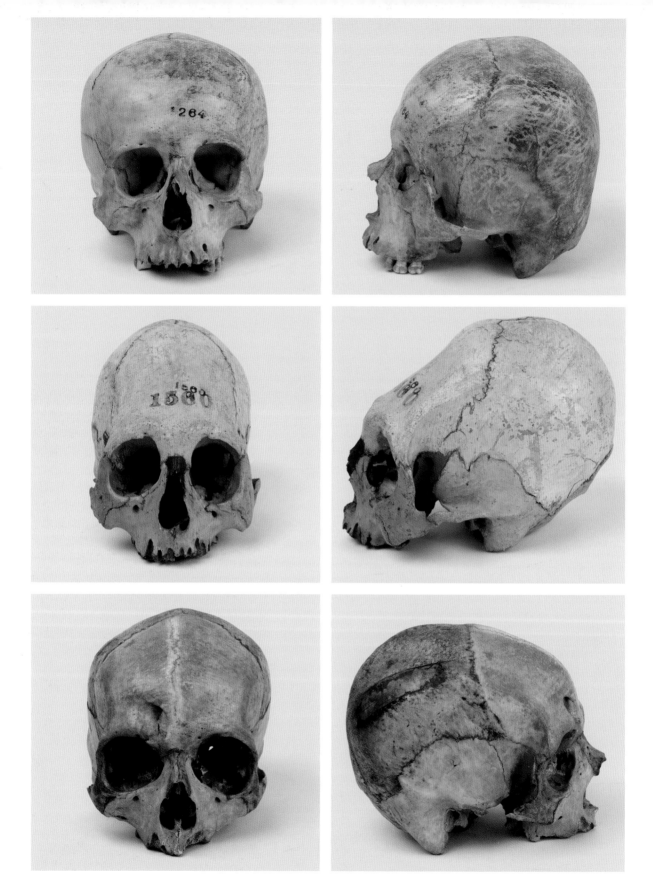

**Skulls of the Andes**
These human skulls (above) date from the 16th century and show evidence of practices common in the Andes, including the flattening or elongation of the skull by cradle boards (top and middle, left and right), and trepanation, or cutting a hole in the skull (bottom left and right), which was sometimes successfully conducted on living people.

**Skulls in anthropology**
Marks and measurements on the skulls and on the images themselves in this series of silver prints, 1904–05 (opposite), suggest that they were used for comparative studies. The comparison of different kinds of skulls was a common practice in 19th- and early 20th-century anatomy and anthropology.

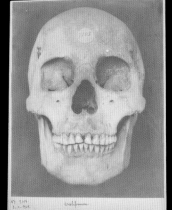
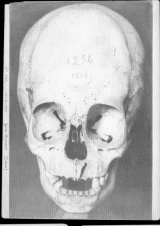
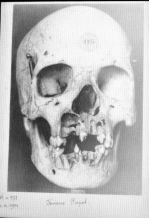
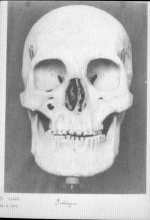

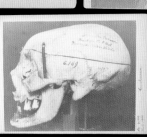
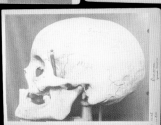
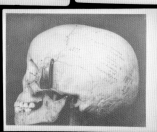

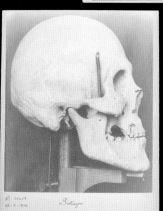
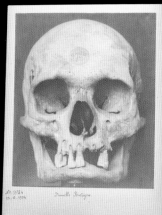
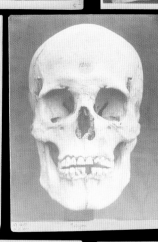
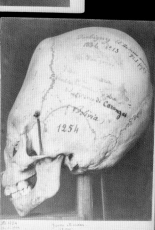

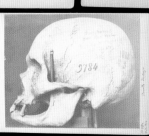
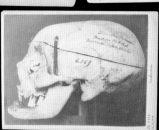
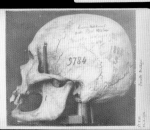

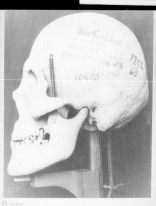
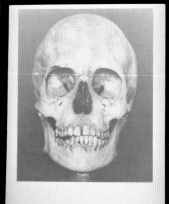
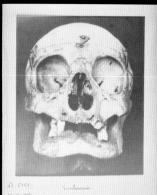
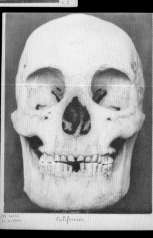

ANDREAE VESALII
BRVXELLENSIS, SCHOLAE
medicorum Patauinæ professoris, de
Humani corporis fabrica
Libri septem

CVM CAESAREAE
Maiest. Galliarum Regis, ac Senatus Veneti gra-
tia & priuilegio, ut in diplomatis eorundem continetur.

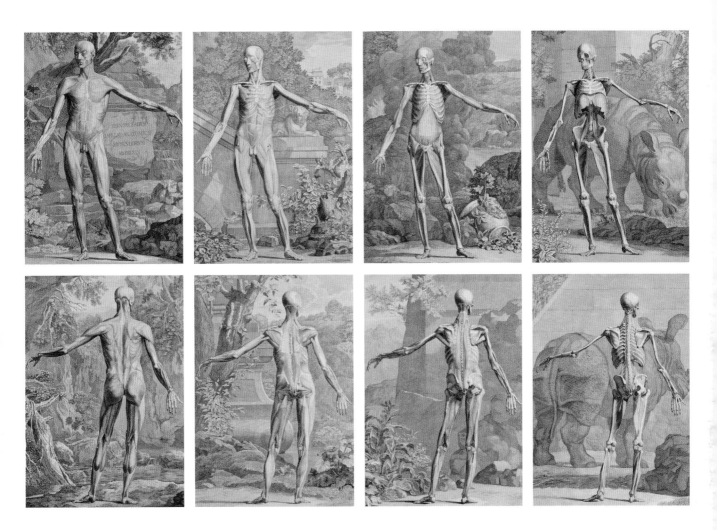

**Vesalius's guide to the human body**
This hand-coloured woodcut frontispiece (opposite) is from Andreas Vesalius's *De humani corporis fabrica*, 1543. The book revolutionized the study of anatomy with its images drawn from real human dissections by Vesalius. Until then, anatomy had been misunderstood because it was based on the work of the Roman physician Galen, who conducted animal dissections.

**Albinus's drawings**
Eight plates from Bernhard Siegfried Albinus's *Tabulae sceleti et musculorum corporis humani*, 1749 (above). Albinus's drawings show the body in various states of dissection, as though alive and animated, in allegorical landscapes that suggest the brevity of life. The images on the right feature Clara the rhinoceros, who was toured around Europe to great acclaim from 1741 to 1758.

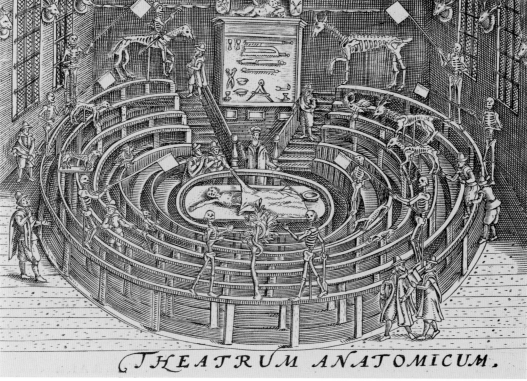

Anatomy as theatre

In the 17th and 18th centuries, human dissections were performed in order to educate and entertain students and the general public. These early 17th-century depictions of the anatomy theatre in Leiden, in the Netherlands, are filled with memento mori imagery, including banners emblazoned with mottoes on the theme of mortality and skeletons posed in allegorical tableaux, such as the skeletal Adam and Eve, who are visible in both images. When dissections were not being conducted, Leiden's anatomical theatre functioned as an early medical museum, making its collections available to the public.

**Guild of Surgeons**

Like other trade guilds in Amsterdam in the 17th century, the Surgeons Guild commissioned paintings of its members and activities, such as *The Osteology Lesson of Dr Sebastiaen Egbertsz*, 1619, by Nicolaes Eliaszoon Pickenoy (top), and *The Anatomy Lesson of Dr Sebastiaen Egbertsz*, 1601–03, by Aert Pietersz (centre). Later in the 17th century, the leading anatomist was Frederik Ruysch, seen here in *Anatomy Lesson of Dr Frederik Ruysch*, 1683, by Jan van Neck (bottom left), and *Anatomy Lesson of Dr Frederik Ruysch*, 1670, by Adriaen Backer (bottom right). Ruysch was famous for developing revolutionary techniques for preserving the human body and for memento mori artworks using human foetal skeletons.

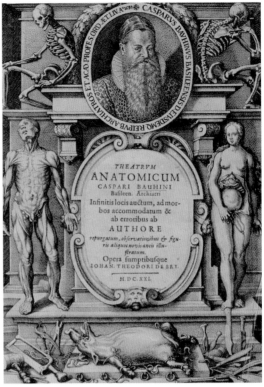

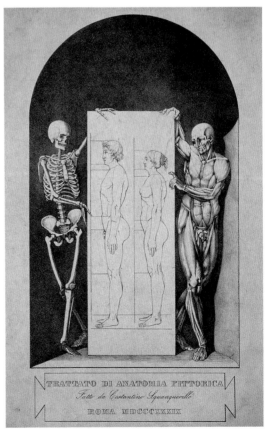

Books of the dead
The frontispieces of 17th-century anatomy books (top) typically juxtaposed the living and the dead surrounded by allegorical symbols. The message in Hans Holbein's Dance of Death, 1554 (bottom left), in *De Doodt vermaskert*, is unequivocal. On the title page of an Italian anatomy book of 1839 (bottom right), a skeleton and écorché demonstrate ideal human proportions.

**Artist anatomists**
Title page by Gilles Demarteau for Charles Monnet's *Etudes d'anatomie
à l'usage des peintres* (A Guide to Human Anatomy for Painters), c. 1770–75.
With the rise of naturalistic artistic representation during the Renaissance,
artists began to study human anatomy. Some artists – most famously Leonardo
da Vinci and Michelangelo – even conducted their own human dissections.

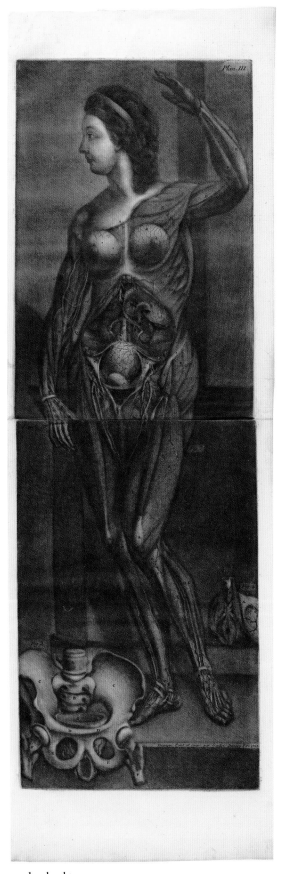

## Under the skin

These four female figures in various states of dissection are by Jacques Fabien Gautier d'Agoty, a French anatomist, artist and printmaker who pioneered a process of colour mezzotint printing for scientific purposes. The use of colour enabled anatomy books to show the different parts of the body, especially veins and muscles, far more clearly than they had before. It also meant that a variety of beautiful effects were newly available to the illustrator; D'Agoty sometimes even coated his illustrations with varnish to enhance their painterly quality. All this serves as a reminder that anatomy in the 18th century was viewed as a fashionable and progressive pursuit appropriate for gentlemen, and that lavishly illustrated anatomy books were luxurious collectibles intended

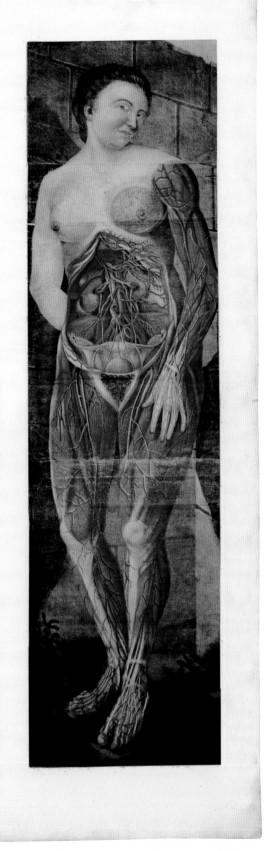

for a non-specialist audience. D'Agoty's son, Arnaud-Éloi Gautier d'Agoty, who went on to create similar anatomical works, famously articulated the problem at the heart of anatomical imagery when he remarked, 'For men to be instructed, they must be seduced by aesthetics, but how can anyone render the image of death agreeable?' Left to right: 'Standing female figure with arms upraised' and 'Standing pregnant woman from side and seated woman with interns open', both from Jacques Fabien's *Anatomie des parties de la generation de l'homme et de la femme*, 1773; anatomical plate, from Jacques Fabien's *Anatomie generale des visceres en situation*, 1752; 'A seated female dissected figure holding a dissected baby', from *Anatomie des parties de la generation de l'homme et de la femme*, 1773.

**Science meets memento mori**

The life-sized écorchés displayed in the Museo di Palazzo Poggi in Bologna were created to demonstrate human musculature. Commissioned by Pope Benedict XIV to serve as the centrepiece for the world's first anatomical wax museum, the four figures were crafted by Ercole Lelli in coloured wax over real skeletons between 1742 and 1751. Lelli had already gained a reputation in northern Italy, not only as a traditional painter of religious themes, but also as an anatomical artist working in wax, having created two life-like wax kidneys and two wooden écorché figures for Bologna's anatomical theatre. Like many artists before him, Lelli sometimes conducted his own

dissections. His display – which also includes an anatomical Adam and Eve and human skeletons posed as angels of death – promoted a scientifically accurate understanding of human anatomy based on dissection while also encouraging a meditation on death as the result of Adam and Eve's original sin in the Garden of Eden. The museum was intended to teach artists, medics and the general public about the divinely rational structure of the human body. Sacred representation and instructional display in equal measure, the exhibition challenges modern lines of demarcation between Church and collection, memento mori and science lesson, body and soul, relic and specimen.

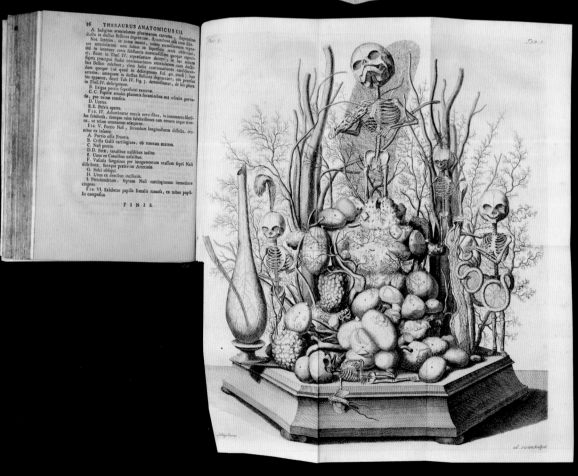

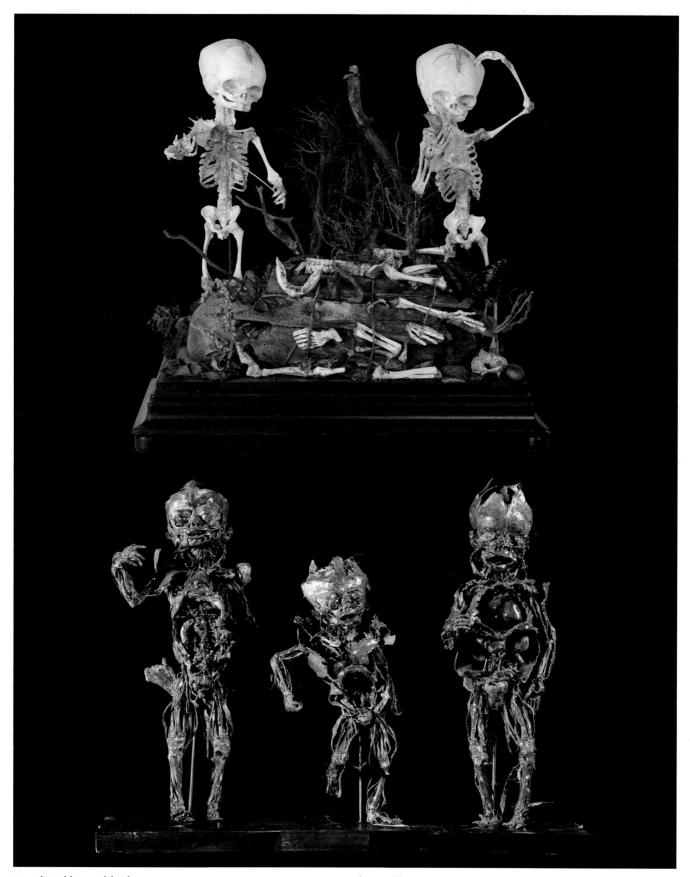

## Ruysch's tableaux of death

Dutch anatomist and artist Frederik Ruysch displayed his specimens and tableaux in a home museum. This guidebook to the museum (opposite) shows two tableaux with foetal human skeletons set into landscapes constructed of gallstones, hardened arteries and other anatomical parts. Ruysch's works were both scientific objects and memento mori.

## The art of human remains

A Ruysch-inspired modern artwork, Michel de Spiegelaere's *Scène Macabre*, 2010 (top), is made from resin and mixed media. Centuries earlier, the artist and anatomist Honoré Fragonard – cousin of painter Jean-Honoré Fragonard – used his own formula to preserve human and animal remains, which he then posed in tableaux. He created these foetuses (bottom) between 1766 and 1771.

## Death in Naples

Giuseppe Sanmartino's *The Veiled Christ*, 1753, was commissioned by the Prince of Sansevero, Raimondo di Sangro, for his Sansevero Chapel in Naples. Some people thought the sculpture was too life-like to have been created by art alone and accused the prince – who was also an inventor, writer and scientist – of using an alchemical technique of 'marblization' to preserve a real human body. Around the same time, the prince also commissioned *The Anatomical Machines*, two real human skeletons overlaid with recreations of the circulatory system and viscera. These models were so accurate that some contemporaries believed the prince had killed and preserved two of his own servants. The models were housed in a room of his palace known as the 'Apartment of the Phoenix,' an allusion to death and resurrection.

**Voyage of despair**
*Heads of Torture Victims* (top left) and *Head of a Guillotined Man* (top right) were both painted by French Romantic painter Théodore Gericault in c. 1819 as preparatory studies for his masterwork *The Raft of the Medusa*, 1818–19 (bottom). The inspiration for Gericault's painting was a disaster in which a French naval ship, *Méduse*, ran aground on a sandbank, thus forcing survivors who had not managed to squeeze into the lifeboats to set out on a makeshift raft. During the thirteen days it took to rescue the craft, all but fifteen of the 150 passengers died, and those who were left were forced to resort to cannibalism. Although this epic larger-than-life-sized painting, which depicts death so vividly, was quite controversial, it was also highly praised at its debut at the Paris Salon of 1819.

**Anatomical Venus**
This life-sized, dissectable wax woman (above) – with real human hair, glass eyes and a string of pearls – was created under the artistic leadership of Clemente Susini in c. 1780–82 to teach the general public about human anatomy. It formed the centrepiece of the Museum for Physics and Natural History, better known as La Specola, in Florence. The Anatomical Venus has seven layers, each anatomically correct element the product of an artist and anatomist working in tandem. Removal of the final layer reveals a foetus in the womb. The Anatomical Venus was so popular that she inspired a variety of spin-offs, including, in the 19th century, the Anatomical Venus (opposite) by French doctor Pierre Spitzner that once toured the fairgrounds of Europe. This example can be dissected into forty parts.

76

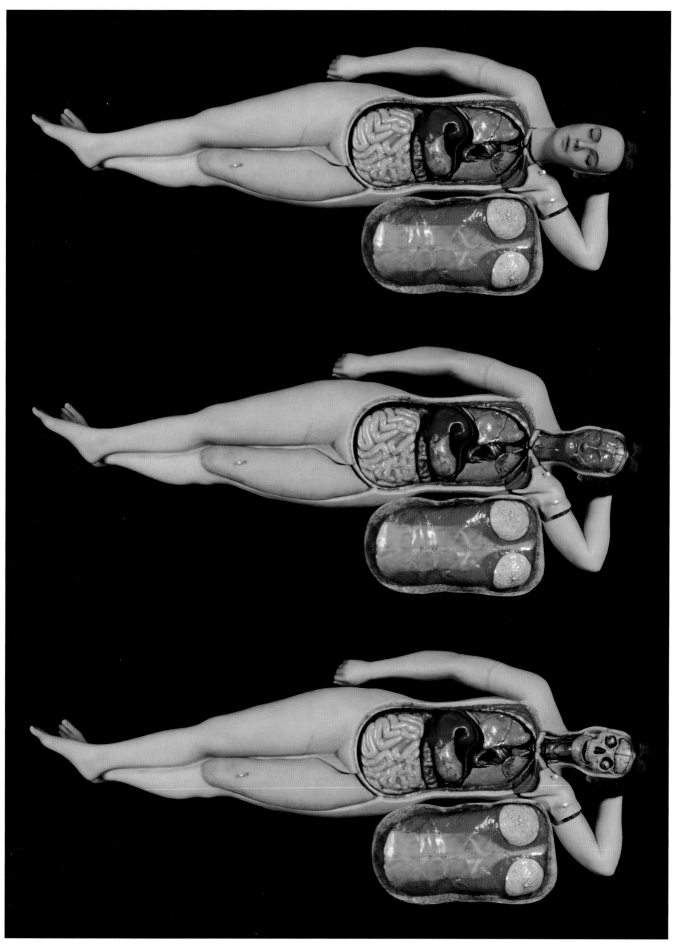

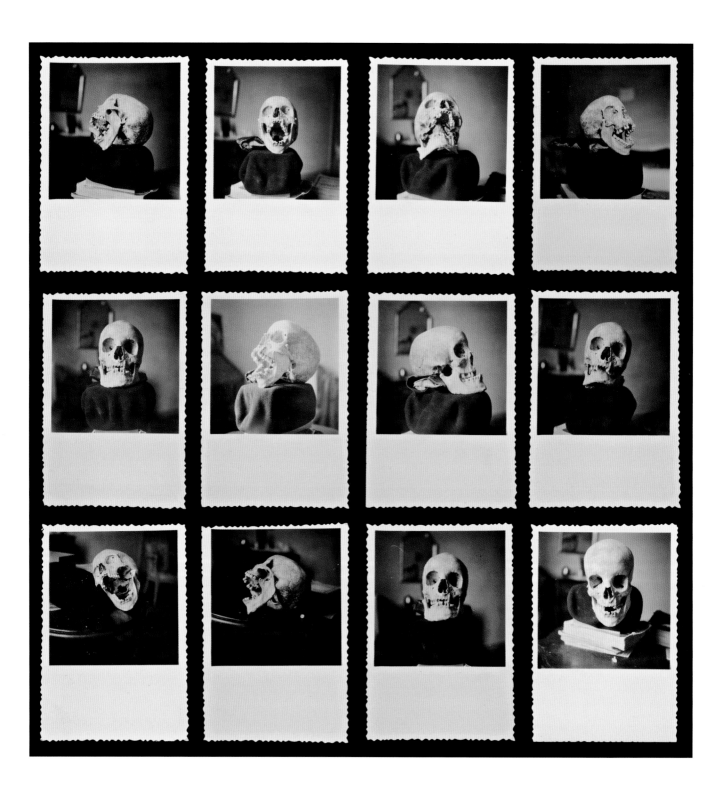

**Death of the unknown**
In this 20th-century series of photographs of a human skull by an unknown
maker for an unknown purpose, we see a skull posed in what appears to be a
private home. On the back of each image is written, simply, 'le Crâne,' (skull).
The final photograph, with the skull posed on a pile of books, is redolent of
a memento mori still life.

*Anatomical Crucifixion (James Legg)*
In 1801, the body of murderer James Legg was, at the request of three artists of London's Royal Academy, nailed to a cross in order to settle a long-standing question about whether artistic representations of the Crucifixion were anatomically correct. His body was then flayed and cast so that the musculature could be studied in detail.

# memorializing the
# DEAD

*Mummifiers, head collectors and death cults*

THE MORTICIAN'S ART

Human relics

*Anatomical Christ*

CATACOMBS AND BONE CHAPELS

The sleeping dead

John Troyer

# playing with dead faces

I grew up playing with dead faces. It's true. In my youth I spent many hours designing deathly grimaces for a skull that my father gave me as a gift. In fact, I clearly remember the day he presented me with the skull and the other materials I would need to build dead human faces – moulding wax, make-up and sculpting tools. Hours would pass as I built noses, eyes, mouths and ears that were then worked onto the skull and blended into the surrounding waxy visage. I was particularly proud of the wounds I made, suggesting a horrible trauma had affected the decedent's face. These memories mark the heyday of my post-mortem facial reconstruction years. I was between six and ten years old.

Building dead faces was completely normal in my house. My father, Ron Troyer, was a faculty member at the Cincinnati College of Mortuary Science during the 1980s and taught courses on cosmetology, facial reconstruction, restorative arts and the general preservation of the dead. He was also a funeral director for more than three decades in the states of Indiana, Minnesota, Ohio and Wisconsin, so I came by my interest in facial reconstruction the old-fashioned way – by asking my dad about his job. Indeed, both my parents recognized my youthful exuberance for making wax faces, so they never tried to stop me. The skull that my father gave me was a standard issue polyurethane 'teaching head' that mortuary science students used in their classes. The more gifted and talented students often built 'historical faces', and I clearly remember seeing busts of Abraham Lincoln and Fagin from *Oliver Twist* in what I called the college's dead head cabinet. It was really just a storage closet with shelves in which students kept their reconstructive projects between classes. I loved staring into the waxy gazes of those multiple free-floating faces on visits to the college.

It seemed only natural, then, that I received my own restorative arts skull, a box of moulding wax and the tools to start building faces. I vividly remember working with the wax to make my art class skull 'come alive' with a dead face.

I could not know it then, but those dead faces and my childhood hobby would help shape my own career development. As it happens, I am the Director of the University of Bath's Centre for Death and Society, the world's only interdisciplinary research centre that focuses on death, dying and the dead body. I specialize in the connections between the dead body and technology (old, new and speculative).

I was no child savant who took facial reconstruction wax and transformed it into an Anatomical Venus, complete with Play-doh organs. I never achieved anything like the 18th-century anatomical waxes on display at La Specola in Florence, or came close to the contemporary waxwork artistry of Eleanor Crook, a proper artist whose lectures and demonstrations on repairing anatomical wax figures always remind me of my youth.

What working with wax did teach me was that in death, most people's faces could be transformed. The entire concept of a 'dead face' changed as I worked the lips into a smile or tried leaving one eye open and one closed. The eyes were always the trickiest anatomical structure for me, since creating a life-like open eyeball with wax and make-up requires real skill. Decades later I would learn about taxidermists using glass eyeballs for animal mounts and think to myself – if only I'd had those for my waxy dead faces.

Twenty years later, during my PhD research on 19th-century post-mortem preservation technologies (photography, embalming, taxidermy, etc.), I realized that my childhood skull was itself part of a long tradition in the handling of dead bodies that changed how 'dead' a dead body looked. During the Industrial Revolution in America in the mid-19th century, funeral practices used many new mechanical tools to modify human biology. In particular, the development of post-mortem photography and of reproducible mechanical-chemical embalming radically altered the modern way of death. An image of a person soon after death could be captured so that they looked 'asleep', while chemically preserving a dead body delayed organic decomposition for extended periods of time.

By technologically removing dead bodies from the everyday experience of human time, 19th-century preservationists unintentionally created a new problem for post-industrial humans – how 'natural' or 'normal' do these preserved faces look? Do we recognize the deceased in death or is this new dead face a poorly crafted shock to the senses? How 'dead' are dead people supposed to look now? And what is a dead face supposed to look like anyway?

My childhood experience of using simple tools to create wax faces eventually opened my adult eyes to how difficult it is to make the dead look real but also a little less dead. I say this as a person who grew up around more dead bodies than I can count, and who paid close attention to the cosmetic and facial work performed by my father on his own dead parents. Grandma and Grandpa Troyer were most certainly dead at their funerals, but they looked good in their caskets. I will go so far as to say that they looked better dead than in the days leading up to their deaths.

A key part of my research focuses on the future of dead body preservation and post-mortem restorative arts, since the rationale supporting any preservative process will eventually change, as it did when embalming became common during the 19th and 20th centuries. In the 19th century, early American embalmers focused on germ theory and hygiene to rationalize the process; by the 20th century embalming had come to embrace the cosmetic enhancement of the dead. Legitimate critiques of the use of embalming emerged during its earliest days, and those have never disappeared. Critics argue that chemical embalming is unnecessary, bad for the environment, unnatural and an invasive process that disconnects grieving family members from the true face of death.

I often remind those working on all sides of the preservation debate that while current embalming technology has been used in roughly the same form for the past 150 years, it too will change. At this juncture in modern First World death practices, I expect to see the development of new preservation systems that are relatively chemically free, non-invasive and semi-permanent. I have no idea who or whom will create these new tools, but the traditional restorative arts used to preserve dead faces are due for an upgrade. What will not change, I think, is the underlying desire of many people to see their deceased loved one dead, but not too dead.

The art and science of dead body preservation was never about using only one technology; it involved a mixture of tools and concepts. Just as 21st-century digital scans of dead bodies for families that do not want any kind of invasive post-mortem examination are slowly replacing the anatomical autopsy, so digital overlays might reconstruct dead faces without using any kind of wax, cosmetics or preservative chemicals. Think of this speculative technology as a new kind of digital death mask.

I still have the skull from my childhood. It is a prized memento mori possession that moves with me no matter where I live. I almost lost it during the mid-1980s when some neighbourhood kids created a haunted house for Hallowe'en, but I managed to get it back. The skull currently sits on a shelf in my house and constantly reminds me of where I have been in my life, and what I will eventually become.

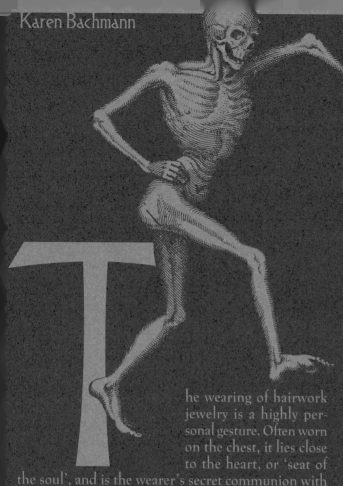

Karen Bachmann

# the power of hair as human relic in mourning jewelry

**T**he wearing of hairwork jewelry is a highly personal gesture. Often worn on the chest, it lies close to the heart, or 'seat of the soul', and is the wearer's secret communion with the departed. One of my favourite pieces, a pendant commemorating the architect Sir William Chambers in the collection of London's Victoria & Albert Museum, is oval in shape and rather large at almost 5 centimetres (2 inches) long and nearly 4 centimetres (1 inch) wide. The frame is made of gold and set within it, under glass, a border of plaited hair encloses a hair 'wheatsheaf' bound with a band of diamonds. The wheatsheaf motif, known as the Vasa crest, is associated with the Swedish royal family (Sir William was Swedish by birth), but it also represents the harvest, the fruit of hard labour and the passing of the seasons. On the back of the pendant, an oval border in plaited hair contains an inscription in seed pearls: 'Sir William Chambers died 8th March 1796. Aged 74'. This pendant is both a public commemoration and a private remembrance of the deceased. We see the inlaid pearl inscription only when the piece is turned over.

In contrast, another piece, from my own collection, is a jet locket with a tied bundle of hair under glass. It is 4 centimetres (1½ inches) long and 2.5 centimetres (1 inch) wide. Unlike the Chambers pendant, this piece is modest: an oval frame of polished jet (commonly used in mourning jewelry), with the interwoven initials 'IMO' (In Memory Of) carved on one side. The upper serifs of the 'I' droop sadly like weeping willow

branches, while the base flares out like a tree trunk. An 'x' in the centre of the 'M' unites all three letters. In addition, the 'M' has a circular motif on each side, giving the overall impression of a locked gate. On the back of the locket, a plain silver bezel contains light brown hair mounted on white fabric and tied with a small piece of yellowed thread. It is not a custom-made piece, but rather a stock item sold by jewelers, in which people inserted the hair of their loved one themselves.

In my career as a fine jeweler, I have created many pieces from precious gems and noble metals. Well-crafted and beautiful such jewelry may be, but it often lacks personal resonance. With an interest in unusual materials gained from my background in sculpture, I found myself powerfully drawn to mourning jewelry combining fine materials with the elemental property of human hair. The jet locket, bought some twenty years ago, was the first piece I purchased. As my collection of mourning jewelry grew, I became fascinated by the history and hidden meanings of the genre. Where did the tradition arise? Why is it so enduring? Why hair?

Mourning jewelry can be traced to the Middle Ages. 'Speaking' reliquaries – receptacles made in the shape of body parts to hold saintly relics – may be seen as not-so-distant cousins of hairwork jewelry. An arm reliquary might contain only one part of a saint, but it was deemed as powerful and holy as the complete body. In *Body-Part Reliquaries and Body Parts in the Middle Ages*,[1] Caroline Walker Bynum asserts that these containers become 'not so much an expression of what is within as a restoration – even redemption – of the body part'. Such reliquaries could act as 'portable altars' – the saint may be entombed in a church, but their dismembered part might travel (such as in church processions) to 'act' on his or her behalf. These human relics (bone, mummified organ, lock of hair, tooth, scrap of fabric, etc.) serve as 'loci of power, indicators and transmitters of power'.[2]

The concept of a relic standing in for an entire person is key to our understanding of the iconography of hair in mourning jewelry. Equally important is the idea of the portability of the relic – it goes where the bearer (or wearer in the case of jewelry) goes.

In the case of mourning jewelry incorporating human hair, the identity of the person to whom the hair belonged is known to the wearer. Aside from some form of engraved name, not obvious to others, the hair represents a private communion between the wearer and the deceased. According to cultural historian Dr Christiane Holm, 'The wearer of remembrance jewelry presents herself as a participant in a hidden intimate network, from which other viewers are excluded. Mourning jewels are exhibited secrets.'[3] The preserved hair, tooth, bit of ribbon, etc. are relics of someone not present; they speak of their intimate connection to the wearer. Without the wearer, they are mere curiosities and seem doubly disconnected – from the body to which they once belonged and from the individual who misses that person.

The emotional value attached to these highly personal relics drove demand for mourning jewelry. During the 17th and 18th centuries, there was an extremely high infant mortality rate, and death was everywhere. The keeping and saving of hair for future use in jewelry or other commemorative craft (such as wreaths) was common. During the Victorian era, the 'cult of the dead' became almost a mania in Britain. Death was everywhere. The death of Prince Albert in 1861 affected Queen Victoria so deeply that she went into mourning for forty years, wearing only black and avoiding all unnecessary public appearances. She had locks of Albert's hair incorporated into various pieces of jewelry, which she wore every day for the rest of her life. This ritual greatly influenced the wider population, and lockets and other articles of jewelry containing hair became the 19th-century version of the portable relic.

Just as a relic is a physical token of a saint's former presence on Earth, commemorative hair jewelry exists to remind us that the departed once lived. It allows the mourner to communicate with the deceased. According to Dr Kathleen M. Oliver, hair acquired the status of a fetish object: 'Because commemorative hairwork jewelry contains a potential sentient part of the decedent and represents a final gift from the beloved, it holds the potential to function as a fetish-ized substitute for the loved one.'[4] The hair acts as a material expression of love that connects the deceased to the bereaved. The hair's corporeality serves as both memento mori and tangible proof that one may exist after death to comfort the bereaved.

Hair does not attain relic status until it is removed from the head. The act of cutting creates a literal and mystical separation between hair and body; it is a rite by which the hair is transformed into personal relic and a model of remembrance. The hair's cut edge represents the transition from natural artefact to cultural relic, when, Oliver says, 'the present presence of the body is anticipated as a future absence.'[5]

The remains that one generally finds in reliquaries (or any other well-preserved coffin or sarcophagus) tend to be bones, teeth, fingernails and hair due to their resistance to decay. Unlike the soft tissue of the body, which starts to decompose almost immediately after death, these body parts may last thousands of years. It is a misconception, however, that the hair and nails continue to grow post-mortem. Dehydration and desiccation of the soft tissues create the false impression of increased hair and nail growth as the skin recedes around the follicles and nail beds. Before the scientific explanation for this, people thought hair and nails were imbued with magical powers. The skin of a corpse could be observed to shrink and lose colour, while the hair and nails remained unchanged. Hair, more specifically, would appear just as it had when the person was alive, imbuing it with relic status as something immortal. Mummified and embalmed remains demonstrate this phenomenon. Hair has the unique communicative power of growing from a living thing, yet being resistant to decay, conveying a sense of immortality. It is dead, yet undead; living, yet unliving. While bones represent the interior of the human body, hair is associated with the outside, by which we recognize a person. Hair is a manifestation of our individuality, with its own colour, texture and style. Long and luxuriant, curly or short, gleaming or dull, the tactile and sensory qualities associated with hair evoke the individual. Eyes may be the windows of the soul, but hair is the body's crowning icon of immortality.

If we can understand hair to be a physical manifes-tation of an absent loved one, we can grasp the spiritual and emotional comfort of wearing that hair. To have a personal relic of someone in an item that may be worn is to keep that person with us at all times. To appreciate hairwork jewelry, it is necessary to under-stand the significance of hair as human artefact loaded with sentimental meaning as well as the importance of wearing the jewelry. The hair has been transmuted from the personal relic of a human long gone, and possibly forgotten, into a wearable icon of everlasting remembrance. To those who love and appreciate the genre, the collecting and wearing of hairwork jewelry keeps alive the original intent of the maker and the memory of the person whose hair is encased, even if that person is anonymous to us. The hair retains its status as a personal relic, even though we may not know the identity of the person revered. We are meant to regard the work with veneration – as it has attained the status of human relic in its reliquary container.

# the anatomy of holy transformation

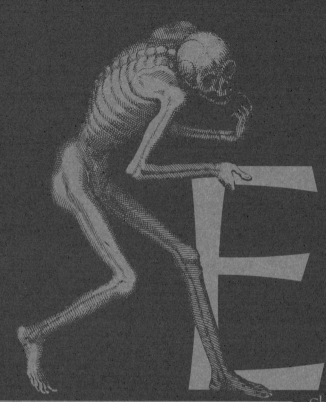

Everyone will have encountered the crucified Christ. Images and statues of the cruelly tortured body are commonplace. They often hang or lie unnoticed, but a believing Christian will see the Son of God, who died to take away the sins of the world and give eternal life, transforming the worst torture into a sign of victory. So what do we see when we look at the crucified Christ, what do we know, and what do we believe, especially when looking at the more extreme representations that exist? The questions are particularly perplexing when we look at the small figures that are the subject of this text – the Anatomical Christs.

So far, I have found nine of these small wax Christ figures. Dating from the 17th and 18th centuries, these tender and delicate models show the usual bleeding wounds of the crucified Christ, but their particularity lies in a small 'door' on the belly, which – when opened – reveals the internal organs of Christ. These organs are depicted without blood and are cleanly arranged in line with the anatomical wax preparations of the period. A window on body parts associated with analytical science, the empirical view on the human body, this miniature construction in the middle of the central symbol of Christianity is like a scandalous, secret little box.

Very little is known about these figures. They are found across Europe, from Berlin to Sicily, but no one knows exactly where and when they were first made, or for what purpose. There are many theories and assumptions. A name that comes up over and over again in attempts to understand the Anatomical Christ is the Sicilian sculptor Gaetano Zumbo (1656–1701), whose work appears to share similar concepts. Zumbo is often credited with being the creator of the first anatomical wax model, made with the help of French surgeon and anatomist Guillaume Desnoues.[1]

Zumbo was regarded as a master carver of wax models of human bodies, living, dead and in a state of putrefaction (after falling out with Desnoues, Zumbo is thought to have conducted his own dissection). Among his works are tiny tableaux reminiscent of the cribs, depicting events in the life of Christ, that are traditionally carved in Sicily, Zumbo's birthplace.[2] However, Zumbo's pieces show grisly scenes populated by the dead and dying. Called *teatrini*, little theatres, or 'plague-boxes', they are in the tradition of memento mori.[3]

One of Zumbo's most famous works is a life-sized, scientifically accurate anatomical head, flayed on one side. Despite being a medical teaching object, the head has a religious air, its angle and shape reminding the viewer of the iconography of Christ. The contrast between Zumbo's theatres of death and the head suggests a connection between medicine and the divine: the decaying flesh of the *teatrini* shows no signs of hope and disintegrates to become indistinguishable from the earth, while the analytical anatomy of the head, the head of the Saviour, shows no signs of pain or suffering. Rather, its expression suggests a knowledge and transcendence beyond the physical, while the small drop of blood on the undissected nasal skin may point to the vulnerability of the purely earthly body.

Zumbo's *teatrini* are displayed in Florence's La Specola Museum, which contains a large number of anatomical waxworks created by the leading practitioners of the art. The male figures in the collection, usually skinless and revealing the bones and musculature that give the body its strength and posture, attributes controlled by will, are reminiscent of Greek heroes and Christian martyrs. They appear as sacred incarnations of a knowledge beyond this flesh. The female figures, named Venus (goddess), Maria (saint) and Eva (human, of flesh and blood), on the other hand, have flawless skin and their bodies are human flesh-caskets of divine incarnation beyond human will and knowledge. They are either dissectable – one can lift their breastplate to examine successive layers of the dissected body – or are in a state of static autodissection, in which entrails gush from huge bloodless openings. Their facial expressions are variously described as erotic, suffering or ecstatic, veering between Eros and Thanatos, life and death, pleasure and pain.[4]

The 'material', the wax, could help put the Anatomical Christs in a context that makes them readable. As an organic material, wax stands close to flesh. Change is inherent in the wax; it is unstable and contradictory, but it is also associated with purity and virginity by virtue of the bee. It was for this last reason, and its ability to mimic flesh, that wax was a symbol for Mary and the incarnation of Christ, for the transformation of the flesh and the body, and the sacrificed body and its resurrection. With its almost limitless plasticity, which allows it to accept any state, colour and texture, the wax pushes the boundaries of materiality. Wax raises questions about boundaries.

While the anatomists violently destroyed the creation of God in order to understand it, the Church used anatomy to reveal the mysteries of the body, the inner organs in which the miraculous transformations of life and death take place.[5] The female and male figures represented two paths to the knowledge of the divine: while the female body made the place of divine transformations visible, the male body pointed to something beyond the visible flesh – the true body of Christ.

The study of human anatomy profited from being placed in a religious context. Curiosity was no longer a sacrilege, a sin against creation. The anatomist cast light on the divine event of creation, and the dissecting table became an altar. Like God, who would unite the pieces of the body at the resurrection, the anatomist reassembled the scattered parts of the body into a true body. Thus, the iconographic echoes of the dead Christ in representations of dissected corpses is not surprising. Christ can be seen as *the* anatomical body.

But what happens when the miracle of divine creation appears as a destroyed body, a decaying corpse, a pure biological thing? The philosopher and psychoanalyst Julia Kristeva describes Hans Holbein's Dead Christ as a body that appears so dead that one wonders how he should ever resurrect.[6] The image leaves the viewer as abandoned as Jesus on the cross. The representation of God is, so to speak, dead, throwing the viewer to the border of insignificance. Our eyes are filled with emptiness, which, like the question from the cross ('My God, why did you forsake me') questions everything.[7] At the same time, this is the place where our flesh is touched – whether by pain or by pleasure.

It is assumed that anatomical figures of Christ were used for private devotions and were often found in private chapels, where the devout used them to imagine the passion of Christ, the ultimate bearing of pain, in *Imitatio Christi* (in imitation of Christ). However, in view of the different representations of Christ on the cross (with a 'pure wound'[8], 'carved up flesh'[9] or with a feminine, delicate and flawless body), the question arises as to what exactly should be imitated. The nature of compassion also varied: sometimes it was as an ecstatic celebration of pain, a masochistic enjoyment, other times it expressed a sense of culpability. Both responses aimed at an experience that was bound to the body while also surpassing it: pain and torture were a means of approaching the sacred in the body.[10] The body, then, is the path through which something can be experienced that cannot be grasped intellectually or symbolically. While being touched, the body experiences something without words, without mediation, that writes itself into the body, into the flesh – similar to God's word becoming flesh in the miracle of transubstantiation.

The bodies of the Anatomical Christ figures correspond to the iconography of Italian crucifixes, which
had long stressed the beauty and delicacy of the Christ
figure. In a remarkable way, however, they also resemble
the female anatomical preparations (the Venus, Maria,
or Eva of La Specola), as well as smaller dissectable ivory
mannekins, most often female, in both the posture of
the body and the representation of the anatomy – the
opening in the torso of the otherwise intact body.

However, here the organs are not placed in an
uninjured, untouched body, but in a body with bloody
wounds that are signs of violence. Therein we can note a
similarity to the figures of Zumbo. Moreover, behind the
'door' in these Christ figures, the organs are presented
symbolically rather than realistically, with the focus on
the ribs, heart and, above all, the intestines, ignoring the
'correct' representation of anatomy known at the time.
The choice of the organs seems to point to the mystery of
transformation. Eve was formed from the rib of Adam,
the mystical transformations (food and water becoming
flesh and blood) take place in the intestines, and in the
heart our lives are written down for God: incarnation,
transformation and writing the transcription of life.
The cavities of the anatomical Christ figures are shown
as bloodless, as in the female anatomical preparations,
and the organs are clearly separated from one another.
Only the heart has an injury, from which a few drops of
blood tread out. If one looks at these organs as tangible
parts of the interior, one sees only 'wrong' anatomy. As
symbolic parts of the body however, they point out to
the miraculous creation and transformation beyond
the human will.

The bloodless anatomy of the creation, which is not
subject to man's will and knowledge, is presented here in
the bloody body, which was killed, to know what and who
Christ was. Therefore, the bloody decay of the human
body does not affect the internal organs, which, moreover, do not reveal themselves as the deepest and visible
interior of man. Rather, in this anatomy – in which
the beautiful outer body disintegrates (as in Zumbo's
figures) – a 'false' anatomy shows that it points beyond
itself, to the miracle of creation, the incarnation in the
destruction: a deeply Christian anatomy.

Out of the grave
Enormous boneyards, or ossuaries, containing heaps of bones removed from
old graves in order to make room for new burials, are quite a sight. These
postcards depict ossuaries in the Old Church Boneyard (top), date unknown,
and the Paco Cemetery (middle), c. 1900, both in the Philippines, and in
Colon Cemetery (bottom), c. 1900, in Havana, Cuba.

(73) Trophy of Head-hunter, Formosa. 臺灣緓阿廳外文生番二股頭人首棚 [不許復製]

## Headhunting

These early 20th-century postcards of headhunting – removing and preserving heads, often of enemies killed in battle – show a practice that was once widespread in many parts of the world. Most scholars believe headhunting was primarily for ritual or ceremonial purposes, but some think it was motivated by a belief that the 'soul matter' (mana) or life-force resided at the base of the head. Many groups of aboriginal Taiwanese, including the Formosa people, engaged in headhunting. Postcards clockwise from top: a skull shelf used by Formosa headhunters to store skulls, c. 1911; a 'tomb of bones' at Formosa, 1911; a headhunter holding a brace of skulls, c. 1911.

90

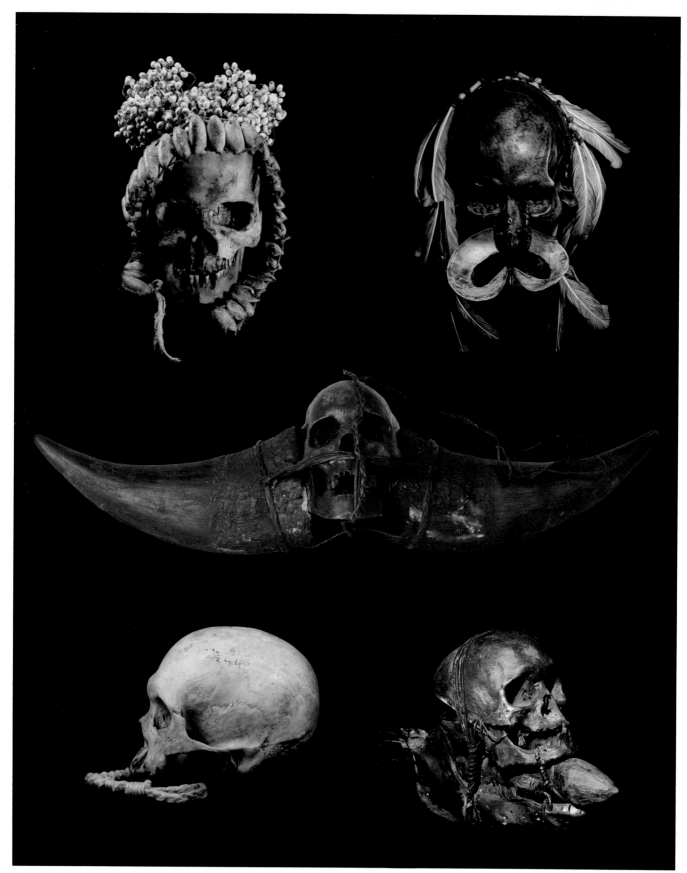

**Skull collection**
The human skull lasts for centuries; it represents that which lies beneath and that which is eternal in us all. Accordingly, the skull has long been used for ritual, religious and metaphoric purposes. In the Western world, it was a popular collectible in the 17th-century cabinet of curiosity, suggesting the memento mori and an easy intimacy with that which frightens us most.

Clockwise from top left: a modern take on the vanitas skull by artist Ryan Matthew Cohn; ancestor skull belonging to the Asmat of Irian Jaya, West Papua, who decorate and preserve the skulls of important relatives; 19th-century headhunter's trophy, Nagaland, India; two headhunted human trophy skulls from the Ifugao tribe of the Philippines. Such skulls, usually acquired during raids on other villages, were believed to have spiritual power.

**Igorot mummies**
These historical postcards show traditional death rituals of the Igorot tribes from Luzon island in the Philippines. The Igorot mummified their dead by salting and smoking the remains, first drawing the legs of the deceased up to the chest (top and middle). The Igorot consult and propitiate the spirits of their ancestors (bottom).

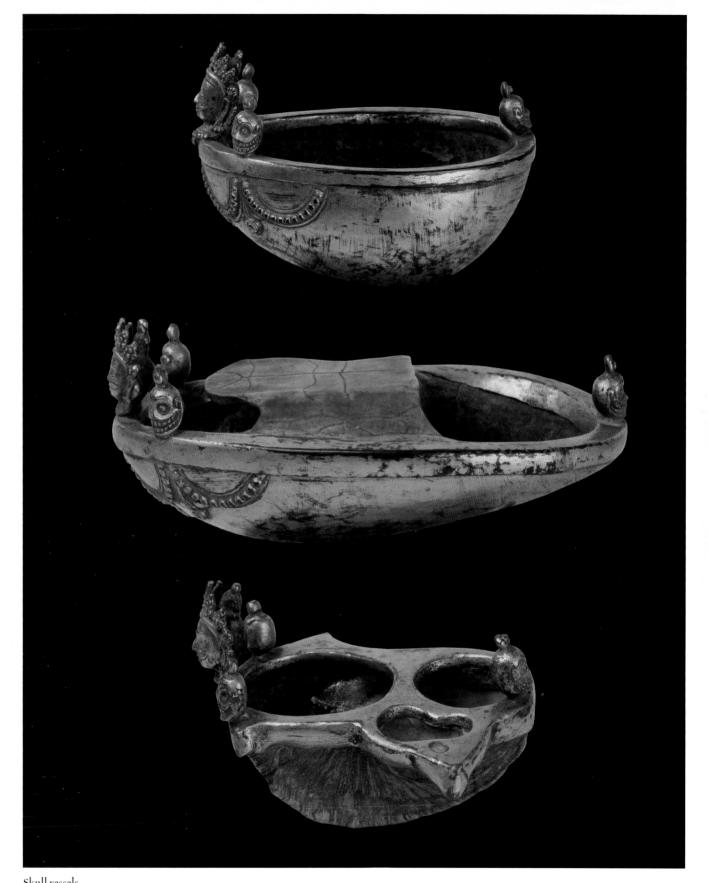

**Skull vessels**
Ceremonial cups, such as these 17th-century examples from Nepal, were made
from a variety of receptacles, such as coconut shells, tortoise shells and human
skulls. Buddhist deities are often depicted holding a *kapal* (skull). Used for
rituals in both Hindu and Buddhist Tantra traditions, skull cups were held
in the left hand and represent wisdom.

**Citipati and Mahakala**
Painted wooden Citipati figures, Nepal, 18th-century (top left and right).
The Citipati, a Tibetan Buddhist deity, is known as Lord of the Cemetery.
Mahakala (bottom), a deity found in Hinduism, Buddhism and Sikhism,
is the protector of monasteries. The five skulls on the crown symbolize the
transmutation of the five afflictions of human nature into virtues.

**Palden Lhamo**
This *thanka* (Tibetan Buddhist painting on cotton) from Bhutan, 18th or
19th century (opposite), shows the wrathful Tibetan guardian goddess,
Palden Lhamo, riding her mule over a sea of blood. This goddess embodies
the destructive aspect of the great mother. She has three eyes and is often
depicted drinking blood from a human skull.

95

Jar burial
It is likely that the images above, of unknown date and origin, document the
practice of jar burial, in which the dead are placed in an earthenware vessel,
which is then interred. The death of the body is viewed as the beginning of a
slow transition from this world to the next; while the corpse is decomposing,
it is believed to be alive and is treated accordingly.

The skull in Mesoamerica
Aztec vessel in the shape of a skull, 1300–1519, painted terracotta. The Aztecs
regarded death as a part of the natural cycle of life. They believed that the
gods had sacrificed themselves in order for humankind to live, and death and
sacrifice to the gods – sometimes human sacrifice – were considered necessary
for life on Earth to continue.

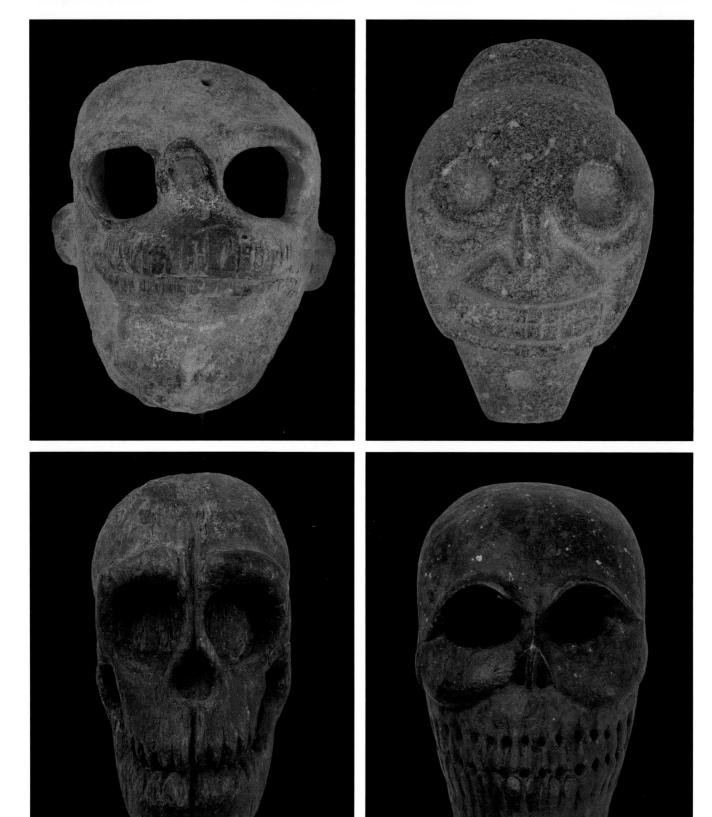

**Universal symbol**

One of the essential characteristics of humankind is a foreknowledge of our own death. Depictions of the human skull are the most direct and iconic symbol of our own mortality and they occur in the traditional arts and rituals of most cultures. Above and opposite are representations of the skull in different media from a variety of times and places, East and West, ancient and relatively modern. Although the need to make sense of our mortality is universal, ideas about what death means – and what happens after we die – vary

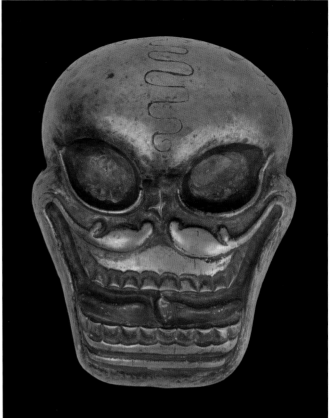

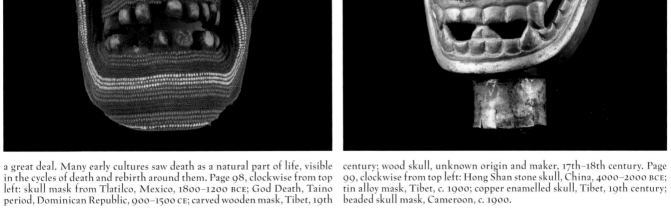

a great deal. Many early cultures saw death as a natural part of life, visible in the cycles of death and rebirth around them. Page 98, clockwise from top left: skull mask from Tlatilco, Mexico, 1800–1200 BCE; God Death, Taino period, Dominican Republic, 900–1500 CE; carved wooden mask, Tibet, 19th century; wood skull, unknown origin and maker, 17th–18th century. Page 99, clockwise from top left: Hong Shan stone skull, China, 4000–2000 BCE; tin alloy mask, Tibet, c. 1900; copper enamelled skull, Tibet, 19th century; beaded skull mask, Cameroon, c. 1900.

**British Columbia's Kwakiutl people**
American photographer Edward S. Curtis is famous for his images of the
Kwakwaka'wakw, or Kwakiutl Indians, of British Columbia. His work is
controversial for blurring the lines between documentary and aestheticized
fiction. These images, taken in c. 1910, were staged in an attempt to recreate
earlier tribal practices related to sorcery and the ritual use of human remains.

From death to life in Haiti
With their sequins and found doll parts, these figures from c. 1970 are sacred objects of Haitian Vodou, popularly referred to as Voodoo. They probably relate to the Ghede, a family of loa, or spirits, embodying death and fertility, whose traditional colours are black and purple. In Voodoo culture, death is seen as the great transition to the afterlife and ultimately reincarnation.

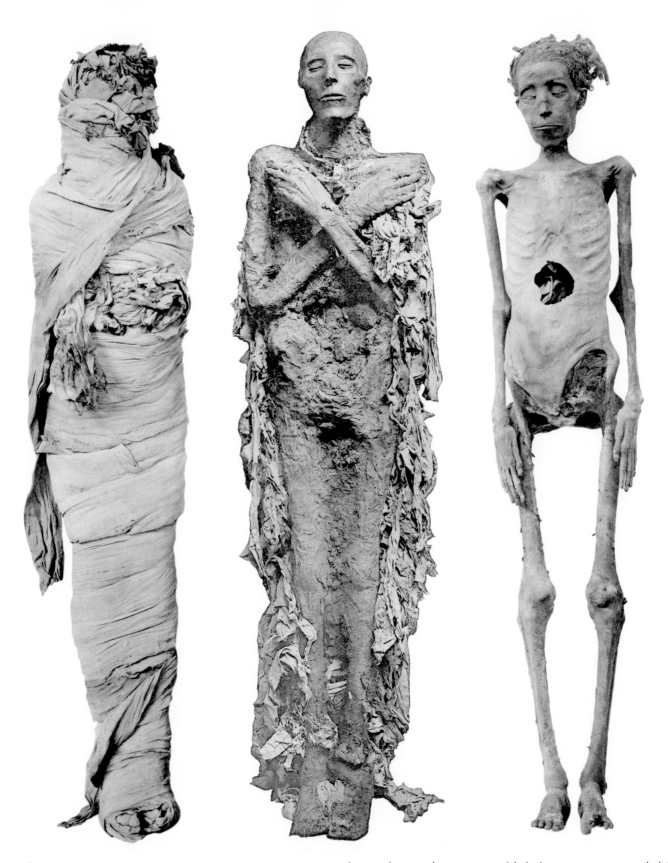

**Death in ancient Egypt**
These mummies are from the Museum of Egyptian Antiquities in Cairo, recorded in Grafton Elliot Smith's *Catalogue Géneral des Antiquités Égyptiennes du Musée de Caire: The Royal Mummies*, 1912. Mummies date back to the earliest Egyptian burials, when the hot sand mummified remains naturally. When the Egyptians began to use tombs, they developed an artificial process of mummification. The preservation of the body was important. Not only did the soul, or *ba*, return to the body at night, but also the remains of the body transformed into the *akh*, an entity that would enable the soul of the dead to survive in the underworld. The body had to be preserved to look as much as possible like it had in life. Left to right: mummy of an unknown woman found in the coffin of Setnakhte; mummy of Seti I; unknown woman.

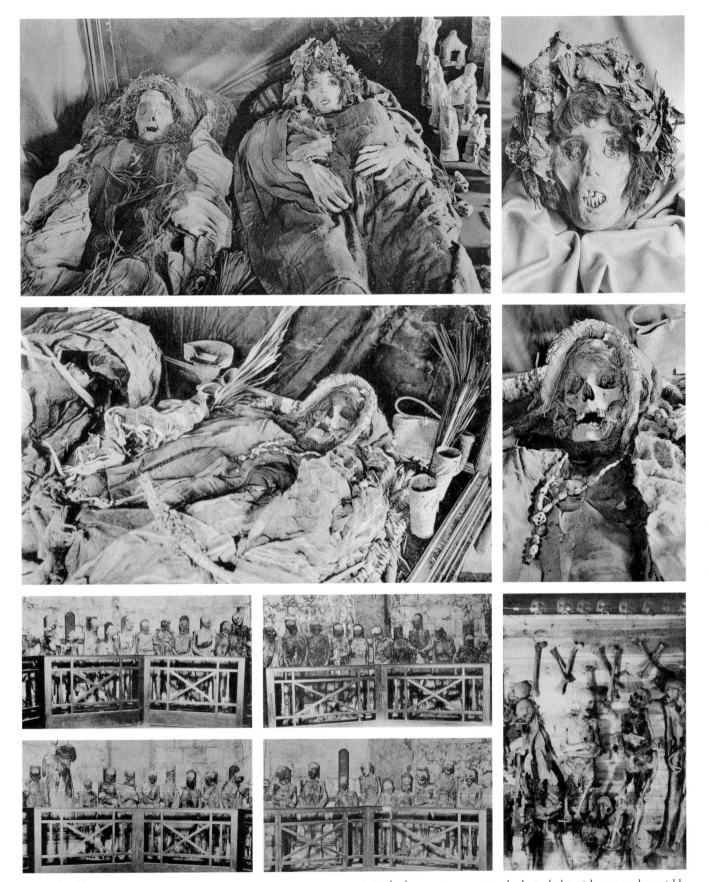

**Postcards of the mummies**

Mummification is often intentional, as in the Egyptian examples (first and second rows), but sometimes it happens naturally due to climate or soil conditions, as in the mummies exhumed from the crypt of the basilica of St Michael in Bordeaux (third and fourth rows, left and centre), which had been preserved by the clay soil. Comprising nearly seventy individuals, the St Michael mummies were put on display in the late 18th century; they quickly became a tourist attraction, drawing the attention of writers and artists such as Victor Hugo, Gustave Flaubert and Théophile Gautier. Propped upright around the crypt, they were given descriptive titles such as 'Buried Alive', 'The Family Poisoned by Mushrooms', 'The African' and 'The General Killed in a Duel'. They were removed from view in 1990 and reburied in a nearby cemetery.

**Death rituals in Toraja, Sulawesi, Indonesia, 1997**
Photographer Linda Connor documents spiritual traditions around
the world. Clockwise from top left: entrance to burial cave (recent
burial); tree with infant burials (behind each patch is a dead or still
born baby); coffins and skulls in a burial cave; skulls in an eroded
coffin; inside the burial cave; and coffins perched on a cliff face.

**African *niombo* funeral sculpture**
A *niombo* (opposite), also called *muzidi*, is an ancestor figure made
by the Bembe people of the Congo, who consider art to be sacred.
The main purpose of the *niombo* was to enable the living to stay in
contact with the dead. It was believed that they housed the spirit of
the deceased, who remained active members of the family.

**Skulls in Tibet**
In Tibet and the Himalayas, ritual objects are often decorated with skulls, such as the trident of hammered brass with gold and silver gilding, c. 18th–19th century, and the 17th-century Citipati panel (opposite).

**Death and Buddhism**
Young monk with death mask, Hemis Monastery, Ladakh, India, 2003 (top); making Buddhist ceremonial masks, Tibet, 1993 (bottom left); Protector Chapel, Tibet, 2003 (bottom right). Photographs by Linda Connor.

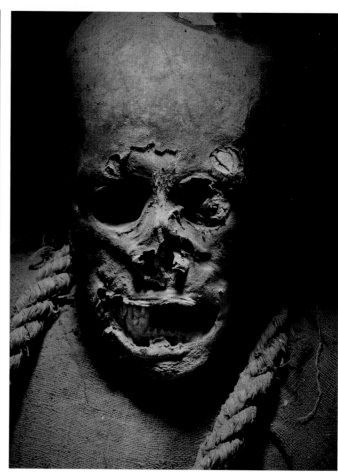
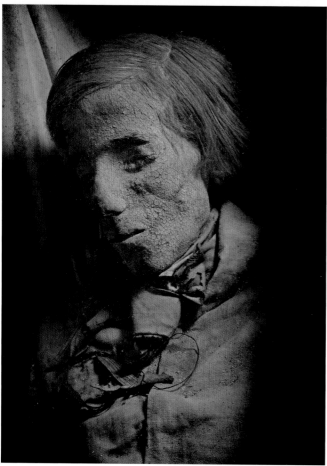

**Palermo's mummies**
The Capuchin catacombs of Palermo, Italy, are filled with the preserved bodies of monks and those rich enough to afford the honour. Carlo Vannini's photographs (opposite) capture the grim beauty of mummies displayed in their Sunday best.

**Palermo's catacombs**
A subterranean cemetery, the catacombs have been a popular tourist attraction since at least the 18th century. These photographs, the bottom one a postcard, depict how this repository of death looked at the end of the 19th century.

## Theatres of Death

Italian artist Gaetano Giulio Zumbo was renowned for miniature wax tableaux, or *teatrini*. Now known as his Theatres of Death, many are on display in La Specola, the museum of zoology and natural science, in Florence. *La peste* (The Plague) (top middle) takes the plague as a subject; *Il morbo Gallico* (The French Disease) (bottom) conveys the degenerative consequences of syphilis; while *La vanità della gloria umana* (The Vanity of Human Glory) (top left) and *Il trionfo del tempo* (The Triumph of Time) (top right) are powerful presentations of traditional memento mori and Triumph of Death themes, in which the dead and the dying are set in rubble-filled ruins. The remarkable veracity of the decay and suffering in the tiny figures was a result of first-hand knowledge: Zumbo conducted his own human dissections. In c. 1700,

he partnered with French surgeon Guillaume Desnoues in the creation of the first anatomical wax model. Cosimo de Medici became a patron and the Marquis de Sade was an admirer: 'So powerful [was] the impression produced by this masterpiece that even as you gaze at it your other senses are played upon, moans audible, you wrinkle your nose as if you could detect the evil odours of mortality.... These scenes of the plague appealed to my cruel imagination.' Zumbo's *teatrini* are also known as his 'plague waxes', as they eloquently expressed the death and destruction wrought by the bubonic plague as it spread through Italy, especially in Milan and Naples. Exploiting the pliancy and subtlety of wax to the full, Zumbo filled his *teatrini* with extraordinary details, from exquisitely moulded entrails to vividly rendered states of putrefaction.

**Catacomb saints**
Between the 16th and 19th centuries, skeletons from the catacombs of Rome were sent to churches around the world, masquerading as saint's relics. These 'catacomb saints' were often decorated with gold and precious stones, such as the examples (opposite) photographed by Paul Koudounaris.

**Spanish funerary robes**
The embroidered appliqué on these 17th-century silk robes (above) includes the skull and crossbones motif. Such imagery was common in the vestments worn by Catholic priests conducting funerals or carrying out other rituals relating to death.

**Chapel of bones**

The Capuchin crypt of Santa Maria della Concezione dei Cappuccini in Rome, seen here in postcards dated between 1870 and 1890, has long been a popular tourist attraction. It is filled with an artistic display of preserved human bones sourced from the exhumed skeletons of some 4,000 friars buried between 1528 and 1870. Some are dressed in robes and arranged in poses.

**Anatomical Christ**

This 17th-century polychrome wax figure (opposite) created by an unknown artist is a Christus Anatomicus, or Anatomical Christ. Little is known about these miniature figures, which have a removable panel in the chest, but it seems likely that they are tools for meditating on Christ's paradoxical nature of being both man and God.

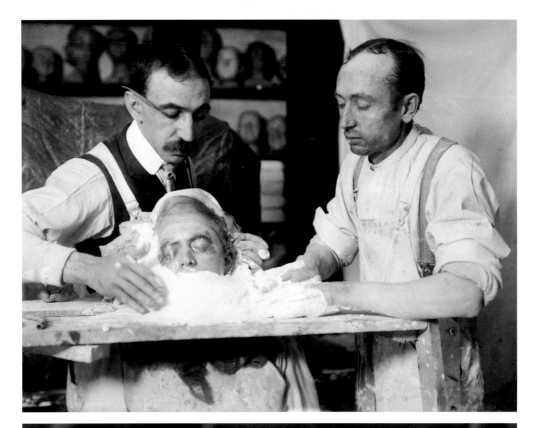

**Death mask**
In a tradition that dates back at least to ancient Egypt, death masks are made by taking a cast of the face of the dead (top). Such masks were used as models for more formal post-mortem portraits but were also mementos in their own right. This mask (bottom) was once believed to be the death mask of William Shakespeare, but it is now considered to be of unknown origin.

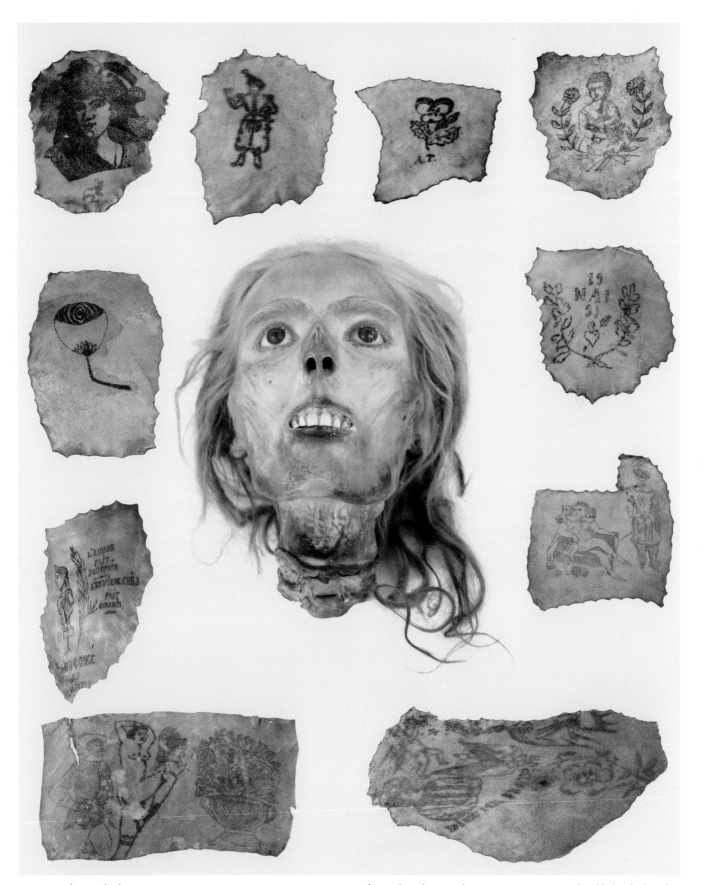

## Preserving human body parts

From the collection of Henry Wellcome, these preserved tattoos on human skin date from the late 19th century. Wellcome purchased them from a Parisian doctor in 1929, as part of a lot of 300 such pieces. The head of a woman (centre) was preserved by Girolamo Segato in the early 19th century. Segato was well-known for creating a process for petrifying human remains (still secret) based on his studies of mummification in Egypt. He created a table finished in what appears to be inlay, but is actually 214 pieces of petrified human remains. This and many of his other works can be seen at the Anatomical Museum of the University of Florence. Segato is buried in the Basilica di Santa Croce; the text on his tomb reads: 'Here lies decayed Girolamo Segato from Belluno, who could have been totally petrified if his art had not died with him...'

**Skull and crossbones**
The skull, with and without crossbones, is part of the classic iconography of the memento mori and was commonly used on grave markers until the 18th century. These examples are from the Camposanto Monumentale, a 12th-century cloister-cemetery in Pisa, and Amsterdam's Oude Kerk. In the Middle Ages, burial grounds were in or near churches, and were meant to urge visitors to pray for the souls in purgatory or contemplate their own mortality. Garden cemeteries on the outskirts of towns were not built until the early 19th century, when expanding cities placed pressure on space and a more secular society did not see the need to be buried near the remains of the saints.

St Nicholas Church, South London
This weathered skull and crossbones from the late 17th or early 18th century
is one of a pair topping the entrance gate to Deptford St Nicholas Church
in London. The mortal remains of playwright Christopher Marlowe, killed
nearby in a pub brawl in 1593, are said to be buried here.

## Mexican death culture

These photographs, taken by Dana Salvo from 1990 to 2004 as part of his series *The Day, the Night and the Dead*, document the unique death culture of Mexico. The country's death-related tradition is Día de los Muertos (Day of the Dead), held on 1 and 2 November. During the festival, believed to be a syncretization of pre-Hispanic and Spanish colonial festivals related to the souls of the dead,

Mexicans build altars to deceased loved ones (above, top right) and make offerings of their favourite food. People also exchange skulls made of sugar and go to the cemetery to clean the graves of their ancestors and to decorate them with candles and marigolds (above, middle row, left). It is believed that on festival days – 1 November for children and 2 November for adults – the boundaries between the living and the dead are more porous than usual.

**Post-mortem nuns in Mexico**
Traditionally, nuns were painted only twice in their religious lives: to commemorate their marriage to Christ, and to mark their parting from the world. They wore crowns of flowers on both occasions, which on their death symbolized their assured resurrection. Portraits were made at the request of the family, who considered it an honour to have a nun as a daughter.

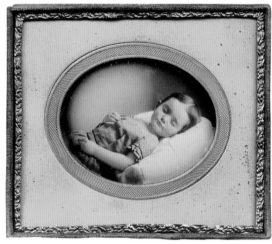

**The sleeping dead**
After the spread of photography in the mid-19th century, post-mortem photographs became popular. More affordable than paintings, they allowed many more people to have a likeness made of their loved one. In the case of a dead child, this was often the only photograph parents had of their son or daughter. Photographers usually placed the dead in a pose that suggested they were sleeping rather than dead, but they would sometimes prop older children or adults upright. Post-mortem daguerreotypes, 19th century (top) (courtesy of the Jeffrey Kraus Collection); hand-tinted ambrotype of an unidentified child, c. 1860 (bottom left) (collection of Jack and Beverly Wilgus); post-mortem photographs, 19th century (bottom centre and right) (courtesy of The Thanatos Archive).

**Skull on grave**

A found photograph by an unknown maker (opposite) shows a human skull placed atop a stone grave marker in an overgrown cemetery. The special treatment of dead bodies via burials and other means links us to the earliest human civilizations and betrays the continued meaning of the body, even in an age that tends to view itself as purely rational.

**Forget me not**

The Victorians revelled in mourning and produced items to commemorate the deceased (top). Women were permitted to wear hairwork jewelry (middle row), containing the hair of the deceased, in the 'second stage' of mourning, which began a year and a day after the loved one's death. Memorial shadow boxes were another form of remembrance (bottom).

## Changing iconography on headstones

These rubbings from early New England gravestones, collected by Edmund Vincent Gillon Jr. and published in book form in 1966, include memento mori images of skeletons, skulls and decaying cadavers, several with an hourglass or a scythe. The winged death's head, symbolizing death and resurrection, was especially common. Such iconography prevailed on headstones until the 18th century, after which changing ideas about hell and the afterlife resulted in less fearsome images, such as winged cherubs, angels, urns and weeping willow trees signifying mourning. This coincided with the changing function of cemeteries; once a place intended to encourage a meditation on mortality and prayer for the dead, they became a relaxing, uplifting site for peaceful contemplation.

**Jewish cemetery in Prague**
The tangle of headstones in the Old Jewish Cemetery in Prague (top and
bottom), which was in use from the 15th century until 1786, reflects both
the permanency of burials in the Jewish faith – graves are not recycled – and
the restrictions on buying new land faced by the Jews. The cemetery is one
of the oldest and largest Jewish cemeteries in Europe.

The
Dance
of
Death

# the personification of DEATH

The Dance of Death through the ages

JESTER, DEMON, TRAVELLER, FRIEND

Death heads in Asia

Eros and Thanatos

A DEADLY FETISH

Death wins all wars

# the dance of death

**M**odern images of the moment of death are predominately photojournalistic in nature, with an incidental documentary aesthetic prevailing. Although we may assume a certain intent in publishing such an image, most likely a desire to induce empathy, this is not necessary for the creation of an effective photograph. In contrast, the late medieval motif of the Dance of the Death, which also depicts the moment of death, emphasizes the allegorical intent of the image: no matter who you are or what your level of privilege may be, death can arrive for you at any moment. The king, merchant, peasant or baby that death ensnares is, in fact, every king, merchant, peasant or baby. The language of the Dance of Death, despite depicting the moment when death comes to claim another victim, is more akin to that of the editorial cartoon or comic strip than the documentary photograph. These images are meant to inspire contemplation and fear, not empathy.

The Dance of Death motifs first appeared in paintings, especially frescoes on the walls of churches or graveyards. The first known Dance of Death, now lost to time, is thought to have been painted in 1424 on the wall of the charnel house, a vault for storing bones unearthed when digging new graves, at Cimetière des Innocents in Paris. The composition, a single horizontal line of figures starting with the most powerful on the left and descending in social station to the right, set the template for future Dances. This composition emphasizes the allegorical and editorial in its very structure. The wealthy and powerful come first and everyone else follows. But death takes them all. The 'dance' depicted is that of the farandole, or community dance, where hands are joined in a line, thus uniting all of society in Death's grip.

Unlike a single, traditional image (rectangle or square), the Dance of Death is 'read' rather than seen. The reader starts at one end and progresses to the conclusion, as with a comic book. From the beginning, the Dance of Death incorporated text, and in

*Clasped in the arms of Death, no one escapes its grip, a fatal one to be sure, but here anguish conceals its own depressive force and displays defiance through sarcasm or the grimace of a mocking smile, without triumph, as it, knowing it is done for, laughter is the only answer.*

**JULIA KRISTEVA ON THE DANCE OF DEATH
IN HER ESSAY 'HOLBEIN'S DEAD CHRIST'**

Page 128
Weimar Dance of Death
Lithographic poster advertising the American release of the 1919 film *Der Totentanz*, from the Century Guild Museum of Art, Los Angeles. In the film, an evil cripple forces a beautiful dancer to entice men to their deaths. The idea of the Dance of Death stretches back to the Middle Ages, and continues to fascinate today.

the case of the Saint Innocents mural also depicted a narrator. At each end of the sequence, the author sat at a desk in a separate book-lined space, or comic panel, if you will. The text in the author panels was contained in unfurled scrolls, again conjuring the comic's modern caption box. Each station in the line of the Innocents mural had accompanying text, most likely painted below the images, as it appears in subsequent and surviving murals throughout Europe. It is fair to assume the text came first, inspired by the 13th-century French literary genre Vado Mori (I prepare myself to die), in which people of various social classes rail in verse against the inevitability of death. But it is the introduction of the mocking voice of Death addressing his victim that gives the text of the Dance of Death mural its mischievous sting:

DEATH:
*Patriarch, it is not by lowering your head only*
*that you can be acquitted.*
*The cross of Lorraine which is so dear to you,*
*Another will receive it: it is all justice.*
*Think no more of honours,*
*You will never be Pope at Rome;*
*You are now called to account (of your acts).*
*The foolish hopes deceive man.*

Death's mocking is then followed by the words of the vanquished lamenting the futility of their striving for position and honour. It is only the hermit who deviates from this and seems to accept his fate.

THE HERMIT:
*Despite a hard and lonely life,*
*Death does not grant a delay.*
*Everyone sees it and must be silent.*
*I pray to God to give me a gift:*
*Let him erase all my sins.*
*I am pleased with all the benefits of*
*which I have profited by His grace.*
*Who is not happy with what he has, has nothing.*

We have only the prints of Guy Marchant's drawings of the Dance of Death in the Cimetière des Innocents to go by, as the mural was destroyed in 1669 in order, it is said, to widen a road. Marchant's drawings were reproduced in a popular pamphlet that enjoyed multiple editions. The pioneering anatomist Andreas Vesalius, author and illustrator of one of the most influential books on human anatomy, *De humani corporis fabrica* (On the Fabric of the Human Body, 1543), is said to have developed his interest in anatomy after examining the bones in the charnel houses of the Cimetière des Innocents. It is easy to imagine the seed

for one of his most famous images from *De Humani*, that of a skeleton contemplating a skull, being planted as Vesalius contemplated the first known mural of the Dance of Death.

The first known picture of a printing press appears in a similar context. An image in *La grant danse macabre des homes* (Lyon, 1499), of which only two copies survive, depicts Death in its familiar skeletal form disrupting a book shop, interrupting the work of a compositor placing type and halting the printing of a book. Contemplating this image, I wonder if the printer could be alluding to a deeper purpose in his work – to cheat Death's erasure of the words of man through the means of reproduction. Pondering the relationship between death and the written word leads to a rabbit hole of associations, from images of Saint Jerome translating the Bible, with only a candle and a skull on his desk, to the popularity of the skull as an image on ex libris, perhaps serving as much as a warning to a book thief as a memento mori.

Most people encounter the Dance of Death in book form, as I did in the dustiest of book stores, Hood Used Books, in Lawrence, Kansas. More specifically, I stumbled upon Hans Holbein's *Dance of Death* (1538), which is the most widely known and reproduced iteration of the genre. I found my copy among bright spines of pop art catalogues and monographs on Impressionism, its black spine with faded gold type standing out in the negative, a slice of darkness among stripes of colour. It is from 1947 and, written in pencil next to the price of $12.50, is 'out-of-print'. But, of course, that applies only to this edition, for Holbein's *Dance of Death* is never out of print and likely never will be (it has recently been reissued as a Penguin Classic). The cover of my copy, also black with gold embossing, depicts Death beating a drum, framed in an oval that contains the words: *Vitas Brevis, Ars Longa* (Life is Short, Art is Long).

Given that my own artistic output at the time leaned towards punkish images of apocalypse and alienation, I no doubt responded to the social critique embedded in Holbein's images. And I must have recognized something of the editorial cartoon, if only in the familiar configuration of a single image with a caption below. Due to the need for a separate vignette for each page in the sequence, the original dance, the farandole, or community dance, is lost. Holbein was doubtless aware of this, given that it is likely he would have seen Guy Marchant's drawings of the Innocents mural, which paired figures but retained the pillars of the charnel house and the joined hands of the dance. Holbein's choice to isolate the figures, imbuing each image with details specific to the individual's station in society, is not insignificant. Indeed, Holbein's other leap forward, to take the Death images out of the symbolic and into the everyday realistic lived space of late medieval life, would not be possible, or at least would be quite clumsy in a single image mural (although it is fun to imagine something akin to a Bruegel crowd composition applied to this theme).

With his emphasis on specifics, Holbein expands what was previously a moral lesson – Death as the great equalizer, putting all social stations on notice – into the realm of social criticism that is tied to the reform ideas of his time. For example, anti-papacy sentiment is expressed in the image of Death coming for the pope. Demons symbolize corruption and Holbein deepens the reformist critique by depicting the king kissing the pope's foot, in contrast to Jesus washing the feet of the poor. A corrupting demon makes only one other appearance, blowing bellows into the ear of the senator to mask the words of the imploring poor man at his shoulder. Such details abound and reward deeper viewing. The nun is distracted from her prayers by a handsome minstrel as a broken hourglass, a recurring symbol of approaching death, lies broken at her feet. The astrologer points to his model of the universe as Death presents a skull, an object considered more worthy of his contemplation. In contrast, the ploughman, unlike the nobles and other powerful characters, who resist or ignore Death, is the beneficiary of Death's help as it implores his horses with a whip towards the setting sun.

One image I return to, which is among ten plates that appear only in later editions, is the idiot fool. Perhaps this one captures my attention because it is hard to identify a modern equivalent, or perhaps there is something in the specific details that I find compelling. His misshapen head, exposed member, finger in mouth and what the text refers to as a 'bladder bauble' makes one wonder if such a fool actually crossed Holbein's path. Unlike many of the other encounters, which are set in urban scenes, the one between the idiot fool and Death takes place in a rocky barren landscape. Death plays the bagpipes and gently tugs on the fool's clothing, while the fool looks quizzical and even entertained, unlike most of the other victims, who regard Death with alarm. Is the fool's lack of concern due to a deficiency of mind or does he, like the hermit, benefit from a life lived without worldly desire?

Holbein's images also contain objects and details contemporary to the time, a feature highlighted in the introduction to my edition. The writer notes the variety of instruments, costumes, furniture, etc., ending with 'Whatever one's profession, business, or special hobby, he is sure to find relevant interesting illustrations in the following pages,' as if trying to ignore that the subject of death is quite relevant enough.

Holbein's *Dance of Death* was first printed in 1538. It was immensely popular. In addition to the eleven editions published in the subsequent twenty years or so, it inspired around 100 unauthorized copies and imitations. Most notable of the subsequent versions influenced by Holbein's imagery are the dramatic and elaborate series by the Baroque artists Rudolf and Conrad Meyer, whose *Sterbensspiegel* was published in 1650. By the 1800s, many examples of the genre return to a stripped-down allegorical form, isolating the figures without backgrounds and eliminating other characters or symbolic props. In one example, a series of delightful 19th-century German ceramics, the context is removed completely. Nonetheless, by virtue of the indomitable structure of the motif and playful text, Death is still the mirthful and mocking equalizer even if the pointed editorial content is subdued.

However, Alfred Rethel's *Auch ein Totentanz* (Yet Another Dance of Death, 1848) marked a departure in the genre. Rethel's Dance of Death is a conservative response to the revolution of 1848, although art historians disagree about Rethel's political leanings. Yet the message is unmistakable. Unfolding in a sequential series with text below, Rethel's Dance of Death recasts Death not as a mocking and mirthful dancer but as a political seducer who manipulates the mob for his own purposes. When printed on a broadside, as it was, the six-panel series would call to mind the classic six-panel structure of modern comics and the visual language of editorial cartoons. For example, the first panel presents vices such as Frenzy, Falsehood and Blood-thirstiness as women, who greet and aid Death as he is woken by the revolutionary cries of 'Liberty, Equality and Fraternity'. The careful viewer will notice Justice tied up in the background.

From here, Death proceeds, in a series of beautifully composed panels, to ride to an industrialized town (wearing an 18th-century coat symbolic of the Enlightenment and a broad-brimmed hat favoured by radicals of the time) and incite the mob to revolutionary violence. In the last panel, Death is revealed in his skeletal nature save for a victor's wreath, triumphantly astride a horse that steps among the corpses – 'all as brothers, free and equal'. Death is again the equalizer, but is using revolution to do his bidding. With its balanced diagonals, historic details and sharp satire, Rethel's Dance of Death harks back to Holbein's aesthetic and message but for entirely different political ends. Although Rethel chose to call it a Dance of Death, the differences in social class are not equalized but championed in the depiction of the perils of revolution.

In contrast, Thomas Rowlandson's *The English Dance of Death* (1815) gives the comedic and social satire possibilities of the motif full rein. Nagging wives, leering husbands, fetching chambermaids and obese drunkards in wheelbarrows are all rendered in grotesque parodies of human folly. A pitiless and delighted Death chases, drags or leads the characters to their inevitable fate. As with Holbein, all social stations are represented, although not in the traditional order, and Rowlandson melds the motif with portions of its obvious cousin, the seven deadly sins. The gluttonous, the vain and the conniving all make appearances, as do some curious modern equivalents such as the quack doctor, the catchpole (tax collector) and the genealogist. Only a few appear noble, such as the recruit, which only serves to show death at its cruellest. In both style and content, it seems that Rowlandson's Dance of Death is the clearest expression of the motif as editorial cartoon.

Despite adopting the title and exploring the social foibles and hypocrisy of Holbein's template, Rowlandson was not slavish in his interpretation. This is true of many modern riffs on the motif. Today, the Dance of Death's most enduring feature, that of the personification of Death, is unleashed in all sorts of forms and permutations, although some themes recur. For example, many of the images in the war-related artwork of the Richard Harris Collection, including works by Goya, Käthe Kollwitz, Otto Dix and John Heartfield, draw on the Dance of Death theme, with antecedents in post-Holbein images of Death taking the soldier as well as Rethel's repurposing. It is, of course, inevitable that the figure of Death and war are linked, and interesting that this is more often in the form of a print rather than an original painting – so much the better for wide distribution.

Perhaps the most curious and inscrutable of the Dance of Death's permutations is that of Death and the Maiden. First appearing in Germany in the early 1500s, the motif is typified by a skeletal figure embracing a naked woman in the bloom of her youth. Erotically charged and tinged with the taboo, it reads like a censored panel of the Dance of Death. It has inspired generations of artists, from Edvard Munch to Joseph Beuys. One modern depiction, attributed to the prolific poster designer Josef Fenneker in 1919, used the image to promote a film written by Fritz Lang that purports to be about a beautiful dancer exploited by a cripple to lure men to their deaths. Like the original mural at the Cimetière des Innocents, the film, titled *Der Totentanz* (Dance of Death, 1912), is lost to time.

In contemplating the original mural and all the subsequent Dance of Deaths, one wonders if they had the intended effect of inspiring a more virtuous populace. One can imagine how the less fortunate classes may have taken pleasure in seeing their oppressors and those lucky enough to be born into wealth brought low by

the great equalizer. Perhaps the effect was less like a photograph that might inspire empathy and more like the editorial cartoon, that tireless tormentor of the corrupt blowhard. It is not hard to imagine a bit of comfort being derived by applying this motif to the least humble and most privileged in today's society. I suspect such an image would go viral much faster than something closer to the cautionary intent of the original Dance of Death. For example, a conscience-prodding image that shows shoppers being chased by Death through a climate-changed landscape may have more power than an image seeking to elicit sympathy by depicting a migrant welcoming Death in the desert. For whatever ends, and whichever side of human nature it appeals to, the adaptability of the Dance of Death comes from a universality that extends beyond content to form. In fact, the single image with a single caption, a form once seen in the mural of a Parisian cemetery, is referred to by contemporary cartoonists as a 'gag' comic. The term not only conjures up the involuntary laugh but also the deathly grip. The mirthful grinning skull is the dark punch line, reminding us that the joke is on us. All of us.

Lisa Downing

# eros and thanatos

*My thoughts are crowded with death
and it draws so oddly on the sexual
that I am confused
confused to be attracted
by, in effect, my own annihilation.*

THOM GUNN,
'IN TIME OF PLAGUE'

ros and Thanatos. Sex and Death. In psychology, philosophy and the arts, this odd couple has become something of a commonplace – almost a cliché, despite the paradox it apparently suggests. What is the nature of the coupling of death and eroticism? Is it a matter of drawing attention to some inherent mortal threat, a consummate deathliness, within the dark heart of sex itself? The term for 'orgasm', borrowed from the French *La petite mort* (the little death) might suggest so, figuring the moment of rapture as akin to self-annihilation. Or, is it that death is, in some way, in and of itself, perversely sexy? Is it that proximity to and contemplation of mortality thrill us, as suggested in Anaïs Nin's short story, 'The Woman on the Dunes' (1979), in which strangers feel compelled to copulate as they watch public hangings in a crowded town square?[1]

The sex-death couple is an enigma. Sexuality appears, at first glance, to be wholly life-enhancing and, indeed, life-giving, if it is understood as designed for and leading to procreation. However, the idea that death is inexorably linked to sex is so deeply rooted and widely represented in Western culture as to suggest that a merely functional understanding is insufficient to the richness, complexity and perversity of human desire. Various theories have been advanced to account for the link. Historically, non-procreative sexual intercourse, masturbation and homosexual sex have been prohibited in the Abrahamic religions, creating a climate of guilt around the 'mortal sin' of pleasurable sex uncoupled from its 'proper' aim. (Even those who have consciously rejected religious faith cannot easily escape these deep-rooted associations, since they are part of the cultural air that we breathe.)

Philosophers of transgression have drawn on the dynamics of eroticism to account for its fatal over-tones. French writer Georges Bataille posited that sexual ecstasy shares qualities with death, as both are

154

states in which the integral boundaries of the self are transgressed and put in danger. In *The Accursed Share* (1988), he writes: 'Anguish, which lays us open to annihilation and death, is always linked to eroticism; our sexual activity finally rivets us to the distressing image of death, and the knowledge of death deepens the abyss of eroticism.'[2] Considering the psychology and metapsychology of human beings in modern culture, Sigmund Freud asserted in *Beyond the Pleasure Principle* (1920) that, alongside the drive to survive, procreate and flourish (Eros or life drive), there exists an opposing principle, the death drive (or Thanatos). While the life drive seeks to decrease tension and to maintain the organism in a state of equilibrium (the pleasure principle), the death drive works in excess of this, seeking to return the human being to our original state of nothingness, of radical unbeing.

Drawing on the opposition between φιλία (love) and νίχος (discord) identified by the Greek philosopher Empedocles, Freud portrayed psychical life as a constant struggle between the two forces of death and Eros. In 'The Ego and the Id' (1923), Freud goes on to discuss the fusion of these drives (*Triebmischung*), which, he claims, becomes manifest in sadistic and masochistic forms of human sexuality.[3]

In dialogue with Freud, and building on his legacy, numerous sexologists and psychoanalysts have drawn attention to the prominence accorded to the taboo of death in some types of perverted sexuality. As I explored in my book *Desiring the Dead* (2003),[4] the perversion of necrophilia, in which the object of sexual arousal is a corpse, was named by Belgian alienist Joseph Guislain in 1861, around the time that representations of morbid eroticism were taken up by writers of the Romantic and decadent movements and by Pre-Raphaelite painters. A century later, American sexologists and psychiatrists would name, define and diagnose yet more deathly sexual perversions or, as the 20th century chose to call them, 'paraphilias'. Psychologist John Money wrote of asphyxiaphilia, in which the practitioner risks death in the pursuit of heightened pleasure by strangling or hanging, often while masturbating, and the presumably rare paraphilia of autassassinophilia, in which the sexual aim is to be murdered for erotic kicks.[5]

Yet, while these rare perversions illustrate the extreme end of the spectrum, the ubiquity of the Eros-Thanatos pair in our erotic imagination runs through the history of artistic representation. Many examples can be found in classical myth. Aphrodite, the goddess of love, is said to have sprung into being from the semen of a murdered man. Similarly, in Egyptian mythology, Isis, the wife of Osiris, the god of death and rebirth, gave birth to her son Horus after impregnating herself with the seed from her husband's corpse. While such

myths can be read as being about the triumph of life over death, it is also possible to read them as foregrounding the idea of death in the erotic imagination. In Greek mythology, Thanatos was the personification of death, who bore away men's spirits after the Fates cut the threads of their lives. Portrayed in classical art as an exquisite, winged youth, bearing a sword and an extinguished torch, he embodied both male beauty and mortality.

However, far from the classical image of death as a beautiful youth, images since the early 1800s have represented death as a wizened or skeletal, implicitly male or masculine, figure. To conjure up the frisson of Eros-Thanatos, and perhaps to inject a note of sadism, they juxtapose this frightful spectre with that of a beautiful, often supine or overpowered, female figure. The gender politics of many modern representations of sex-death are hard to ignore. Indeed, several feminist writers claim the linking of death and sexuality reveals a masculine fantasy of power and literalizes patriarchal dominance. In her comprehensive study of representations of eroticized dying or dead female bodies in art, *Over Her Dead Body* (1992), Elisabeth Bronfen argues that the fearful modern male imagination dealt with the threat of female emancipation, and the increasing presence of women in the social sphere, by portraying girls and women as ultimately passive via this repeated artistic trope.[6]

It is possible, perhaps, that death and sexuality often occupy the same discursive and visual space precisely because they both continue, to some extent, to be cultural taboos – things we avoid discussing in polite company. In Freud's essay 'Our Attitude Towards Death' (1915), he describes the tendency, especially in peacetime, to hide death from our everyday gaze, in order to minimize its threat. Several commentators on Western culture, most notably Philippe Ariès, have written about this. In his historical account of attitudes towards death (1974), Ariès asserts that culture understood mortality in mystical terms, and as both redemptive and inevitable, death has become shameful in the largely secular modern period. Ariès goes on to claim that the rich history of eroticizing death finds its pathological apotheosis in the modern fascination with erotic violence; he contends that death has become 'admirable in its beauty'.[7]

Given the thanatic qualities of much erotic art, visual culture may be the site where we can see most clearly the problematic relationship between desire and destruction that has informed thought, imagination and representation since the earliest times, and that continues to thrill, delight and shock us in equal measures today.

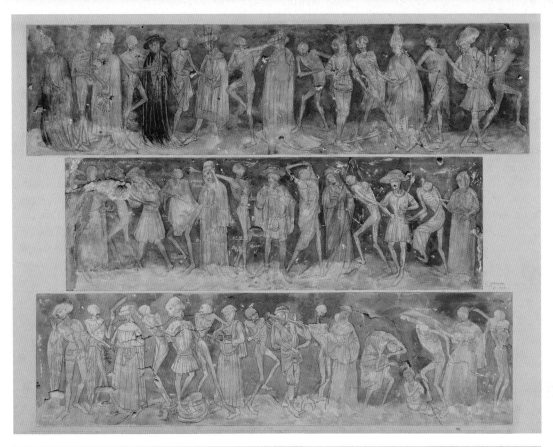

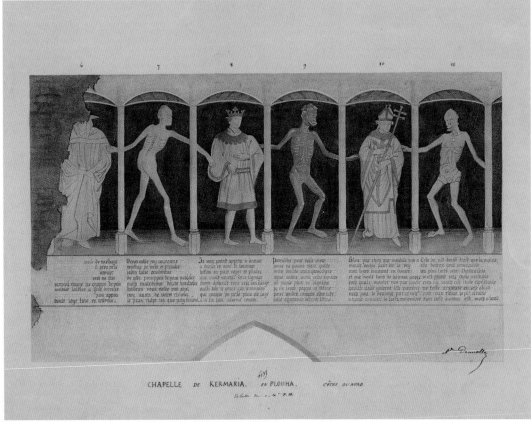

CHAPELLE DE KERMARIA, EN PLOUHA. CÔTES DU NORD.

**Skeleton on a plinth**
The sense of whimsy and personality in this etching of a yawning skeleton (opposite), created by an unknown artist in the 17th or 18th century, is typical of depictions of death at this time. Such personifications suggest a capricious figure who might come at any time regardless of age, health or social status.

**Warnings on the walls**
The Dance of Death first appeared in frescoes on the walls of cemeteries. The fresco at Abbaye de la Chaise-Dieu in the Auvergne (top), dates from c. 1470; the 1861 watercolour (bottom) is of a late 15th-century or early 16th-century fresco in the Chapelle Kermaria an Iskuit, in Plouha, France.

137

**Death's procession**
Peeter van der Borcht's Dance of Death, c. 1535–1608 (top), shows mummies representing clergy, kings, soldiers, nobles, scholars and merchants. Symbols of their standing in life, including snakes and skulls, litter the ground alongside traditional emblems of the transience of life.

**Dance of Death in Bern**
These lithographs from *Todtentanz von Niklaus Manuel*, 1850 (bottom), depict Wilhelm Stettler's 16th-century paintings of the now-lost frescoes which once graced the cemetery walls of a Dominican monastery in Bern. The frescoes were destroyed in 1660.

**Pigouchet's book of hours**

Books of hours were part of private Christian devotion in the Middle Ages. They usually contained a mix of prayers, psalms and texts and, when made for the very wealthy, were often lavishly illustrated. This book of hours, created by Philippe Pigouchet in c. 1500, presents a Dance of Death, with Death coming for the cardinal, the pope, the theologian and a variety of other figures.

The sequence was probably intended in the tradition of the memento mori, to urge the reader to contemplate the brevity of human life in order to live a more pious life in preparation for God's Final Judgment. There are also images of Christ's death, resurrection and Final Judgment, depicting the ambivalent Christian attitude towards death, wherein physical death offers the possibility of eternal life. Upper left is an Anatomical Zodiac Man, illustrating a form

of medical astrology – or iatromathematics – in which parts of the body were linked to the movement of the moon and stars and astrological formations. Aries, for example, was associated with the eyes, adrenal glands and blood pressure; Virgo with the abdomen and its many organs; and Sagittarius with the legs or thighs. Similar ideas were shared by the ancient Babylonians and Egyptians.

**Basel's Dance of Death**

Matthaeus Merian's *Totentanz der Stadt Basel* (Dance of Death of the city of Basel) of 1649 (above and opposite) was based on Basel's famous Dance of Death mural (demolished in 1805), which had been painted on the wall of the Dominican monastery's cemetery in c. 1440 after an outbreak of plague. The Black Plague first hit Europe in 1348–49 and reoccurred throughout the 17th century. By the late 14th century, it had reduced the populations of some European towns and cities by as much as 70 or 80 per cent. In the wake of such large numbers of causalities, and the reduction in priests, traditional death and burial rites were not always maintained. The increasing popularity of such imagery coincided with this societal shift.

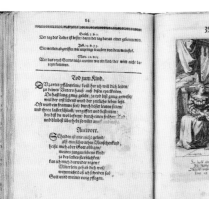

**39. Kind.**

**38. Zwey Liebende.**

---

128     Cantus. a. 4.     2. Toni.

Traurigkeit hat mich umhüllet/ und mein herz mit angst erfüllet/ da der bott auf mich zulieff ij mit dem schwartzen ij mit dem schwartzen todten brief/ mit dem schwartzen ij mit dem schwartzen todten brief/ mit dem schwartzen todtenbrief. Du grausamer herzenklopfer/ du grausam merklopfer/ lebensfeind und athem- und athem stopfer/ muß ich dann so eilend reisen/wilst mir keine/wilst mir keine frist erweisen/ frist er-

Tenor.

Traurigkeit hat mich umhüllet/ und mein herz mit angst erfüllet/ da der bots auf mich zulieff ij mit dem schwartzen todten brief/mit dem schwartzen/schwartzen schwartzen todtenbrief/ mit dem schwartzen todten brief. Du grausamer herzen- klopfer/lo pfer/lebensfeind und athem- und athemstopfer/ muß ich dann so eilig reisen/muß ich dann so eilig reisen/wilst mir keine frist er-

2. Toni.     Altus. a. 4.     129

Traurigkeit hat mich umhüllet/ hat mich umhül- let/ und mein herz mit angst erfüllet/ da der bott auf mich zulieff mit dem schwartzen todten- brief/ mit dem schwartzen todtenbrief/ mit dem schwartzen todtenbrief/ mit dem schwar- zen/ mit dem schwartzen todtenbrief/ mit dem todten brief/ mit dem/ dem todtenbrief. Du grausamer herzenklopfer/ lebensfeind und athemstopfer/ und athemstopfer/ muß ich dann so eilig/muß ich dann so eilig reisen/reisen/ wilst mir keine/wilst mir keine frist er-

Bassus.

Traurigkeit hat mich umhüllet/ und mein herz/ mein herz mit angst erfüllet da der bott auf mich zulieff ij mit dem schwartzen todtenbrief/ mit dem schwartzen/ schwartzen todtenbrief/ mit dem/ mit dem/ mit dem schwartzen/ schwartzen todtenbrief/ mit dem schwartzen todtenbrief. Du grausamer herzenklopfer/ lebensfeind/ und athem- und athemstopfer/ muß ich dann so eilend reisen/ eilend reisen? wilst mir kei- ne frist erwei-

---

**53. Todts ungewißheit.**

**48. Spiler.**

Sije X. p.12.

Heut König, morgen Tod. Und wann der Mensch stirbt, so fräßen
Ihn die schlangen und würme.

1.

**Conrad and Rudolf Meyer**
The frontispiece (above) of *Todten-dantz*, 1650, by Conrad and
Rudolf Meyer represents death as a transi, or figure of a rotting
cadaver, holding a frayed banner emblazoned with the book's title,
author and publication details, while an angel heralds the Final
Judgment of the people below. The visual tradition of the Dance of

Death originated as a cemetery fresco; Hans Holbein the Younger
translated the idea into print with forty-one woodcuts published
in book form in 1538. Noted for their detail and characterization,
Holbein's *Dance of Death* has remained in print ever since. It went
on to inspire a number of other book versions of the Dance of
Death, including the one seen here.

MORTALIVM NOBILITAS

Emifit eum Dominus Deus de paradiso voluptatis, ut operaretur terram, de qua sumptus est. Gen: 3.

Sedentes in tenebris & in Vmbra Mortis

**Wenzel Hollar**
First published in 1651, this hand-coloured Dance of Death by Wenzel Hollar probably dates from 1816. In the largest image above, we see Adam and Eve being expelled from the Garden of Eden as Death, a personified skeleton, plays a fiddle – a reminder that Adam and Eve ushered death into the world.

Perditum Pastorum... & defice erent
... ... ... Sicut oues.

Laudaui magis mortuos quàm viuentes
Eccle. 4

Est via quæ videtur homini recta, nouissi-
ma autem eius deducunt hominem ad mortem.

Væ qui dicitis malum bonum, & bonum malum:
ponentes tenebras lucem, & lucem tenebras; ponentes amarum in dulce, & dulce in amarum.

Medice, cura te ipsum... 4

Cum fortis armatus custodit atrium suum...
si autem fortior eo superueniens vicerit eum, uni-
uersa eius arma auferet, in quibus confidebat, &c.

Me & te sola Mors separabit.

Ducunt in bonis dies suos, & in
puncto ad inferna descendunt.

Qui congregat thesauros lingua men-
dacii, vanus & excors est, & impingetur
ad laqueos Mortis. Prouerb. 21 23

Stulte, hac nocte repetunt animam
tuam: & quæ parasti cuius erunt.

Corruit in curru suo.

Quid prodest homini, si vniuersum Mun-
dum lucretur, animæ autem suæ detrimen-
tum patiatur. Matth. 16. 27

Hon... in...
pu... propijetur multis miseris: qui quasi flo-
s... & conteritur & contemnitur, nil dilati, &c.

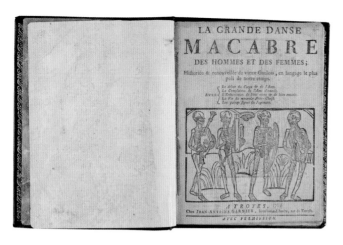

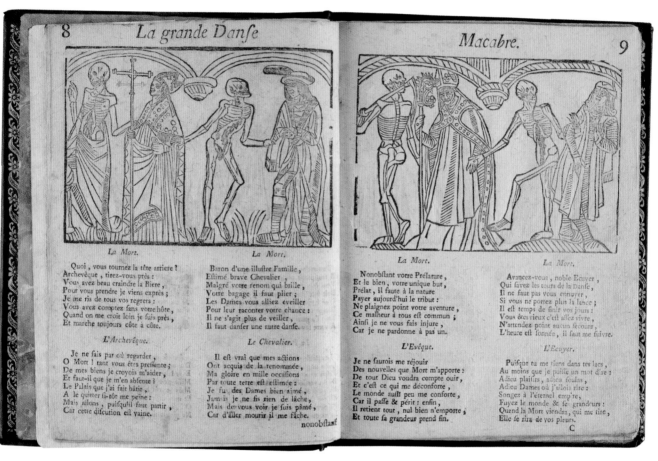

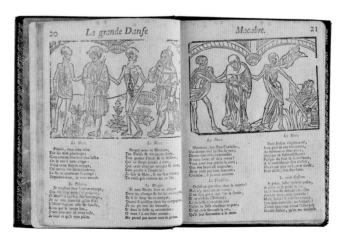

**Musical tradition**

This French Dance of Death by Jean-Antoine Garnier, dating from 1728, is introduced by a group of jaunty corpse musicians, reminding us that the Dance of Death was also a musical tradition, stretching back at least to the late 16th century. The genre was revived by Romantic composers such as Modest Mussorgsky, Franz Liszt and Camille Saint-Saëns in the 19th century.

La Mort. · La Mort.

La Mort. · La Mort.

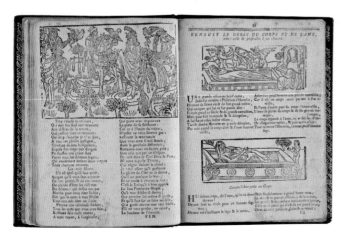

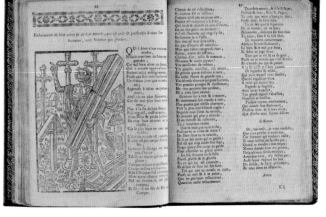

## Social satire

In *The Dance of Death Modernised*, 1808, by Isaac Cruikshank, after the cartoonist and humorist George Moutard Woodward, the Dance of Death tradition is exploited as a vehicle for social satire. As is usual for the genre, Death comes for people from all walks of life, but in this case, its victims vehemently protest their fate or attempt to bargain with Death. The preacher, for example, promises never again to mention death or the devil in his sermons if he is spared, and the lawyer claims exemption from death 'by the statutes'. Meanwhile, the miser promises to go contentedly with Death if he spares his money, and the lady of fashion demands that the 'filthy wretch' stops being so boisterous with someone of her stature. Only the beggar does not protest his fate.

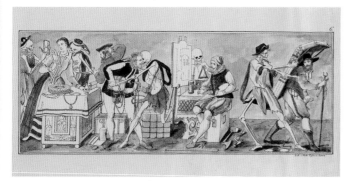 

**Mirror on Human Frailty**

The etchings from *Todten-Tanz oder Spiegel menschlicher Hinfalligkeit in acht Abbildungen* (Dance of Death or Mirror on Human Frailty...), 1838, are based on a series of seven Dance of Death oil paintings created between 1610 and 1615 by Jakob von Wyl. The title page information is framed by an ornate neo-Gothic facade with skeletons hiding in the niches. In the first image (top right), a scantily clad Adam and Eve, ashamed of their nakedness, are being driven out of the Garden of Eden by an angel brandishing a flaming sword; Eve still holds the fatal apple from the Tree of the Knowledge of Good and Evil in her hand, while skeletons trumpet and beat on a drum with bones. Von Wyl's original canvases can still be seen at the Ritterscher Palace in Lucerne.

Tod zum Schultheiß. / Der Schultheiß.

Tod zum Kardinal. / Der Kardinal.

Todt zum Kirbeypfeiffer. / Der Kirbeypfeiffer.

Tod zum Kauffmann. / Der Kauffmann.

Tod zum Narren. / Der Narr.

Tod zum Blutvogt. / Der Blutvogt.

Tod zum Wucherer. / Der Wucherer.

Tod zum Jüngling. / Der Jüngling.

Todt zum Koch.

Dance of Death figurines
In 1822, Anton Sohn translated the Dance of Death into sculptural form with forty-two hand-painted terracotta figures (pages 152–55). Referred to collectively as the Zizenhausener Totentanz (Zizenhausener Dance of Death), they are based on Matthaeus Merian's illustrations of the famous mural at the cemetery of the Dominican monastery in Basel. The colourfully painted figures were intended for display in the home. Each figure is 14 centimetres (5½ inches) tall and has a printed label around the base relating a dialogue between Death and his victim. In the figure above, Death seems ready to take what appears to be a young mother, despite the child clinging to her skirts. Death cheekily grabs her breast, perhaps as an allusion to other intimacies between death and the vulnerable body.

Das Beinhaus.    Der Tod zum Schulter.    Der Tod zur Kayserin.    Der Tod zum Wirth.

La Mort aux Spectateurs.    La Mort au Savetier.    La Mort à l'Impératrice.    La Mort à l'Aubergiste.

Der Tod zum Graf.    Der Tod zur Edelfrau.    Der Tod zum Narr.    Der Tod zum Kirbeseyffer.

La Mort au Comte.    La Mort à la Dame.    La Mort au Bouffon.    La Mort au Musicien.

**Death and the fool**
These lithographs from Hieronymus Hess's *Totentanz*, c. 1843, were copied from 17th-century watercolours of Basel's famous 14th-century Dance of Death fresco. Only the fool (bottom row, second from right) looks happy to see Death, who appears to him as a jester, evoking the tradition of the sacred fool, in which he who appears foolish is secretly the wisest of them all.

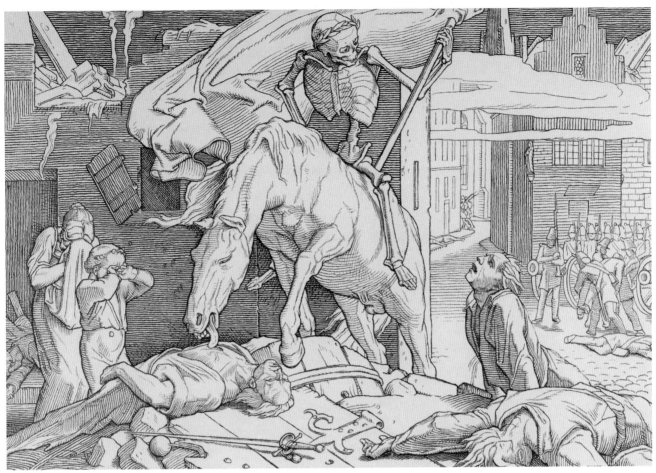

## War and the Dance of Death

In *Auch ein Todtentanz* (Another Death Dance), 1849, German history painter Alfred Rethel used the concept of the Dance of Death as a form of political critique. It was inspired by the Belgian insurrections of 1848, which were among a number of revolts sweeping Europe that year. Although titled a Dance of Death, these images really belong to the Triumph of Death tradition, a genre that began around the same time, in which Death tramples bodies callously and indiscriminately underfoot. Rethel's series demonstrates the versatility of the genre, which can be wielded as a tool for the contemplation of mortality, a social satire or even a grim commentary on war. In the main illustration above, Death rides his steed over the bodies of the dead; in the small image top left, Death receives the sword of justice.

**Spreuer Bridge cycle**
Gebrüder Eglin's *Der todtentanz gemälde auf der Mühlenbrücke in Luzern* (The Dance of Death on the Mühlenbrücke in Lucerne), 1893, documents a Dance of Death painted on sixty-seven triangular panels set into the rafters of Lucerne's Spreuer Bridge. Dating to the 17th century, the cycle was painted under the direction of Kaspar Meglinger. The panels can still be seen today.

Ob ich zwar bin das haupt der welt
Ein Bapst an Gottes statt erwelt — Niclaus Katzenhofer, der Zeit
Gulbherr das 3t.Mal Landvogt
im Ergow — Kumpt der Tod furt mich mit grus
Von meinem ampt zum Tempel us. — 3.

Wo ist mein Künig mein Künigrich?
Mein Hofgesind, wer streit für mich? — Jost Kündig, des innern Raths
und Fr. Anna Dererin. Renoviert 1797. — Do der Tod trängt, das Herz mich engt
Sich jederman von mihr abwendt. — 8.

Eingas umb dich wünst Haupten thändt
Do dich der grösst Sturm anrinnt. — Der Würffel Wh dn sin win
von sil Gwalter verwalter
Hauptmann zu Wyl im Toggen im 15 12. — Zug uff den Schanz, lass andere ganz;
Der Tod füll zu und dich umschanzt. — 26.

Gutterager, du hast gsezget vill
Der Güter, darumb ich auch will — Melchior Balthasar, der Izt
Gutterager — Dich selbs fraagen wie ein Wuhr
Und empacken in ein Tootenbahr. — 31.

Goldschmid, du hast uf mit Manier
Gossen u. gschmelzt din silbergschir. — Landvogt Bernhardt
Fleckenstein — Glesch wie du gossen, naßt auch werden
Gschmelzt ein armen gschür der erden. — 39.

Wann die Natur uit hilff der Kunst
So ist das Pflanzen alls, umfunst. — Johann Ludwig Peyer im Hof
Gwardt Leutn in Lotterunge
Fr. Anna Maria Englin. — Der wir wilt du dein dir Läben
Das dir selbs nimb, widergeben. — 44.

Gewiß ist der Tod, ungwiß sein Zeit
Ungewiß sein, gwiß ist der Streit. — Hans Schiffmann
Renov. 1794. — Und mag auch niemand werden kund
Was wir erwarten alle Stund. — 61.

Das letzte Gricht voll forcht u. zitter
Macht uns den Tod so herb u. bitter. — Hans Rudolff von Meggen
Caspar Studer — Des höchsten gwalt u. zornig ghellt
Ogt keiner weist wie der Baum fellt. — 63.

159

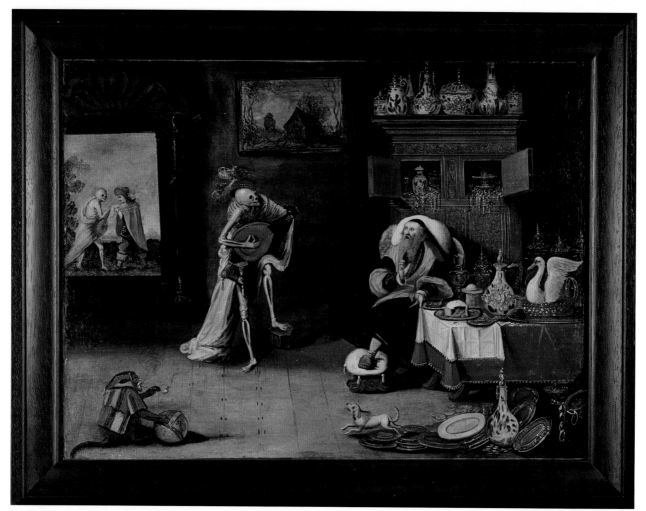

## Moral lessons

Death coming for the rich man was a popular theme in the 17th century. Here, in a painting by an unknown 17th-century Flemish artist (top), a finely costumed Death serenades a man surrounded by art, silver and piles of gold coins while a pipe-smoking monkey in what appears to be a jester's costume suggests that Death has the last laugh. Two paintings by Flemish artist Frans Francken the Younger show similar encounters. In *A Voluptuary Surprised by Death* (bottom left), Death gives a wealthy young man a letter that reminds him of an earlier agreement to sell his life in exchange for the earthly riches and pleasure he currently enjoys. *Death Playing the Violin* (bottom right) depicts Death serenading a wealthy man, with one foot resting on an hourglass.

*Frolicking Skeletons*
Kawanabe Kyōsai's 19th-century painting *Frolicking Skeletons* portrays merry skeletons playing music, arm wrestling, tight-rope walking and dancing on a hillside. Kyōsai, who also created more conventional illustrations of skeletons for his 1887 treatise on painting, was not only renowned as an iconoclast, but was also a virtuoso painter in the tradition of Hokusai. He was known for artworks inspired by Japanese folklore and was the first political caricaturist in Japan, which made his work popular with the Japanese public but attracted the disapproval of the authorities. Kyōsai led a wild life and was a great lover of alcohol; he was said to have produced his best work while under the influence. His eccentricities, lifestyle and work made him a legend in his own time.

**Dicing with death**
Gamblers play dice with Death and play cards at a table while
Death looks on in these illustrations (top) from Abraham a Sancta
Clara and Christoph Weigel's *De kapelle der dooden, of de algemeene
doodenspiegel* (The Chapels of Death, or the General Mirror of
Death), 1764.

**Commemorating an emperor**
*Allegory on the Death of the Emperor Ferdinand*, c. 1657 (bottom), was
constructed by Daniel Neuberger from mixed media, including
wax and glittering sand. In the centre, Emperor Ferdinand III
lies on his funeral bier. The surrounding skeletons, one holding
an hourglass, mourn the emperor's fate.

Le tems présent.

le tiers État. la Noblesse. le Clergé.
C'est ici que les premiers sont les derniers.

Le tems passé.

le tiers-État. la Noblesse. le Clergé.

## The French Revolution

These prints show comparative views of French society before and after the Revolution through the fates of three groups of French society: the clergy, the nobility and the rest of the people, termed 'the third estate'. In the bottom image we see *Le temps passé* (times past), in which the third estate has been reduced to a skeleton by the decadent nobleman and the fat clergyman. In *Le temps present* (top), after the Revolution, the disenfranchised clergy has been turned into a skeleton. Printed in 1790, a year after the Revolution began, these images suggest that the new order restored life and equality to the people at the expense of the clergy and the ruling class.

**The skeleton tradition**
These 19th-century engravings show animated skeletons engaging in typical human activities such as singing, dancing and painting. In one image, two skeletons sculpt a skeletal bust, while another admires a skeletal version of the famous Venus de' Medici. These whimsical and lighthearted images by an unknown artist mock human pretensions in the face of certain death. With their wit, warmth and topicality, they also evoke Mexican artist José Guadalupe Posada's satirical *calaveras*.

**Illustration for Goethe's *Balladen***
This etching by Sepp Frank was created for Johann Wolfgang von Goethe's
poem 'Der Totentanz' (Dance of Death) in a 1919 edition of *Balladen* (Ballads).
The poem tells the story of a group of skeletons who rise from their graves
to dance at night. One of the skeletons loses his shroud, which is picked up
by the warder. Without the shroud, the skeleton cannot return to the grave.

**The wages of sin**
Pieter Bruegel the Elder's *The Triumph of Death*, c. 1562 (top), is perhaps the most famous example of the Triumph of Death genre, which has its roots in the Dance of Death. Bruegel filled the dismal devastated landscape with lovingly detailed vignettes of death and destruction. An army of skeletons marches on the living while Death, riding an emaciated horse and wielding a scythe, forces them into a giant coffin. No one is spared, whatever their station in life. In a Triumph of Death fresco by an unknown Italian artist, c. 1446 (bottom), Death as a cadaver rides a decomposing horse, wreaking havoc in his wake.

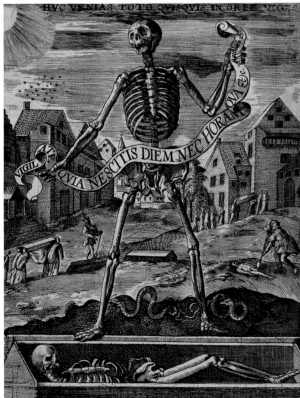

**Death conquers all**
The Latin phrase *Sic transit gloria mundi* (Thus passes the glory of the world) flies on the banner at the top of Cornelis van Dalen the Elder's 17th-century engraving of the same name (top). The early 17th-century image of a skeleton holding a banner reading *'Vigilate quia nescitis diem'* (bottom left) is a reminder of mortality from Matthew 25:13:

'Therefore keep watch, because you do not know the day or the hour.' Abraham Allard's *An Allegory on the Vanity of Death: Kings Examine the Skeleton of King Croesus*, late 17th or early 18th century (bottom right), draws on the myth of Croesus. Famous for his wealth and power, Croesus was a popular symbol of the vanity of human life in art and literature.

**Death's arrows**
Cupid and Death accidentally mix up their arrows in this 1793 illustration for 'Cupid and Death' from *Aesop's Fables* (top left). Rodolphe Bresdin's *La Comédie de la Mort* (The Comedy of Death, 1854, top right), an allegorical meditation on the futility of human life, depicts a surreal landscape peopled by despondent humans, rejoicing skeletons, demons, owls and bats. *Death on a Rampage*, by J. Barra (bottom), is probably from the early 17th century. In this take on the Triumph of Death, Death is a winged skeletal horseman who tramples a king, a laurel-crowned man (the laurel signifying the achievement of earthly fame), a young man and a naked woman.

**Love vs. Death**
This illustration of Aesop's fable 'Cupid and Death' comes from *The Fables of Aesop Paraphras'd in Verse: Adorn'd with Sculpture and Illustrated with Annotations*, 1668. The fable was supposed to explain the mysteries of the old falling in love with the young, and why death sometimes takes the young and healthy.

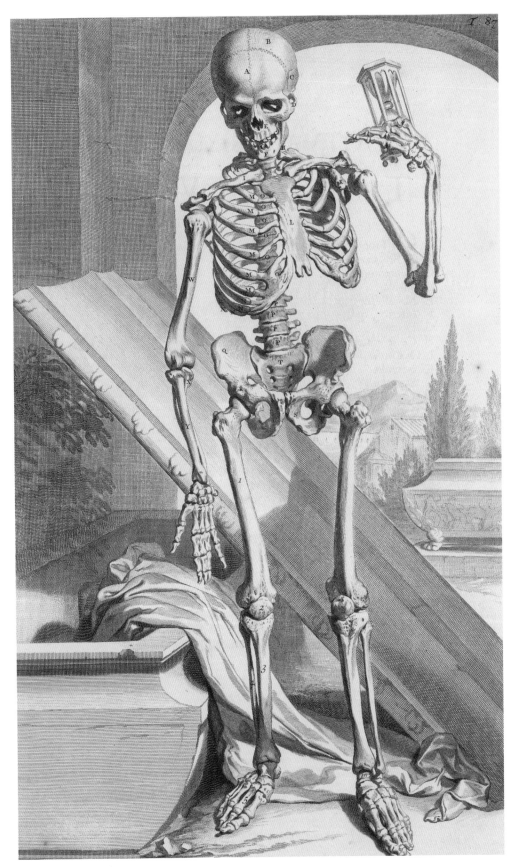

**Anatomically correct**
This illustration by Gerard de Lairesse for Godefridus Govert Bidloo's
*Anatomia humani corporis...*, 1685, functions equally as a scientifically accurate
portrayal of the human skeleton and a religiously inspired meditation on
death, using the visual language of allegories of death or memento mori,
such as the hourglass.

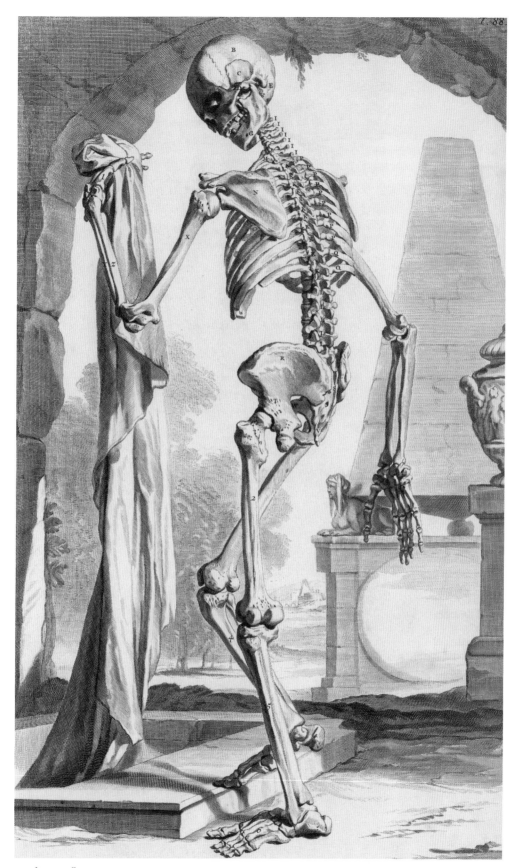

**Vesalius's influence**
Gerard de Lairesse's illustrations were influenced stylistically by Vesalius's
ground-breaking *De humani corporis fabrica* of 1543, which also utilized
memento mori allusions and animated skeletons posed in landscapes. The
allusion to the tomb in an anatomical atlas also acknowledged that most
anatomical knowledge comes from the study of the dead body.

Death chases Adam and Eve from the Garden of Eden

Johann Weichard Valvasor's *Theatrum Mortis Humanae Tripartitum*, 1682, with illustrations by Andrej Trost, begins with a Dance of Death, proceeds to the deaths of famous historical figures, and ends with sinners being tormented by demons in a variety of ways. The animated skeletons on this frontispiece represent death, Adam and Eve, and the trappings of their original sin.

# THEATRUM
# MORTIS HUMANÆ
## TRIPARTITUM.

I. Pars.   Saltum Mortis.
II. Pars.   Varia genera Mortis.
III. Pars.   Pœnas Damnatorum continens.

### Cum

## FIGURIS ÆNEIS ILLUSTRATUM

### Das ist :

 **Schau-**  **Bühne**

## Deß Menschlichen Todts in drey Theil

1. Theil   Der Toden-Tantz.
2. Theil   Underschidliche Todts-Gattungen.
3. Theil   Der Verdambten Höllen-Peyn/vorstellend.

Mit schönen Kupffer-Stichen geziehrt vnd an Tag
gegeben.

### Durch
## JOANNEM WEICHARDUM
### Valvasor / Lib. Bar.

*Cum Facultate Superiorum, & speciali Privilegio*
*Sac. Cæs. Majest.*

Gedruckt zu Laybach / vnd zu finden bey Johann Baptista
Mayr / in Saltzburg / Anno 1682.

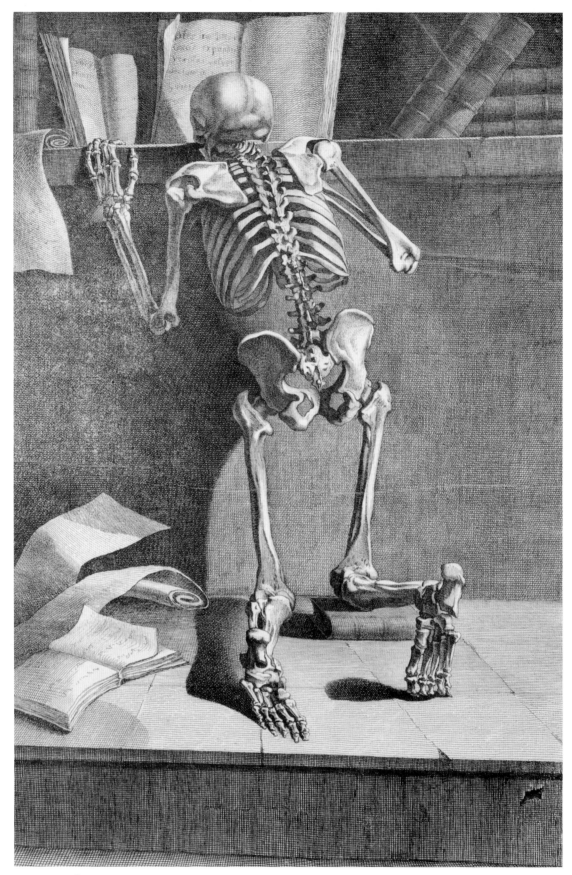

**For artists and anatomists**
French artist Jacques Gamelin intended his self-illustrated book *Nouveau recueil d'ostéologie et de myologie dessiné d'après nature* (A new collection of bones and muscles drawn from nature) of 1779 to be of use to both artists and scientists.

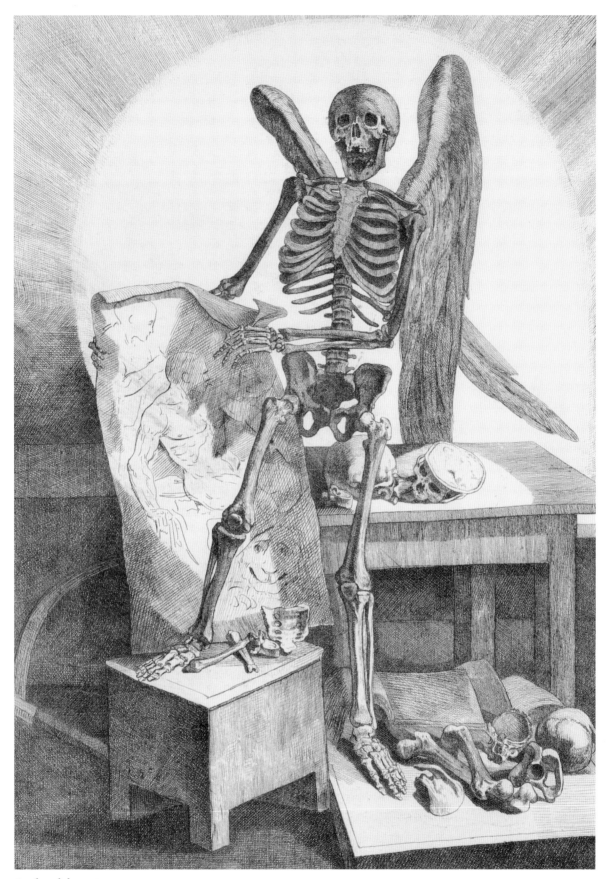

**Death and the artist**
Gamelim conducted his own dissections of executed criminals in order to make
his illustrations. In the etching above, an angel of death mocks the human
folly of perfecting art in the face of certain death.

**Death waits for no one**
The two figures urge viewers to contemplate their own mortality: a fruitwood memento mori skeleton with bow and arrow from the early 17th century (left) and Wolfgang von der Auwera's *Allegory of Time/Kronos*, 1736–56 (right). The personification of time in Greek mythology, Kronos symbolized mortality in European art and was the root of 'Father Time', who also wields a scythe.

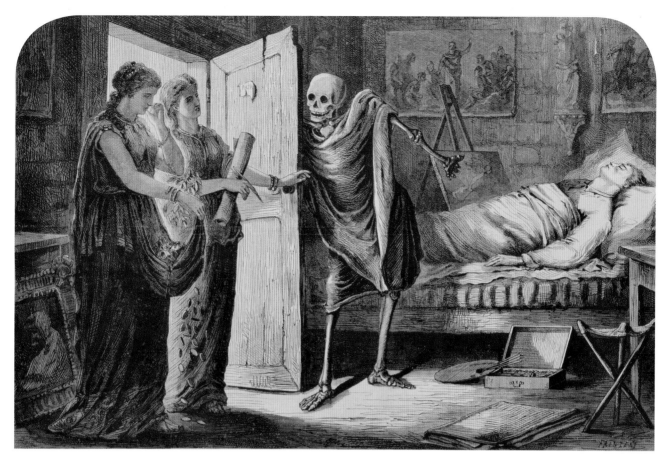

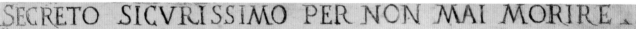

SECRETO SICVRISSIMO PER NON MAI MORIRE.

QVANDO LA MORTE VERRA' PER PIGLIARTI, SVBITO LE SOFFIARAI
IN FACCIA, MA AVERTI BENE NON MAI TI FERMARE, PER CHE SE
TI FERMI SVBITO SEI MORTO.

MI TE FE. 1706.

**Death at the door**
An 1871 engraving titled 'Too Late' (top), published in *Harper's Weekly*, depicts Fame and Fortune paying a visit on a poor and starving artist who is languishing in obscurity. When they arrive, they are ushered in by Death, a skeleton dressed in black, who has sadly arrived first.

**Just blow**
Giuseppe Maria Mitelli's print of 1706 (bottom) satirizes the gullibility of those seeking to escape death. When Death attacks a man with his scythe, the man blows at him. The text advises that when death comes for you, you should blow in its face, but the second you stop you will be dead.

**Death and the young couple**

In Rembrandt Harmenszoon van Rijn's print *Death Appearing to a Wedded Couple from an Open Grave*, 1639, a figure of Death emerges from an open grave and makes his presence known to a young couple. He appears to be gesturing at the young man, who does not seem overly worried, while the woman holds a flower, a symbol of the ephemeral nature of youth, beauty and life. Although not technically a Dance of Death, the picture evokes the tradition. Death was no stranger to Rembrandt; he lost a son in 1635, at only two months, and two daughters who survived little more than a month. His wife also died early, probably of tuberculosis. Only his son Titus survived into adulthood.

**Death the stalker**
Clockwise from top left: *Death to the Virgin*, 1785, by Johann Schellenberg; 'The Old Man and Death', from a version of *Aesop's Fables*, 1793; *Couple Surprised by Death*, 1568, by Frans Menton; illustration from Jean de La Fontaine's, *Fables choisies*, 1755–59; Abraham a Sancta Clara and Christoph Weigel's *The Chapels of Death, or the General Mirror of Death*, 1764.

## Mortals perish

In Hieronymus (Jerome) Wierix's engraving of a young semi-naked couple threatened by Time and Death, 1610–20 (top), the woman sees herself reflected with Death in Time's mirror, a reminder that beauty cannot last the ravages of time. Death surprises a young naked woman admiring herself in the mirror in

*Mortalia Facta Peribunt* (Death Surprising a Woman), c. 1530–80 (bottom left), suggesting the foolishness of vanity in the face of certain death and the judgment to follow. The theme continues in the lithograph *Abuela* (Grandmother), 1997 (bottom right), a contemporary take on vanity and death by the American artist Luis Jiménez.

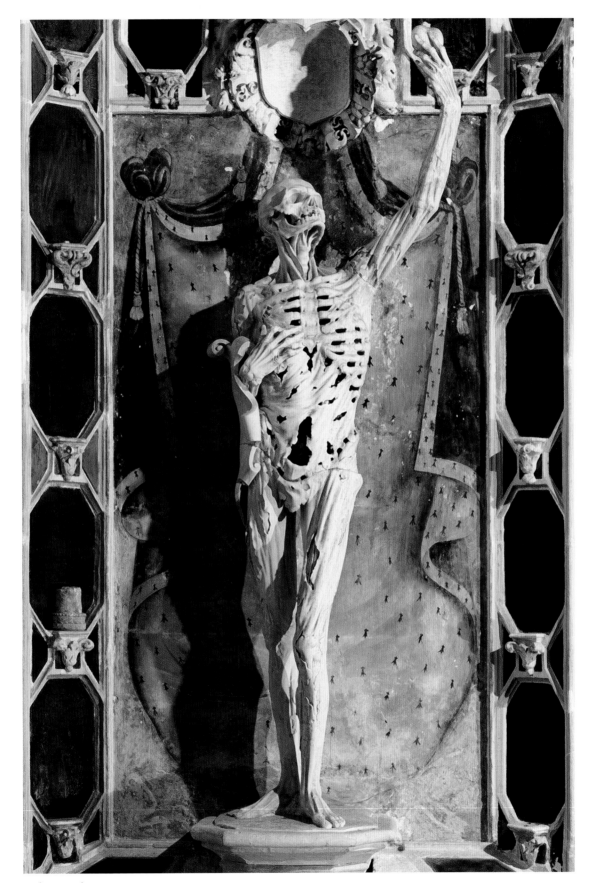

**Cadaver tomb**
When René de Chalon, Prince of Orange, was wounded in battle, legend has it that he asked for a funerary monument in the form of a transi (decaying corpse) on his deathbed. This figure, created by Ligier Richier in 1547, once held the prince's preserved heart in its raised hand. The use of transi for tomb sculpture is not uncommon, but such figures more usually lie prone.

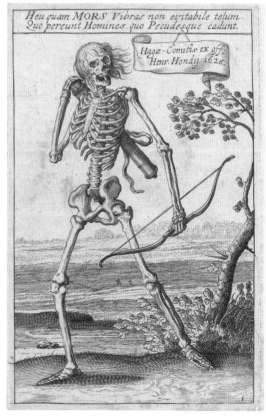

Heu quam MORS Vibras non evitabile telum
Quo pereunt Homines quo Pecudesque cadunt.

Hagæ-Comitis ex off.
Henr. Hondij 1625.

**Battle cry**
Death takes up arms in these three works: 'The Triumph of Death on Time'
from *The Triumphs of Petrarch*, c. 1539, by Georg Pencz (top); *Les Cinq Morts*
(The Five Deaths), a series of etchings by Stefano Della Bella, c. 1648 (bottom
left); and Hendrik Hondius's etching of a skeleton with bow and arrow after
Teodoro Filippo di Liagno, 1625 (bottom right).

**War and the Triumph of Death**
These allegories on the destruction and futility of war draw on traditional Triumph of Death imagery. In *Victory* (top), an illustration by Alfred Fredericks from *Harper's Weekly*, December, 1870, Death rides a plodding skeletal horse across a landscape strewn with the bodies of dead fighters, a laurel wreath of victory on his head and a tattered flag flapping in the wind. In William Strang's *War*, 1893 (bottom), an uncanny Death figure beats a drum, flaming torch in hand, while buildings burn around him. This grimly satirical image contrasts the pomp and heroism of war with its senseless destruction.

## Triduum of the Dead

Paolo Vincenzo Bonomini painted *Cycle of Scenes of Living Skeletons*, early 19th century, for the Church of Santa Grata Inter Vites in Bergamo, Italy, to mark the Triduum of the Dead. This three-day Catholic festival dedicated to the souls of the dead begins on All Saints Eve, on 31 October, continues through All Saints Day, when the saints are remembered, and ends on All Souls Day, when all Christian souls are prayed for. The artist, who was popular for his caricatures, depicted in skeletal form common social types of the era, including the military man, the monk, the fashionable young couple and the painter, which is a self-portrait. Left to right: imperial guard with drum, cooper, friars wearing white tunics, painter and his wife with dwarf, and husband and wife nobles.

**Besnard's Death figure**
French artist Paul-Albert Besnard was a popular portrait painter in the late 19th and early 20th centuries. He produced an idiosyncratic series of prints (opposite and above) devoted to the intersections of Eros and Thanatos and the tradition of the Dance of Death, with Death depicted as a skeleton paying a call on the unsuspecting. Most of these images were created in c. 1900.

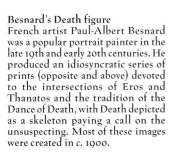

**Death comes to town**
James Ensor, whose idiosyncratic work went on to inspire the Surrealists
and the Expressionists, tries his hand at the Triumph of Death trope with
*Death Chasing the Flock of Mortals*, 1896. Like much of Ensor's work, this
image of Death descending on the inhabitants of a picturesque town conveys
a combination of the carnivalesque, the grotesque and the comic.

**World War I**
These nine images from *Une Danse Macabre* (A Dance of Death), a collection of twenty colour prints produced by Swiss artist Edmond Bille in 1919, present a modern take on the classic Dance of Death genre. Rather than focusing on Death taking people of every station, it becomes a meditation on war, most likely inspired by the horrors of World War I.

# LA DANSE MACABRE

LITHOGRAPHIES DE MAURICE BERDON

# einTotentanz

von

Alfred Kubin

# die BLÄTTER mit dem TOD

Bei Bruno Caffirer · Berlin 1918

# Der Krieg

von Otto Dix

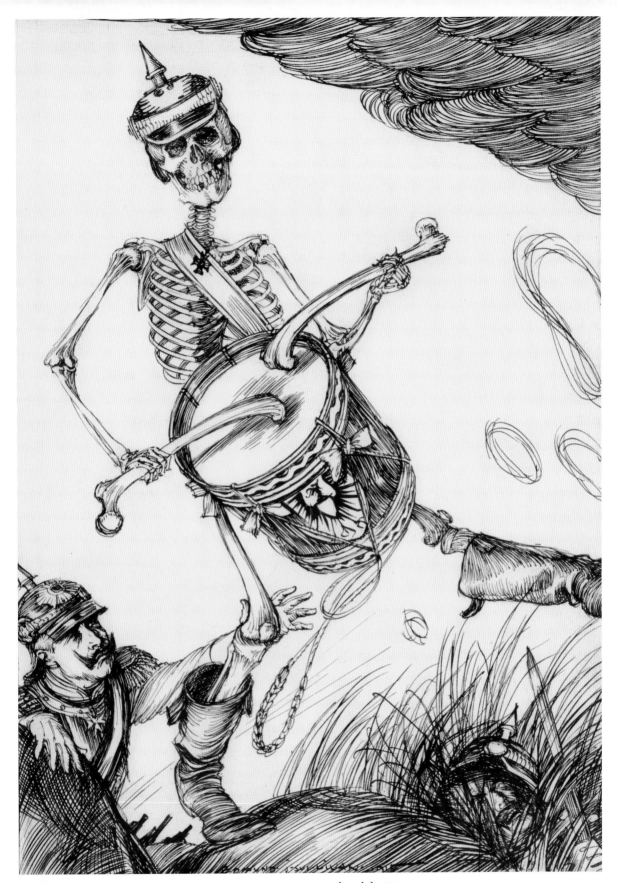

**Deadly warnings**
Death prevails in these 20th-century takes on war (opposite): *La Danse Macabre*, 1931, Maurice Berdon; *Ein Totentanz* (cover), 1918, Alfred Kubin; *Ein Totentanz* (frontispiece), 1918, Alfred Kubin; and *Der Krieg* (War), 1924, Otto Dix, from a cycle of illustrations inspired by Dix's experiences as a volunteer soldier in World War I.

**Death and the Kaiser**
In 1915, E. J. Sullivan published *The Kaiser's Garland*, a critique of Prussian militarism during the arms race that preceded World War I. A series of images by the author satirizes the political situation and bellicose personalities of the time. This illustration is titled 'The Path of Glory'.

**Aus der Bücher-Reihe der**

**SS-Totenkopf-Standarte „Oberbayern"**

**Nazi symbol**
This ex libris, or book plate, was used by the SS-Panzer-Division Totenkopf, one of the armed divisions of Nazi Germany during World War II. Totenkopf translates as 'death's head,' which also formed the division's insignia.

**Death and the herd**
In a take on the Triumph of Death, American artist Edward Hagedorn's *The Herd*, c. 1935–43, shows a menacing skeleton with a whip looming over a throng of terrified people. The hills in the distance are covered with graves.

GATEWAY TO STALINGRAD

November 25, 1942

PROBLEM BEFORE THE CONGRESS

January 7, 1941

WITNESSES FOR THE PROSECUTION

April 30, 1945

NEW RULER OF THE WORLD

October 30, 1938

Death and World War II
Pulitzer Prize-winning artist Daniel R. Fitzpatrick, who worked for the
*St Louis Post-Dispatch*, produced these cartoons during World War II. His
images are credited with helping to change public opinion about Nazi Germany
in the USA and persuading America to abandon its isolationist stance and
enter the war in Europe.

# ATOMKRIEG NEIN

MOUVEMENT SUISSE DE LA PAIX · SCHWEIZERISCHE BEWEGUNG FÜR DEN FRIEDEN · MOVIMENTO SVIZZERO PER LA PACE

**Nuclear war**
The iconic poster Atomkrieg Nein (Atomic War No), 1954, by Hans Erni, was created during the race for nuclear supremacy between the Soviet Union and the United States. In this simple yet powerful image, the Earth has transformed into a skull with Europe exploding in a mushroom cloud. The text at the bottom reads 'Swiss Movement for Peace'.

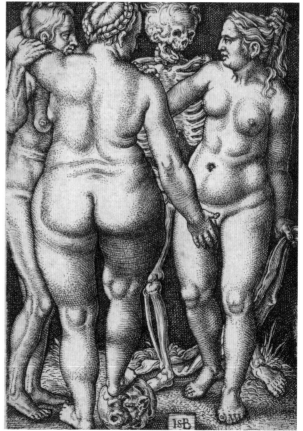

Death and the Maiden
The theme of Death coming to seduce a beautiful young woman in the Death
and the Maiden tradition has its roots in the Dance of Death but possesses
an amplified erotic tension, as captured in Hans Baldung Grien's painting
*Death and the Maiden*, c. 1518–20 (opposite). This concept is also the theme
of the 16th-century engravings (above).

**Eros and Thanatos**
Four images depicting the theme of Eros and Thanatos, sex and death (clockwise from top left): *La possession*, 1900, Albert Besnard; naked woman on a skull, c. 1500; *Two Nude Women with a Skull and Hourglass*, 16th century, Ludwig Krug; *Death Taking the Young Mother*, c. 1814–16, Thomas Rowlandson.

*La Belle Rosine*
In Antoine Wiertz's painting of 1847 (opposite), a young naked woman in the full flush of life unknowingly contemplates what she will one day become. Rosine was the name of the young woman who posed for the painting; the label on the skull reads 'La Belle Rosine'.

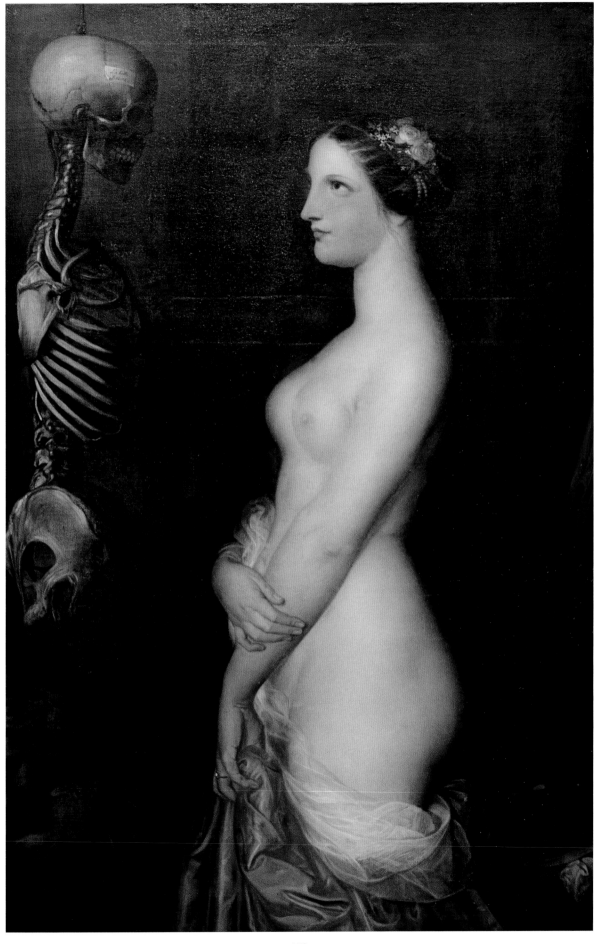

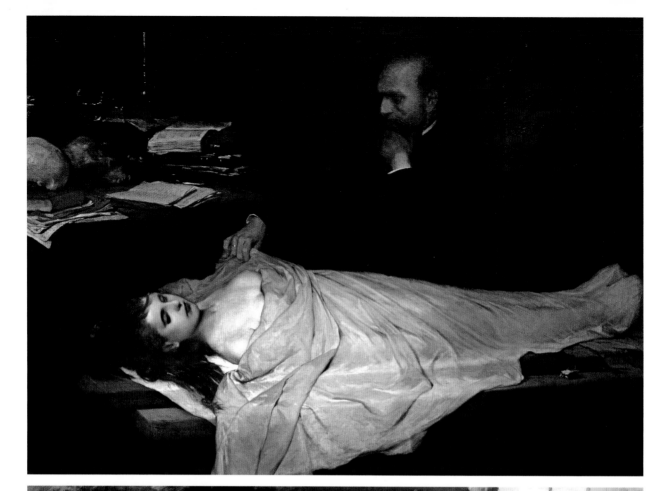

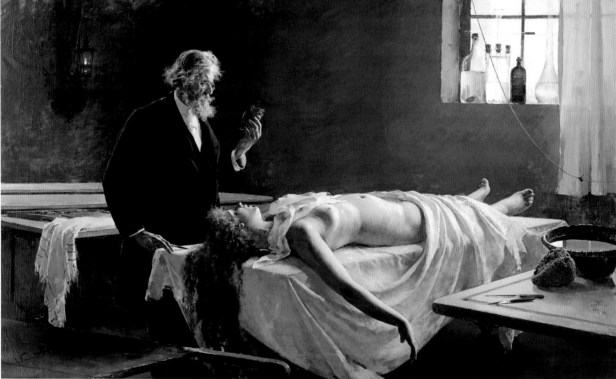

## The beautiful dead

These 19th-century paintings highlight the troubling erotic implications of a doctor in private possession of a beautiful corpse. This was a common subject at a time when dissection of any cadaver was still controversial, in part because of the illicit means often used to obtain bodies. In *The Anatomist* (top), 1869, by German painter Gabriel von Max, an anatomist gazes down thoughtfully as he pulls the veil from a beautiful cadaver, the moth by her legs and the skull on the desk both symbols of mortality in the vanitas tradition. Spanish painter Enrique Simonet Lombardo uses the anatomical dissection as a metaphor for the heartlessness of a beautiful woman in *¡Y tenía corazón! (Anatomía del corazón)* (And she had a heart! (Anatomy of the heart), 1890 (bottom).

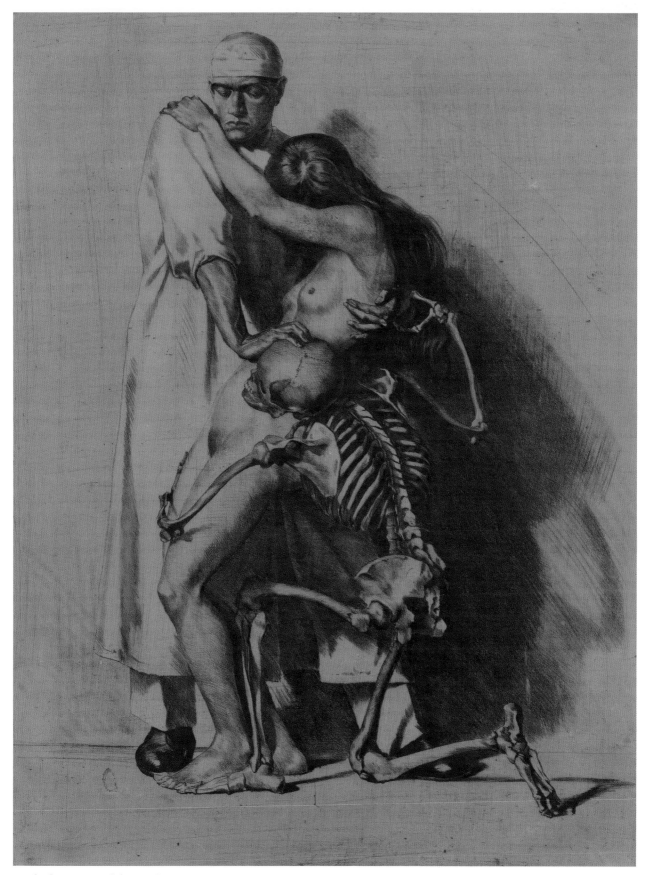

Death, the Doctor and the Maiden
The Death and the Maiden trope is given a modern twist in Ivo Saliger's
*Physician Struggling with Death for Life*, 1920. Here, in a graphic representation
of the heroic ideal of medicine triumphing over death, a young doctor uses
all his strength in his attempt to liberate a naked young woman from the
clutches of death, which is personified as a human skeleton.

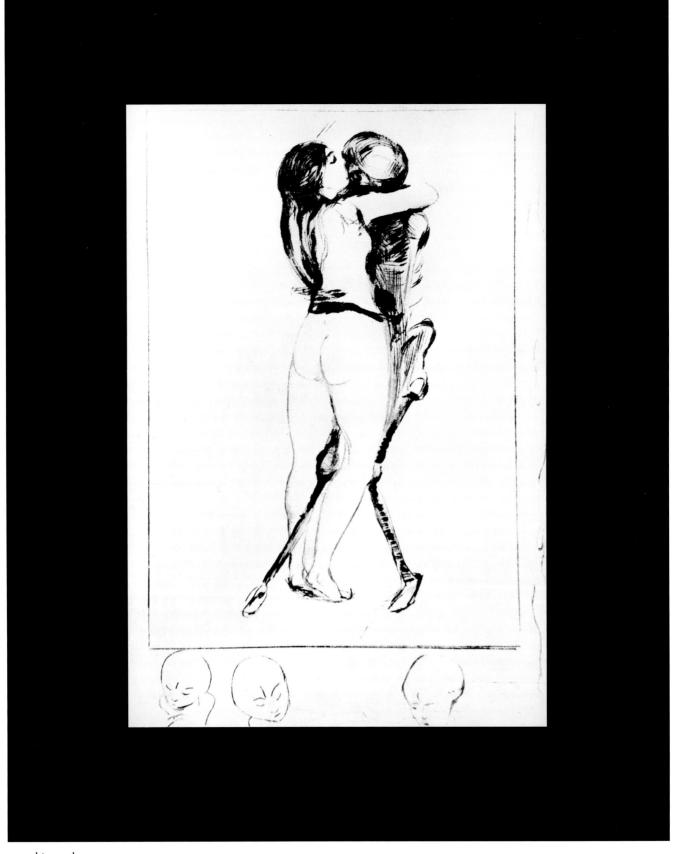

**Munch's Maiden**
In Edvard Munch's *Death and the Maiden*, 1894, the young woman appears quite amenable to Death's advances. Sketchy images of sperm and foetuses decorate the frame, suggesting the triumph of life over death, or the 'death' implicit in sexuality and the creation of new life.

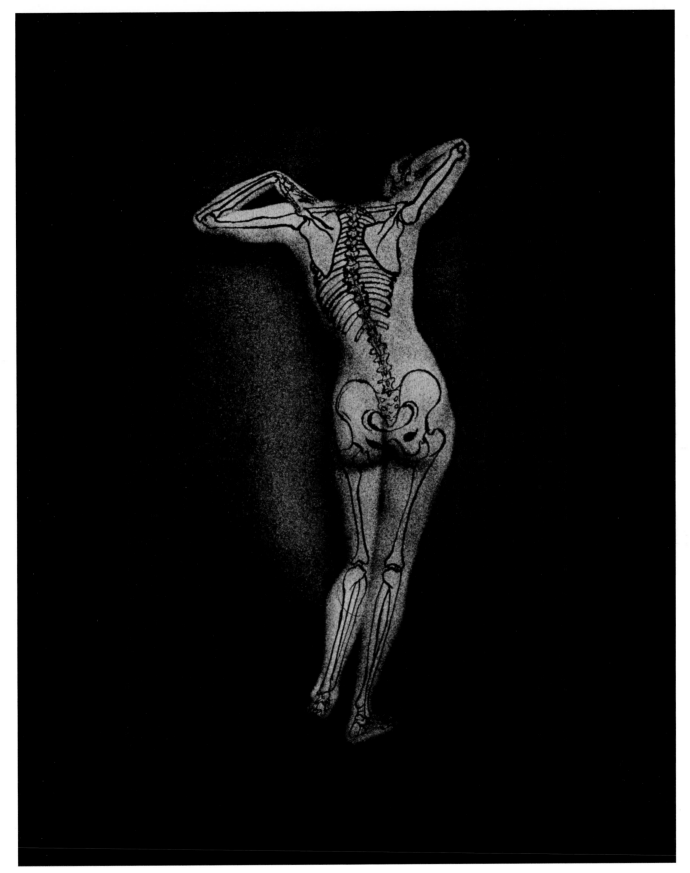

Death as the Maiden
*Nu au squelette* (Nude to Skeleton), 1930, by Hungarian-French photographer Ergy Landau, is a variation on the Death and the Maiden theme. Here, Death becomes the Maiden rather than her seducer. The implication is, as in the vanitas, that the seeds of death reside in the living.

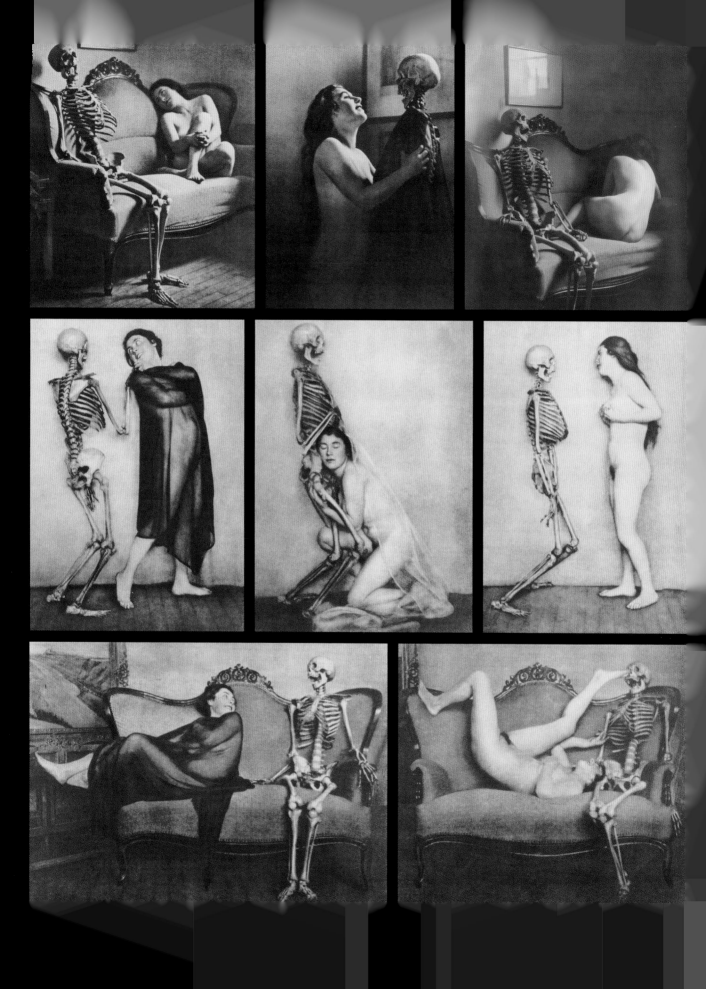

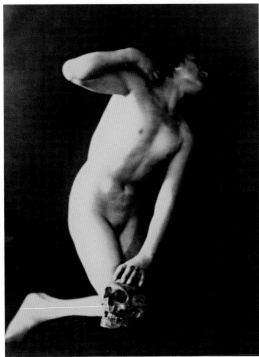

**Flirting with Death**
Eight images (opposite) from *Narre Tod Mine Spiegesell* (Fool Death, My Playmate), a portfolio of photographs on the Death and the Maiden theme, c. 1922, by Franz Fiedler. The photographer poses his model with a human skeleton in a variety of romantic and suggestive scenarios.

**The skull and the nude**
Eros and Thanatos in the form of photographs of nudes with skulls (clockwise from top): *Untitled #33* (smiling nude with skull to her right *[Salome]*, early 20th century, František Drtikol; photograph of a veiled nude with a skull, mid-20th century, unknown photographer; *Untitled (Nude Man with Skull)*, 1925, František Drtikol.

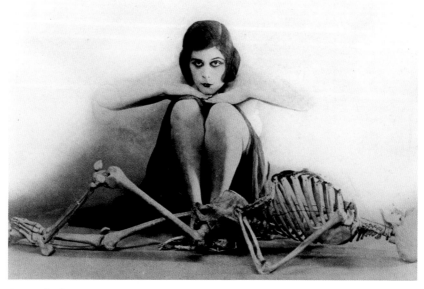

**Femme fatale**
These publicity stills of Theda Bara are for the film *A Fool There Was* (1915). The film – like the Kipling poem on which it was based – was about the destructive allure of the femme fatale, a popular theme in the late 19th and early 20th centuries. Starlet Theda Bara's real name was Theodosia Burr Goodman; her stage name, concocted by her studio, was an anagram of 'Arab Death'.

## Death and the Maiden updated

In *Untitled (Mujer sobre buró/Woman on Bureau)*, Mexican artist and tattooist Dr Lakra demonstrates the continuing relevance and fascination of the Death and the Maiden theme. Many of Dr Lakra's artworks, including this one, are in the form of vintage photographs, which he embellishes with his own drawings. Here, he uses an erotic photograph of a naked woman admiring herself in the mirror and turns it into a take on – and critique of – the Death and the Maiden tradition. The snake wrapped around her body reminds the viewer of the serpent in the Garden of Eden which persuaded Eve who in turn persuaded Adam to eat of the forbidden fruit, thereby leading to their banishment from paradise and introducing mortality to humankind.

# symbolizing

# DEATH

*Cohabiting with dead things*
MEXICAN DAY OF THE DEAD
The worship of Santa Muerte
*Vanitas paintings*
SMOKE, BUBBLES, CANDLES, BOUQUETS
The skull in art and advertising

# Evan Michelson

# collecting death

*Is not impermanence
the very fragrance
of our days?*

RAINER MARIA RILKE

I have in my collection a fragile, deathly little scene: a miniature 19th-century gravesite diorama underneath a glass dome. The gravestone, tall, wax-coated wooden obelisk, is beautifully inscribed with these words (translated from the French):

*Josephine La_____
Wife of John Wood
Deceased on the 1st of August, 1886
aged 60 years.*

Like the gravestone, the fence posts that surround the gravesite are also made of wax-coated wood. The coffin itself is of paper. Everything else – the weeping willow, the fence railing, the greenery and even the tiny floral wreaths are made of human hair in various colours, carefully wound around thin wire and artfully twisted. When the dome is lifted, the musty sweet smell of wax and the faint warm tones of antique wood escape, overlaid with the powdery smell of great age. The effect as a whole is simultaneously delightful and sombre, and it transfixes me. It always has. From the moment, many years ago, when I first spotted the strange little assemblage sitting unattended and in poor repair at a flea market, it has moved me immeasurably.

Page 208
Self-portrait with Death
*Self Portrait with Death Playing the Fiddle*, 1872, by Swiss symbolist Arnold Böcklin. The presence of Death lurking over his shoulder has caused the artist to pause in his work.

This particular object is deathly on several levels. It is a model of a gravesite, constructed partially out of human hair, and it probably contains the hair of the recently deceased as well as hair from assorted family members and even friends. The little scene speaks volumes about the sentimental excesses of the Victorian age, about the superstitious significance often given to human remains, about the decorative possibilities of grief, and about the poignancy of forgotten remembrance.

The dome has taken its place in my collection, surrounded by other eerie or melancholy things. These objects reside in my very old house. This is a home in stasis; an interior that feels hushed, no matter how many people are chatting and drifting through the rooms. The stillness comes, in part, from the accumulated hours, days and more than 130 years that have passed since the house was built, from the age of the horse and carriage to the age of the Internet. It also comes from the many bits and pieces of people, animals (and more than a few insects) that adorn its weirdly angled interior. This is, in many ways, a memorial home, a frame for the deathly and disconsolate. Yet visitors find it welcoming, serene and inspiring. Death can (under certain circumstances) be the most animating company of all.

Society's disapproval of cohabiting with an excessive number of dead things appears to be deeply woven into the fabric of human history. By the early 20th century morbid holdovers from the past, such as elaborate expressions of mourning or preserved animals, had almost completely disappeared from the domestic sphere. Even in the mawkishly sentimental 19th century, Charles Dickens's magnificently morbid Miss Havisham was a tragic and dysfunctional figure; more than a century passed before she emerged as a Gothic icon. The 19th-century penchant for taxidermy (often in the form of a beloved pet, a trophy animal or a natural history diorama) became instantly stuffy, dated and déclassé in the modern, brightly lit and brutal wake of World War I. By the time Alfred Hitchcock's Norman Bates made his film debut in *Psycho* (1960), a preoccupation with taxidermy was already effective shorthand for a dangerously unhinged mind.

In the cold hush of a church, decorated bodily relics transport the pilgrim; in a domestic setting, such things tend to create an air of unease. In an anatomical museum, articulated human remains are elevated to an art form that fascinates and enlightens in the service of science. In the parlour, they proclaim a more nebulous sensibility. In a natural history museum, taxidermy informs; in a bedroom, stuffed animals are an awkward audience at best. One or two hairwork shadowboxes was an appropriate number for the average Victorian home; several rooms-full become a sepia-tinged indicator of a decidedly mortal preoccupation.

Yet the material culture of death has never been so treasured or domesticated as it is now; collectors of the loved and lost are legion and their collections are varied. Some people collect sentimental odes to strangers, such as needlework, paintings and funereal sculpture; others the hardware of mortality, such as coffins, mourning clothes and paraphernalia, hearse finials, draperies and the like. Post-mortem photographs depicting the recently deceased in coffins, laid out in parlours or propped up on porches also contribute to surroundings that exude the profound, solemn, weighted company of eternity.

Many people decorate with anguish. Anyone who has ever been in close proximity to death knows that disease, decay and the slow fading away of a life have a terrible lingering heft. The moment of death can bring release, and caring for the dying can be one of our greatest acts of love, but for most people proximity to human death is nearly unbearable. Sudden, unforeseen death (by accident or homicide) is equally dreadful, with an added dose of shock. So why would some people choose to live with the collected grief of others? Likewise, in an age of ever-increasing sensitivity to the emotional lives of other animals, why has taxidermy once again found favour in public and private spaces?

Once you eliminate collectors who seek shock value or novelty, who are overcompensating, or who are working out serious emotional issues, one is left with the vast majority of collectors for whom the form and function of stasis, death, loss and mourning truly resonate. Those of us who are at home with loss find comfort in the stillness and endless mystery that lingers around the dead. Graveyards and natural history museums are traditionally places of observation and thoughtfulness. In a place of burial, we are surrounded by silent others. All we can know of them is what is written on their stones, but we are invited into their lives, as strangers, to know them, and to know that they were loved. Likewise, when confronted with taxidermy we can be witness to these animals, creatures that were usually torn from life through violence. We collectors feather our nests with things that are familiar yet strange, beautiful and melancholy, comforting and menacing all at once. Through the act of living with and looking at these things, we surround ourselves with a complex aesthetic of wonder.

It is that act of observing and wondering that allows us to enter into the lives of these things, and into the lives of others. Through these objects we find empathy for people and creatures that are remote and unknowable through time and space. Freed from the didactic, clinical setting of the museum or gallery, human and animal remains become expressions of personal individuality; these objects become a part of one's own life, a part of a personal altar to something we seek to understand. In this way an object lives again, creating another narrative in relation to the objects surrounding it.

Likewise, time transmutes the grief of others into something beautiful and strange. Post-mortem images, hairwork wreaths and wax bouquets all speak to the reality of lives lived and lives lost. The further back we go, the murkier the shadows that surround the dead; mystery increases with the passing of the years. The material culture of death, charged with the ultimate urgency of love, resonates. Like art, these strange and beautiful objects take us out of ourselves and into the minds of others.

Ultimately, the aesthetic of death and mourning hovers at the edge of our understanding, and tests the limits of our imagination. I find great comfort in being a caretaker of strange and beautiful objects, and letting them tell their stories. Collecting the dead and deathly is a way of conferring a modicum of immortality, of paying witness to the lives, deaths and loves of others. It enriches the living mind through empathy and, in an abstract way, keeps the memory of others alive.

And so back to my little graveyard scene. I have often wondered how long Mr Wood and his wife Josephine were married. I have puzzled over whose practised fingers worked the hair painstakingly through those fine wires (the work lacks a certain refinement, seeming more like the labour of a loved one than a paid professional). I wish to know if this little scene resembles the actual burial place, or if it is simply a model using the conventional funereal iconography of the day. The dome has been on public display, and strangers have reported that they cannot forget it, that they are inspired by it, that they are delighted to have made its acquaintance, that they, too, have been pondering the lives (and not merely the deaths) of Josephine and her family.

The gravesite needed a fair bit of restoration when I found it, so I have handled all the hair, twisting the wire back into shape and gently piecing together tiny shards of antique wax. I have had physical contact with the tangled tresses of Josephine and her mourners; such restoration work is a strange but by now familiar way to commune with deceased strangers. I hope someday to pass the dome on to someone else who will look after it, fall under its spell, and become a part of its story. The little scene is illuminating; it is familiar; it is strange; it feels like home.

Eva Aridjis

# death in ancient and present-day mexico

**M**exicans have a very particular relationship to death that began in pre-Hispanic times and continues through the present with the celebration of holidays such as the Day of the Dead and the existence of the cult of La Santa Muerte, or Saint Death. For many Mexicans throughout the ages, death has not represented the end of life, for they believe the dead can communicate with the living while the living can communicate with Death or death deities. This belief that the dead are still active has often been treated lightheartedly, as can be seen in José Guadalupe Posada's familiar engravings of skeletons dancing.

Before the Spanish arrived in Mexico in 1519, there was widespread human sacrifice. Dead souls were believed to endure perilous journeys through the underworld after leaving the surface world. The Mayas, Aztecs (or Mexicas), Olmecs, Toltecs, Zapotecs and other Mesoamerican civilizations each had their own belief system, all of which were polytheistic and connected to nature. They had gods of rain, fire, wind, the sun, the earth, maize (corn) and death. In fact, there were many death gods – both male and female – and these deities were usually depicted as skeletal figures.

Pre-Columbian art tended to depict gods and the religious ceremonies honouring them, as well as people, animals and plants. Popular forms included imposing stone temples decorated with monumental and brightly painted sculptures and filled with ornate pottery and metalwork in gold and silver. While very little metalwork has survived (the Europeans melted it down for currency), the temples and sculptures unearthed at hundreds of archaeological sites have provided a wealth of information about the religious and everyday life of these civilizations, including their relationship with death.

The concept of life-death duality was central to pre-Hispanic cultures. It came from observing that there was a rainy season during which everything bloomed, and a dry season during which everything died. Just like the seasons and the agricultural cycles associated with them, death was a natural stage of existence that came after life but also before it. Life and death were two parts of an endless cycle, and in order for there to be life there had to be death, as well as killing and sacrifice.

For Mesoamericans, human sacrifice was a means to maintain world balance and harmony. In exchange for life, humans needed to acknowledge and repay the gods that made life possible. In the Aztec Legend of the Five Suns, the gods sacrificed themselves so that mankind could live. The Aztecs sought to repay this debt to the gods with dogs, rabbits, quail, insects, flowers, beans and paper. But human sacrifices were the greatest offering; the temples and pyramids on which these sacrifices took place were crammed with offerings of treasures and the remains of humans and animals.

The Maya likened the cycle of death and regeneration to the life cycle of maize. According to the Quiché Maya text Popol Vuh (Book of the People), the gods fashioned the human race, the people of maize, to supply them with nourishment in the form of prayer and sacrifice. The offering of nourishing human substance could be obtained through human sacrifice or through penitential bloodletting. Self-sacrifice was common and people would offer maguey (agave) thorns tainted with their own blood, while kings offered blood taken from their tongues, ear lobes or genitals.

It is estimated that the number of people sacrificed in central Mexico in the 15th century was as high as 250,000 a year. Aztec sacrifices took place on specific days, and each god required a different kind of victim. It is often assumed that most of the victims were conquered foreign warriors or low status locals, but Aztec slaves were a major source of victims. These were not a permanent class but rather individuals from any level of Aztec society who had fallen into debt or committed a crime. Prisoners of war who were sacrificed had varying social status, and most of the child sacrifices were of local and noble lineage, offered to the gods by their own parents.

It was common procedure for a sacrificial victim to be taken to the top of a temple and laid on a stone slab by four priests. A fifth priest would then slice open the victim's abdomen with a ceremonial knife, grab the heart and pull it out. Before and during the killing, an audience in the plaza below would stab, pierce and bleed themselves as a form of ritual self-sacrifice, while others sang, danced or played music. The victim's body was then thrown down the temple steps, while their still-beating heart was placed in a bowl held by either a statue of the god being honoured or by a chacmool – a reclining stone figure with a vessel or bowl on its stomach. Chacmools were thought to link the physical and supernatural realms and were painted using a wide range of colours.

All ancient Mexicans believed in the afterlife, which began when a soul left the surface world and journeyed back to the underworld, from where it had come at birth. Many bodies were buried in foetal or sitting positions, suggesting that death was associated with a return to the womb. Cremation was also common, and the remains were stored in jars and buried. Whether a corpse was buried or cremated depended on how the individual in question had died.

In all pre-Hispanic cultures, rich offerings placed in tombs further confirmed belief in an afterlife. Real and ceramic dogs frequently accompanied the dead, as an animal companion was considered necessary for a journey in the afterlife. The Xoloitzcuintli, a breed of hairless dogs that dates back 3,500 years, were considered sacred by Aztecs, Mayas and Toltecs and their remains have been found in many tombs.

Mesoamerican beliefs varied according to region and era, but there is little evidence that human morality affected the afterlife in any of these cultures. For the Aztecs, the key to one's afterlife was the manner of death itself. The Aztec afterlife was stratified, with thirteen layers of heaven and nine of the underworld. Warriors who died in battle or by sacrifice went to a paradise in the east of the sky, while women who died in childbirth went to a paradise in the west. People who died from a lightning strike, drowning or disease went to Tlalocán, a paradise presided over by the rain god Tláloc. Even suicides inhabited their own stratum in the sky.

Most Aztec souls entered the underworld, where they faced a four-year journey to Mictlán (Land of the Dead). The nine layers of the underworld through which they passed, represented in numerous nine-level pyramids, had many obstacles. The dead had to cross rivers, pass through colliding mountain ranges, endure winds that cut like obsidian knives, evade flying arrows and confront wild animals that would open their chests and eat their hearts. To aid souls on these perilous journeys, the dead were cremated with their dogs and worldly possessions, such as a woman's weaving kit and fabrics or a man's bows, arrows and fishing nets.

The dead finally found rest upon reaching the ninth level, Mictlán, ruled by the gods Mictlantecuhtli and his wife Mictecacihuatl. Mictlantecuhtli was usually depicted as a skeleton wearing head ornaments and paper banners, owl feathers and a necklace of human eyeballs. During the Aztec festival of Tititl, a man impersonating Mictlantecuhtli would be sacrificed to this god, always at night and while incense burned. Mictlantecuhtli was also the god of the Dog, because of the association between dogs and the underworld. His wife Mictecacihuatl, believed to have been sacrificed as an infant, watched over the bones of the dead and presided over festivals honouring the dead. She was represented with a defleshed body and an open mouth, which swallowed the stars during the day.

For the Maya, one was tested after death by the gods of the underworld themselves. The Maya underworld, known in Quiché as Xibalba (Place of Fright), began with passage through a cave or still water that led to various other levels. Many of these were hot and steamy sites of decomposition and decay, inhabited by foul-smelling gods of death. Mayas overcame death by outwitting these gods, and the victors would rise to the night sky and become heavenly bodies. The best surviving account of a journey of this type can be found in the Popul Vuh, in which the Hero Twins outwit the gods of death and retrieve the ashes of their dead father and uncle from the underworld.

The Maya underworld had at least two rivers and a large city with buildings and a ball court. The city was home to six deadly houses through which visitors had to pass: Dark House, which was pitch-black; Rattling or Cold House, full of bone-chilling cold and rattling hail; Jaguar House, where hungry jaguars awaited; Bat House, filled with dangerous, shrieking bats; Razor House, containing blades and razors that moved about on their own; and Hot House, filled with fires and heat.

Although the Mesoamerican underworld was a place of fright, it was not like hell in the Christian world, or a place where sinners went. The underworld was the destination of all those who escaped violent death, and hence of most souls. The Spanish friars generally translated the word for Christian hell as 'Mictlán', but threats of an eternity in Mictlán had little effect on the Mayas as they believed all souls must go there.

Both the Aztec and Maya underworlds were inhabited by various gods of death. In addition to Mictlantecuhtli and Mictecacihuatl, the Aztec goddess Coatlicue was associated with death. Known as the Mother of Gods or the Earth Goddess, she was said to have given birth to the moon, the stars and to Huitzilopochtli, the god of the sun and war. Most representations of Coatlicue emphasized her deadly side, as the Earth who consumes everything that lives and represents both the womb and the grave. Coatlicue is usually portrayed with a face formed by two serpents and wearing a skirt of snakes and a necklace made of human hearts, hands and skulls. The Maya equivalent of Mictlantecuhtli is today known as God A or Cizin (flatulent one). Cizin is also the name for the devil. He was usually depicted as a skeletal figure with a horizontal black band across his eyes; he appears in both Classic and post-Classic Maya art and codes as a deity of violent sacrifice (such as decapitation).

It was not only the gods who exerted powerful influences upon the living. Ancient Mexicans believed that deceased ancestors could send punishing diseases or serve as intermediaries between the living and the gods, so it was important to hold festivals honouring them as well.

In the Aztec calendar, a month consisted of twenty days, a period of time called a veintena. There were eighteen veintenas in a year, and each one was an agricultural festival during which specific gods were honoured. There were festivals for dead children and others for dead adults, and during these festivals the living communicated with the deceased through offerings of food and flowers. This pre-Hispanic festival honouring the dead still exists, and is now known as Día de los Muertos (Day of the Dead).

Preparations for the Day of the Dead in present-day Mexico begin early. Tombs are swept before offerings are laid out, and on the night of 1 November the living stay up late, talking to their deceased relatives and filling them in on the events of the past year. On 2 November, cemeteries swell as people adorn graves with flowers, burning candles and incense. A band of musicians will play anything from funeral marches to tropical tunes to liven up the visiting souls, and the air hangs heavy with the sweet fragrance of copal, a pre-Hispanic incense. Tables in family homes are transformed into altars bearing the photographs and favourite dishes of the deceased, as well as candles and images of Christ, the Virgin Mary and Mexican saints. Toys are put out for dead children, and alcohol for the adults. In bakeries all over the country, skulls and crossbones decorate *pan de muertos* (little loaves of bread baked for the occasion), while sugar and chocolate skulls grin mischievously from the windows of shops. Aside from the edible artefacts, there is a profusion of puppets, masks and figurines depicting Death as a laughing skeleton who dances, rides bicycles and plays musical instruments.

The Day of the Dead has its roots in pre-Hispanic culture, but it also integrates elements of European culture such as All Souls Day, which commemorates the souls of Christians who have died. The Franciscan and Augustian monks who arrived shortly after the conquistadors managed to convert Mexican Indians to Christianity relatively quickly, perhaps because the Catholic reverence for saints, with their specially designated holidays featuring elaborate religious processions, was similar to festivals the Mesoamericans held for their gods. By 1537, nine million Indians had been baptized and dozens of churches had been built, employing Mexican Indians as labourers and sometimes using stones from demolished 'pagan' temples.

During the colonial period which lasted from 1521 to 1821, architecture went from Gothic to Baroque and painting remained highly European in its style. As many of the artists were Spanish-born friars, their subject matter was extremely religious with depictions of the life of Christ, the Crucifixion, angels and saints. After Mexico won its independence from Spain in 1821, the arts moved towards a neoclassical style, and Mexican artists began depicting Aztec Indians and scenes from the conquest in their paintings. Then, in the mid- to late 19th century, there was a return to European styles. In *Allegory of Death*, painted by the Mexican artist Tomás Mondragón in 1856, a woman faces the viewer, her body split in two. The left side of her body is youthful and well-dressed, while the right side is a skeleton with little bits of flesh being eaten by worms. The words *Este es el espejo que no te engaña* (This is the mirror that doesn't deceive you) are written in the bottom corner of the painting, as if to state that when confronted with death, one's true self shall be reflected. This memento mori would have served to remind the viewer of his or own mortality and inevitable death, and that beauty is fleeting.

Mexican culture is full of memento mori, from the Day of the Dead *pan de muertos* and sugar skulls to *calaveras* (skulls), which are literary compositions in verse form in which an individual who is alive is described as if he or she were dead. Intended to be amusing, these *calaveras* are exchanged by friends.

Manuel Manilla (1830–95) and José Guadalupe Posada (1852–1913) were two Mexican engravers whose iconic works were printed for mass distribution as broadsheets, posters and cartoons. The most recurrent image in both artists' work – the skeleton engaged in everyday activities – embodied the repressed urges of society and reflected a preoccupation with mortality. Their work was part memento mori, with skeletons dancing, eating or working, and part political satire, depicting politicians, revolutionaries and high-class individuals. Posada's famous *Calavera Catrina* (1913), translated as The Dapper Skeleton or Elegant Skull, shows an ornate hat sitting on the head of a grinning skeleton. The work mocked the styles of elite women in the late 19th century, and is the most recognizable Mexican skeleton image in history.

Diego Rivera and his partner Frida Kahlo – the most important Mexican artists of the 20th century – were inspired by death as a figure in both pre-Hispanic art and Mexican folk art. Rivera claimed that Posada was the most important Mexican artist, and he even described himself as 'the son of Posada and the Catrina'. In his famous mural *Dream of a Sunday afternoon in Alameda Central Park* (1946–47), Rivera painted himself as a young boy standing next to Posada and the Catrina,

as if he really were a child out for a stroll with his parents. Rivera's mural *Day of the Dead* (1924) shows a crowd gathered around food stalls including several children wearing skull masks, flanked by Day of the Dead bread and sugar skulls and against a backdrop of skeletons playing guitars. His painting *Day of the Dead* (1944) shows an Indian family gathered around the grave of a deceased relative, burning candles and copal. Both works signify Rivera's enduring interest in the festival, both as a symbol of Mexican culture and in its role of honouring the dead.

Kahlo also created many paintings that featured death as a central theme or subject, a preoccupation with death having been triggered by a brush with it at the age of eighteen. While Kahlo was travelling on a bus in Mexico City, the bus was hit by an electric trolley and the handrail from the streetcar entered her left hip and exited through her genital area. She barely survived and spent two years convalescing. It was while bedridden that Kahlo started to paint. The first paintings she made that depicted death were portraits of deceased individuals she had known. *The Deceased Dimas* (1937) pictures Rivera's three-year-old godson on his deathbed, while *The Suicide of Dorothy Hale* (1939) depicts the American socialite Dorothy Hale's suicide in graphic detail (Hale threw herself out of the window of a tall building in New York City), jumping, falling and lying bloodied at the foot of the building. In *Girl with Death Mask (She Plays Alone)*, from 1938, Kahlo paints a little girl wearing a skull mask, believed to be a self-portrait of the artist as a young girl. The portrait serves both as a reference to the Day of the Dead, when it was common for children to wear masks such as these, and as a memento mori, reminding the viewer that even a child will wear the face of death one day.

Kahlo's later paintings about death reflect a preoccupation with her own death, painted at a time when she suffered from numerous health complications and spent much of her time bedridden. In *The Dream* (1940), Kahlo depicts herself sleeping in bed with a giant skeleton, or figure of death, sleeping above her. In *Thinking about Death* (1943), the artist paints herself with a skull and crossbones contained in a circle in the middle of her forehead, a pictorial representation of having death on the mind. The lush leaves pictured in the background most likely reference ancient pre-Hispanic beliefs that death leads to rebirth and life.

Through the Day of the Dead and other manifestations of popular culture in Mexico, children are exposed to the idea of death early. In *la lotería*, a children's game similar to bingo, one of the cards in the deck is La Muerte. Here, death is represented as a skeleton, and a female figure. A similar and very important representation of death in present-day Mexican culture is La Santa Muerte, a female version of the grim reaper who is also considered a saint. The cult of La Santa Muerte has exploded throughout Mexico since the beginning of the 21st century. Today, she enjoys millions of devotees both in Mexico and wherever there are large Mexican communities, such as the southwest of the United States.

La Santa Muerte is associated with healing, protection and safe delivery to the afterlife. Since her followers are essentially asking her not to take them, or to give them a peaceful death, she is worshipped by many people who are in danger of dying: sick people, old people, criminals such as drug traffickers, prostitutes, policemen, people in prison or who work at prisons, and people living in dangerous neighbourhoods. Her followers claim that La Santa Muerte does not discriminate – she will take the rich and the poor, the good and the bad, the young and the old. There are also many gays and transsexuals who worship her, as she is popular among those who do not feel accepted by the Catholic Church.

The worship of La Santa Muerte is considered satanic by the Catholic Church, so devotees worship her at public altars erected on the street or in the safety of their own homes, where they offer alcohol, confectionary, cigarettes, apples, money and jewelry to representations of her made out of resin or plastic. Although people dress her up in different costumes to please her or to celebrate different holidays, La Santa Muerte is always depicted as a skeleton with a hood and a scythe.

The cult of La Santa Muerte was born from a syncretism between pre-Hispanic and Catholic beliefs. In line with the former, she represents the close relationship between the dead and the living and is a welcoming physical figure. (The afterlife is not connected to morality in this cult.) And in Catholicism, she is worshipped as a saint: people clasp their hands to pray to her, they kneel before her and the Masses recited for her are Catholic prayers.

The Day of the Dead festival, the engravings of Manilla and Posada, the paintings of Rivera and Kahlo, and the cult of La Santa Muerte all have their roots in pre-Hispanic representations of death: Death as a physical figure (or god) who is part of everyday life, and/or death as a natural phenomenon that is not the end of life. In both ancient and contemporary Mexican culture, death is an important part of life that can be both embraced and celebrated. *¡Viva la muerte!* (Long live death), as many Mexicans would say.

**Death in disguise**
Albrecht Dürer's unusual engraving *The Coat of Arms with the Skull*, 1503,
depicts a wild man ( a traditional figure in German folklore) caressing a young
bride (signified by her crown). The skull on the shield in the foreground,
which mirrors the angle of the young woman's face, suggests that the man
is Death in disguise.

**Vanitas paintings**

Carstian Luyckx's *Allegory of Charles I of England and Henrietta of France in a Vanitas Still Life*, 17th century (above), was intended as a meditation on the brevity of the life of King Charles I, who was beheaded at the age of forty-four. Heavily symbolic, vanitas paintings remind the viewer of the vanity of earthly pleasures and achievements in the face of certain death.

**Bubbles, shells and flowers**

In these 17th-century vanitas paintings (opposite), an assortment of objects symbolizes the transience of worldly pleasure, possessions and achievements, urging viewers to live a more pious life in preparation for the Final Judgment. Clockwise from top: *A Vanitas*, 1669, by Evert Collier; *Vanité au buste*, 1655, by Johann de Cordua; *Vanitas Still Life*, 1655–70, by Jan van Kessel.

## Rise of the vanitas

The vanitas genre was widespread in the 16th and 17th centuries, especially in the Netherlands and Flanders. Part of a long tradition of artistic still lifes (also called *nature morte*, or 'dead nature'), vanitas became popular in Protestant nations where sacred images, seen as idolatrous, were being purged from the

churches in the wake of the Reformation. Artworks for the home, such as portraits and still lifes, began to contain religious and moralizing themes, drawing on the tradition of painting skulls and other symbols of mortality on the reverse sides of Renaissance portraits (see page 225). Taking its name from the biblical phrase 'Vanity of vanities, all is vanity' (Ecclesiastes 1:2), the vanitas

shows the futility of earthly possessions, pleasures and glories in the face of inevitable death. Common symbols include the skull, representing mortality; flowers, musical instruments and coins to signify the fleeting nature of pleasure; hourglasses and clocks to represent the passing of time; and burning candles to indicate the ephemeral nature of existence. Opposite, clockwise from top: *Vanitas Still Life with Bouquet and Skull*, 1642, by Adriaen van Utrecht; *Vanitas – Still Life*, 1668, by Maria van Oosterwijck; *Vanitas Still Life with the Spinario*, 1628, by Pieter Claesz. Above, clockwise from top left: *Still Life with a Skull and a Writing Quill*, 1628, by Pieter Claesz; *Allegory of Vanity*, 1632–36, by Antonio de Pereda; *Vanitas Still Life*, 1660, by N. L. Peschier.

**In the beginning is the end**
These 17th-century paintings of babies with skulls tell us that birth is also the beginning of the end, while the child sleeping on a skull may represent Christ. Clockwise from top left: *Allegory of Transience* by a follower of Hendrick Goltzius; *Vanitas – Allegory with Putti in Landscape*, Dutch School; *Vanitas*, follower of Luigi Miradori.

**Man is a bubble**
Roman writer Marcus Terentius Varro's expression 'homo bulla' (man is a bubble) inspired a popular vanitas trope, seen here in *Allegory of Vanity*, an engraving published by Pieter de Jode II in the 17th century (opposite, top), and in *Quis evadet?* (Who will be spared?), 1594, by Hendrick Goltzius (opposite, right).

VITA QVID EST HOMINIS? flos, vmbraq, fumus, arista
Illa malis longa est, illa bonis breuis est.

HODIE MIHI, CRAS TIBI.

Petrus de Iode sculpsit.

QVIS EVADET?

HG
1594

Flos nouus, et verna fragrans argenteus aura
Marcescit subito, perit, ah, perit illa venustas.
Sic et vita hominum iam, nunc nascentibus, eheu,
Instar abit bullæ vaniq́ elapsa vaporis.

F. Estius

Placebo domi
no in regione
uiuorum. ps. Dilexi qm. an.
Heu me quia incolatus me
us prolongatus e. ps. Ad dnim.
a. Dominus custodit te ab om

**Office of the dead**
This ink on vellum illuminated manuscript from c. 1450, featuring an image
of death as a skeleton, is from an office of the dead, a set of prayers important
to medieval rituals associated with the dead. Commonly included in books
of hours, they were read to the dying as part of what is known as extreme
unction, one of the last rites.

**Death is hidden**
Sometimes skulls were painted on the back of portraits. The back of a diptych portrait of Jean Carondelet, 1517, by Jan Gossaert (Mabuse) (top) shows a skull and the sitter's coat-of-arms; the front (not shown here) depicts Carondelet praying. *Portrait of a Man*, 1535–55, by Barthel Bruyn the Elder (bottom), has a skull on the reverse.

**Death in the family**
Pages 226–27: *Sir Thomas Aston at the Deathbed of His Wife*, 1635, by John Souch, shows Sir Thomas resting his hand on a skull while one of his children holds a cross. The fashion for deathbed portraits and post-mortem portraits began in the Netherlands. The Latin inscription on the black velvet pall reads: 'He who sows in flesh reaps bones'.

Qū spem Carnē seminat Metet ysëa.

227

**Holbein's anamorphic skull**

*The Ambassadors*, 1533, by Hans Holbein the Younger (above) is crammed with the books and instruments of learned men, but at the foot of the painting Holbein painted an anamorphic skull, a symbol of mortality suggesting the vanity of human endeavour. Common visual tricks in the Renaissance, anomorphs need to be viewed from a certain angle for the distortion to disappear.

**The Greek view**

*Self Portrait*, c. 1647, by Italian artist Salvator Rosa (opposite) shows Rosa inscribing Greek letters on a skull resting on a book by the Roman stoic philosopher Seneca. Seneca's statements on death included: '[Death] has both preceded us and will in turn follow us. Whatever condition existed before our birth, is death.'

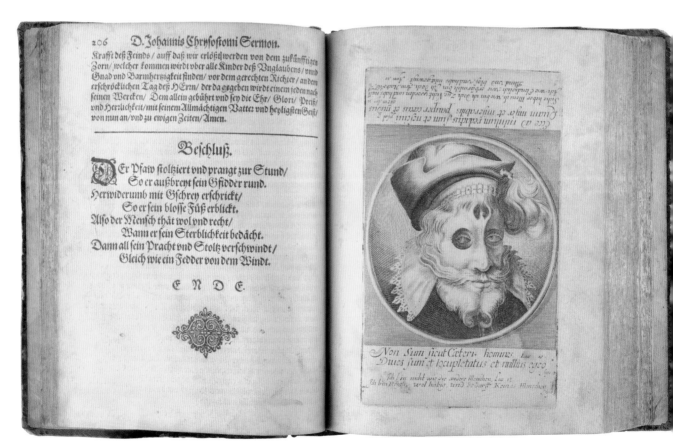

**Death in Seville**
*A Pair of Allegories of Mortality,* 17th century, by a follower of Don Juan de Valdés Leal (top), shows two skeletons in the robes of royalty; one wears a laurel wreath, a symbol of fame and recognition, and the other a king's crown. The macabre figures are similar to the ones in Valdés Leal's *In Ictu Oculi* (In the Blink of an Eye), 1670-72, painted for Seville's Hospital de la Caridad.

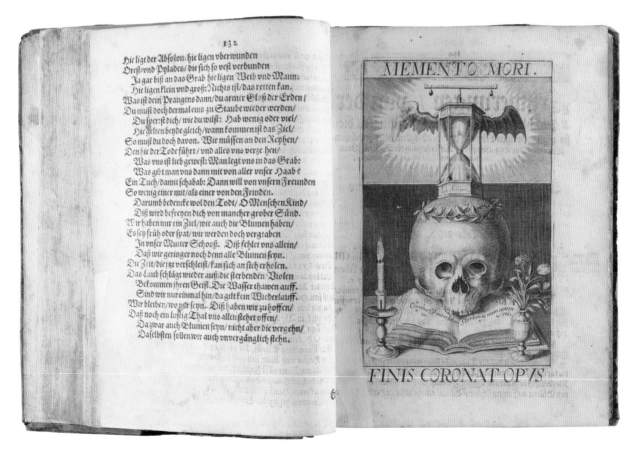

**Remember you must die**
Conrad and Rudolf Meyer's *Todten-dants*, 1650 (bottom, left and right), is one of many books on the Dance of Death published in the 17th century. The image opposite can be viewed in two ways; right side up, it is the portrait of a man; upside down, it is a grinning skull. Above is a classic memento mori symbol of mortality: a human skull topped with an hourglass with bat's wings.

231

## Vanitas busts

These late 17th-century vanitas busts – the one on the left of a military man in armour, from Italy, and the one on the right of a man in a fashionable wig and cravat, from France or Italy – suggest the vanity of earthly life and endeavours in the face of inevitable death. Terracotta busts were sometimes made as models for tomb monuments.

## Skulls in architecture

Memento mori symbols were also incorporated in architecture, especially churches, monasteries and convents. The marble skull peeking out of a shroud (centre), 17th-century, is from France; the carved Renaissance lintel (bottom), in limestone accented with gold leaf, is English and dates from c. 1580.

**Memento mori calligraphy**
This calligraphic sheet with memento mori text and imagery is signed 'Marie Garnier, 1757'. It was probably an exercise sheet for practising or demonstrating skills in calligraphy. Like embroidery or cross-stitch samplers, such exercises were usually performed by young women, and the use of memorial or memento mori imagery was uncommon.

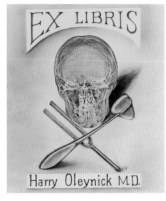

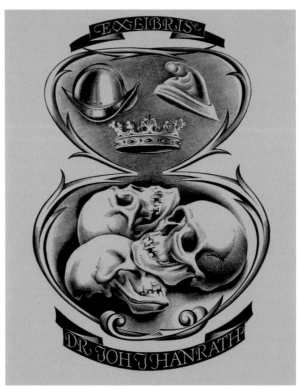

## Ex libris and death

The use of book plates, or ex libris, a term that comes from the Latin for 'from the books of,' dates back to 15th-century Germany. These decorative labels are meant to identify the owner of the book and usually include the name of the person or collection along with mottos, coats-of-arms, family crests and other symbols of identity. In past centuries, when books were expensive, ex libris were common. As is evident in the examples above and opposite, they often incorporate death-themed imagery, perhaps because the contemplation of death is considered the work of the wise, and book collectors were seen as members of the intelligentsia. Books were also symbols of mortality in the vanitas still life, the accumulation of knowledge being seen as a worldly activity that was ultimately futile.

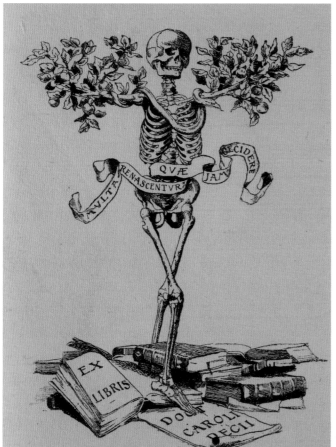

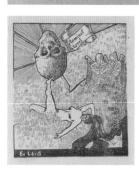

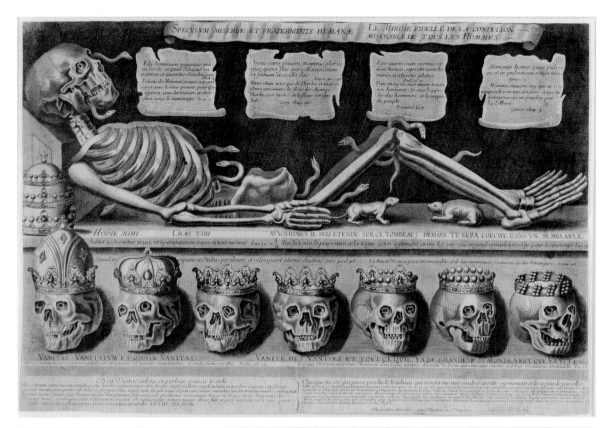

## Message from the tomb

A snake winds through the skull of a decomposing corpse in *Allegory of the Transience of Life*, c. 1440–1504, unknown artist (opposite). Above the corpse, Moses holds the Ten Commandments, a reminder that biblical laws are the key to salvation. Like other such allegories, the image urges viewers to be pious in preparation for Judgment Day.

## Skulls in crowns

In these similar images, a transi (rotting cadaver) from 1782 (top) and a skeleton reclining on its bier, c. 1680 (bottom), are surrounded by skulls in crowns, representing different sorts of earthly powers. In the image at the foot of the page, memento mori symbols include the artist's paintbrushes.

**Wise owls and bookworms**

Many of these ex libris, which feature skull or death-themed imagery, also include a book, a reference to the purpose of the ex libris and a symbol of mortality, too. In the ex libris of D. H. Christ (above, third row, right), an owl – a symbol of wisdom, the night and death – sits on a skull while a snake winds through the skull's eye sockets; in the background, a ghostly cross hovers over more books. The book plate for Ernst Kremling (opposite, top row, third from left) also shows an owl atop an open book, but this time with enigmatic bat-winged figures hovering behind. In the ex libris for Franzisci Thalivitzer (above, top row, third from left), a skeleton is chained to what appears to be its burial slab while a skull and an owl sit on the bookshelf above.

Auch dieses wird vorübergehen, sei's Gram, sei's Lust,
Wer kam, der nicht vorübergehen zuletzt gemußt?
Drum tröste dich in allen Wehen, gieb dich zur Ruh
Wenn diese nicht vorübergehen, so gehst doch du!

Ex Libris M. v. B.

EX LIBRIS
FRANCIS W. BALEY

BUCHEIGNER
ERNST
KREMLING
HS

· EX LIBRIS ·
· VICTOR v. HACKER ·

Ex
Libris
Ernst Rosenfeld.

EX LIBRIS
Dr. FREDERICI

EX · LIBRIS
OSCAR · MICH.
HENRIQUES

ES LEBE · DAS · LEBEN
EX · LIBRIS · DR. HANS · REISCH

EX LIBRIS
OTTO HERSCHAN

EX
Libris
NOLENTIS

EX LIBRIS
WILHELM TRIEBE

EXLIBRIS BUSCHKE

Ex Libris
Otto Lemcke

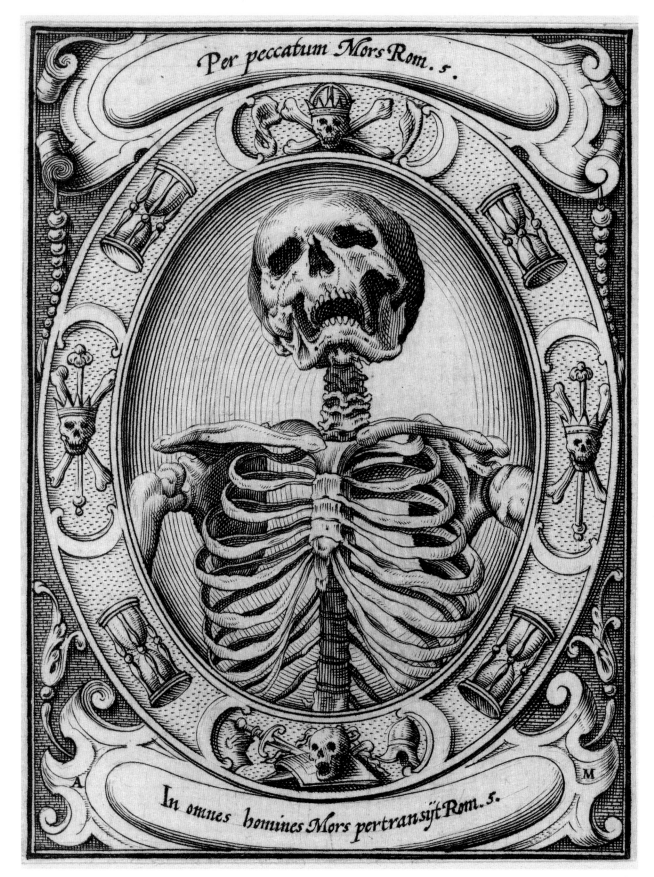

Per peccatum Mors Rom. 5.

In omnes homines Mors pertransijt Rom. 5.

The bones speak
A print made by Alexander Mair, c. 1605 (above), from a series of six memento mori engravings, draws on the biblical verse Romans 5:12: 'Therefore, just as sin entered the world through one man, and death through sin, so death spread to everyone, because all have sinned.' Philips Galle's engraving, c. 1570 (opposite), includes the motto *Mors* *ultima linea rerum* (Death is everything's final limit). The Latin at the bottom of the engraving, from Prosper of Aquitaine, translates as 'Death makes sceptres and hoes equal. Death, the final boundary of things. You flourish in wealth, and boast of the society of the great and powerful; you rejoice in the beauty of the body and the honours which men pay to you.'

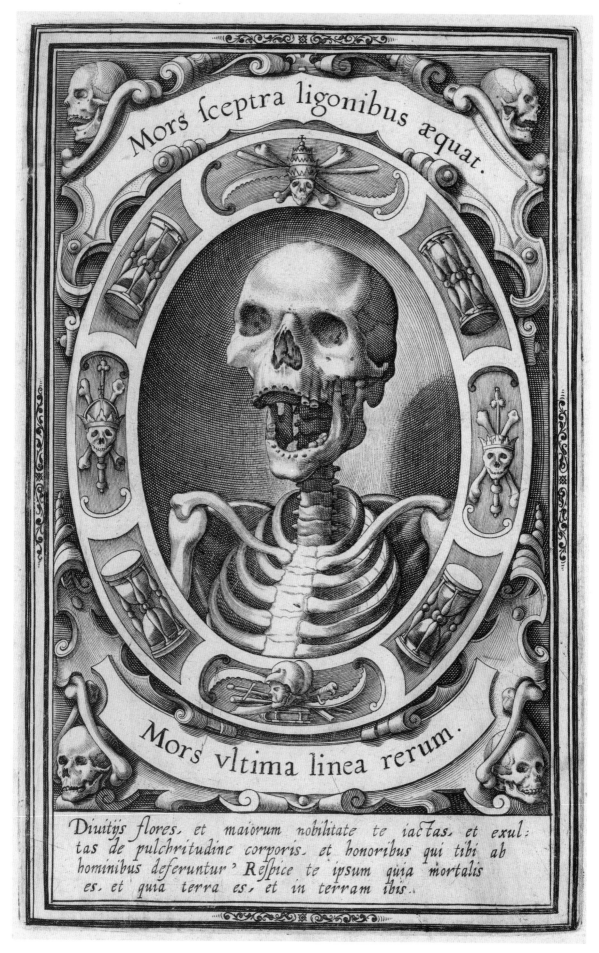

Mors fceptra ligonibus æquat.

Mors vltima linea rerum.

Diuitijs flores. et maiorum nobilitate te iactas. et exul:
tas de pulchritudine corporis. et honoribus qui tibi ab
hominibus deferuntur? Refpice te ipfum quia mortalis
es. et quia terra es. et in terram ibis.

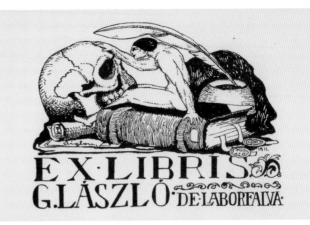

PAUL BOURGET

THOMAS LOWRY

D.H. ZIEBLER

EX LIBRIS
NORBERT L.
LEDERER

ALBERT MAYER EX LIBRIS

Ex Libris          Dr. Waehmer

Ex Libris          D' VAN DEN CORPUT.

EXLIBRIS A.BUSCHKE

## Reading the ex libris

Pasted inside a book, the ex libris is a relatively private and affordable art form, which may explain the many erotic examples. A few of the book plates above combine erotic imagery with symbols of mortality. In two images (above, second row, left), Death is wooing a beautiful young woman. In another (opposite, second row, left), Death plays his fiddle while a naked young woman swoons against his black robe. In Emil Morath's book plate (above, top left), an enigmatic figure of a naked boy with wings – perhaps an allusion to Greek mythology's Psyche, the personification of the soul – wrestles a snake, a symbol of immortality and rebirth, as it emerges from a skull, which is topped by an owl and sitting on a pile of books. A similar figure can be seen in the ex libris of A. Bosco (opposite, second row, right).

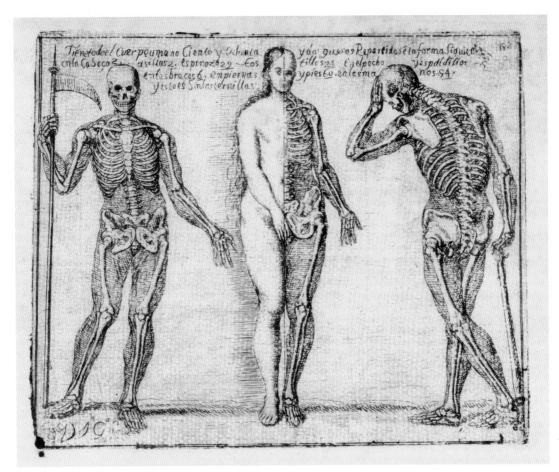

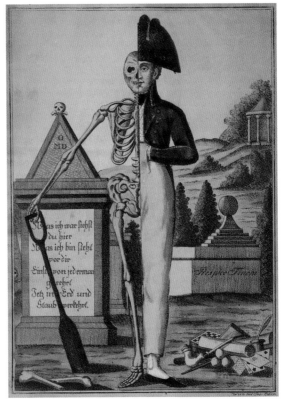

## The half-dead

Depictions of the body in two halves – one young and fashionable and the other
a skeleton or corpse – were a particularly graphic commentary on the vanity
of life: José García Hidalgo's *Three Skeletons: Death, Woman, Man*, 1693 (top);
an etching attributed to Valentine Green (bottom left); and an 18th-century
depiction of a half-human half-skeleton man in a graveyard (bottom right).

**Youth and death divided**
The half-dead figure was a popular theme of small memento mori intended for display on a table or in a cabinet. British waxes (left and right) depict a Regency-era man and woman as half-fashionable young people and half-skeleton. The *Viererkopf* (memento mori), c. 1650 (centre), comprises four heads divided in two: on one side is an infant; the other side transitions from youth to death, the latter represented by the skull. The object was meant to communicate the idea that dying begins at birth.

**Wages of sin**

These paintings of finely dressed half-skeletons, mainly by unknown artists, take a familiar memento mori theme that was popular through the 18th and 19th centuries. In *Alegoría de la Muerte* (Allegory of Death), 1856, by Mexican painter Tomás Mondragón (top left), a half-woman half-skeleton stands at her dressing table in front of a cemetery; a thread divides the painting, and

a text (not seen here) reads: 'This is the mirror that does not deceive you.' In the coloured etching of a nobleman, 18th century (bottom right), the subject stands before a plinth inscribed 'The Wages of Sin is Death' (St Paul's Epistle to the Romans); the 'sins' – dice, games, cards, an invitation from Lord Bauble – are scattered at his feet. Behind him is the landscaped parkland of a grand 18th-century house.

**A meditation on decay**
One side of this 18th-century vanitas tableau in wax resembles Queen
Elizabeth I of England; the other half is a bare skull crawling with
insects, snails and reptiles, representing the decay of the body in the
grave. The text is drawn from Ecclesiastes 1:2 in the Bible: 'Vanity of
vanities, all is vanity.'

MIrad de Dios la bondad
Su amor, su ser su prudencia
Su sufrimiento, yclemencia
Aun con vèr nuestra maldad:
Contenplad la eternidad:
Lo promto de la jornada:
Que està la hora ceñalada,
Y que la mejor criatura,
No es mas que podre vasura,
Sombra, polvo, viento, ó nada.

Hombre, pues eres mortal,
y pues penfar bien no quieres
aquello mifmo que eres,
si quiera pienfalo mal.
Aun afsi harà efecto tal,
que llegando à conocer
la inconftancia de tu sèr,
configas, sin mas tardar,
un tan pronto hacer penfar,
que fea penfar, y hacer.

La tierra es mi sentro,
y todo en esto para;
mira, reflexa, repara,
lo que ensierro dentro

**Polyptych of Death**
A panel from *Poliptico de la Muerte*, or Polyptych of Death, painted by an unknown artist in Mexico in c. 1775 (above). Other panels show a man on his deathbed struggling between the forces of good and evil and the Final Judgment. The polyptych was probably made by the Spanish to indoctrinate the indigenous populations in Mexico in the Catholic view of death.

**Death as a winged skeleton**
Giuseppe Milani's allegory on death (opposite) portrays death as a winged skeleton in tattered rags swinging a scythe atop a ruin in the classical style; below lie a pile of bones, architectural fragments, symbols of the vanity of life and earthly achievements and glories. A candle, another symbol of mortality, burns in the foreground.

Der Tapffere Huſſaren Obriſt Herr Iohann Daniel von Menzel
wurde Aº 1744. d. 25. Iuny am Rhein auf der ſo genanten Maulbeer Inſul beij dem recognoſcieren
von denen Franzoſen erſchoſſen.

Ich Sinne Tag und Nacht mein Deſſein auszuführen,
Drum reit ich an dem Rhein ſo offt recognoſciren,
Ihr Söhne! die ihr euch denckt Ehre zu erwerben,
Komt, Lieber in Gefahr, als ohne Ruhm zuſterben.

Mon Colonel woihn? will Sie die Rhein paſſier?
par bleu mein Mousqueton er mack Sie ubbich reſtier,
dock weil Sie kom su nah, ⟨hb ick Sie tod geſchoß,
jeſzt kan Sie nit mehr reit, drum freut Sick die Franſoß.

Mon Ami, avec moi a la danse
C'est pour vous la juste recompense.

**Death and the soldier**
In Gabriel Bodenehr's *Portrait of the Soldier Johann Daniel von Menzel with Death*, 1715–79, Death – dressed in the uniform of a French soldier – is shown disarming the Austrian general. Von Menzel died in battle in 1744, during the war of Austrian succession, in which Prussia and France challenged Habsburg power. This is probably a post-mortem portrait dramatizing his death.

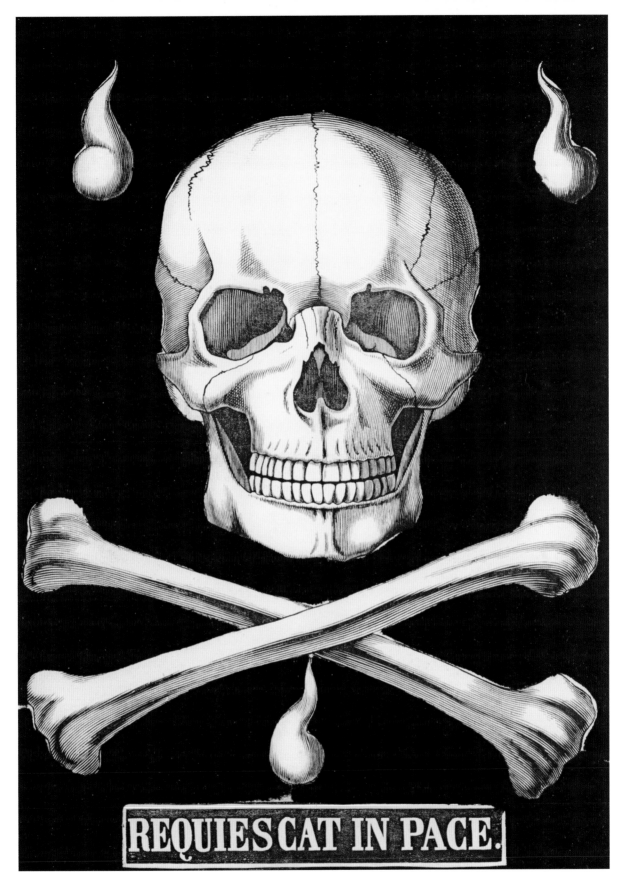

**Rest in peace**
A print of a skull and crossbones, with the words *Requiescat in pace*, 1828–66. The term, better known as RIP or Rest in Peace, is commonly seen on headstones or other memorials of the dead. It has its roots in *Dormit in pace* (He sleeps in peace), which was used in early Christian catacombs to suggest that those who die in the Church are united with Christ.

**Memento mori in ivory**
In the 16th century, the memento mori moved from the church or the cemetery to the home, with the creation of artworks and objets d'art such as the carved example opposite by an unknown maker from c. 1640. It shows a skeleton standing among symbols of earthly glory, highlighting the futility of vanity and worldly pleasures.

**Hand on skull**
Portraits of individuals holding a skull while ruminating on mortality were common in the 17th century. Clockwise from top left: monument to William Aubrey, 1658, by Wenzel Hollar; portrait of Margaretha van Lotharingen, 1660, by Pieter van Schuppen; *St Jerome Holding a Skull*, 1606, by Crispijn de Passe; *Penitent Magdalene*, late 17th century, by Arnold de Jode.

O Mensch ge=
denk an den Tod.

Es ist ein guter und heilsamer
Gedanke für die Verstorbenen
zu beten, damit sie von ihren
Sünden los werden.

## Skull as trompe l'oeil

This 18th- or 19th-century memento mori by an unknown artist on lacquered wood panels (opposite) takes the form of a preacher's altar. The front is flanked by two skulls, in the centre is a trompe l'oeil of a skull in a niche, and the attributes of death are represented in the lower part. It is thought that the work is from the Lucerne area of Switzerland.

## Death by letter

Symbols of death on envelopes are usually placed for a political purpose. In these examples from the USA, death is linked with secession, a reference to America's Civil War, and abolitionism. Two of the envelopes – 'The Watch on the Rhine–Zero Hour' (third row, left) and 'The Last Territorial Demand' (top right) – poke fun at Adolf Hitler.

**Japanese memento mori**
*Okimonos* (ornaments for display) were created as part of a Buddhist tradition of meditations on mortality and have much in common with the memento mori of Christian culture. The snake is a common symbol of rebirth, and Izumi Sukeyuki's *Curious Snake Exploring a Skull*, 1900–10 (above), made from carved and inlaid wood, is an expression of the Buddhist understanding of the soul and its reincarnation after death. The Japanese ivory *okimonos*, c. 1800 (opposite), by an unknown artist, shows a monkey perched atop a head. This might be a reference to what Buddhist tradition refers to as 'the monkey mind' – the restless, unpredictable, capricious mind that meditation and discipline seek to tame. *Okimonos* of this nature were once popular as lucky charms in Japan, especially among Samurai and gamblers.

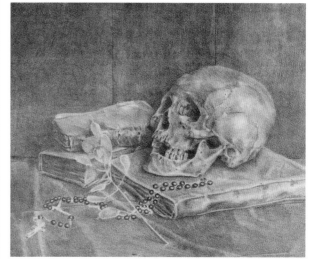

**Skull as muse**
Although bones – and the skull in particular – symbolize mortality, they also represent the endurance of the body (bones lasts for centuries) and our common humanity. Anton Derkzen von Angeran's *Still Life with Two Skulls and a Book*, 1909 (bottom left), and the depiction of a skull with book and a rosary by an unknown artist (bottom right) are classical takes on the traditional vanitas still life, with the skull as a central symbol of human mortality. *Two Skulls* (top) painted by French symbolist artist Julien-Adolphe Duvocelle, c. 1898, takes the iconography of the skull as a point of departure for a more ambiguous and idiosyncratic artwork. Duvocelle used the idea of a staring eyeball in another work titled *Ogling Skull*.

**Vanitas tradition in photography**
*Nature Mort* or *The Sands of Time*, c. 1855, a stereoscopic daguerreotype by
Thomas Richard Williams, is littered with symbols of mortality. At the
time it was made, the medium of photography was relatively new, and not
surprisingly the work has a painterly feel. When viewed through a special
viewer, the image appears to be three-dimensional.

**Hairwork commemorations**
This glass dome containing a hairwork graveyard scene, dated August 1886, is from the collection of Evan Michelson (see pages 210–11). In the 18th and 19th centuries, human hair was used in a wide variety of arts and crafts. It could be woven, plaited, glued into sheets or even dissolved into an ink to mimic sepia. Many such pieces were memorial in nature and utilized the hair of a dead loved one; others were sentimental and expressive of the bonds of friendship or family. Because human hair will last for centuries, and is so intimately related to our individuality, it was seen as an ideal material from which to fashion sentimental keepsakes and memorials. The art of hairwork found its greatest expression in the mid-19th century, when the art of mourning reached its zenith.

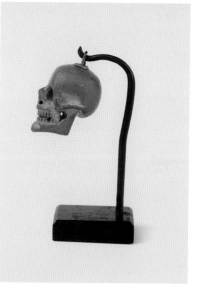

**Everyday memento mori objects**

The pocket watch in silver skull case (top left) was made in Germany by J. C. Vuolf c. 1665. Hinged at the back, the lower jaw and bottom of the skull case opens to reveal the dial. Across the front of the skull case is inscribed '*vita fugitur*' (life is fleeting) and an hour glass and the inscription '*incerta hora*' (the hour [of death] is uncertain) is engraved on the back. The two silver 'vinaigrettes' c. 1701–1800 (bottom left) housed vinegar-soaked sponges the scent of which could be inhaled through holes in the top when passing through foul air. A pipe in the shape of a skull 1840–1910 (top centre) features glass eyes and white teeth and the memento mori-themed cups 1901–70 (bottom right) are copied from a Roman pair. The memento mori circular box (centre right) dates from c. 1830, while the skull pendant (top right) is contemporary.

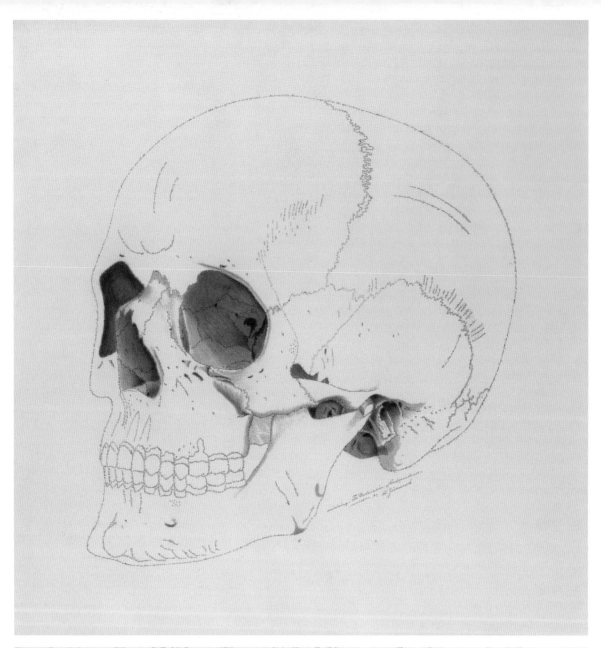

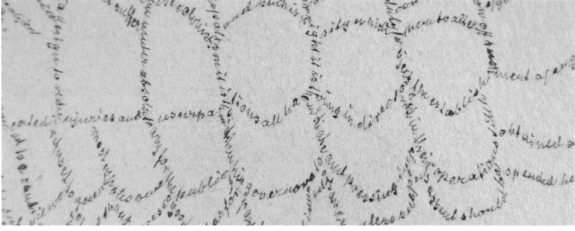

**Writing exercise**
This late 19th-century cursive writing exercise (above), signed 'Fr. Ziekersch', uses the text from the US Declaration of Independence to form the shape of a skull. In the 19th century, when cursive script was an art to be mastered, such exercises were not uncommon.

**The skull as warning**
These 20th-century metal signs from India, caution against high voltage. The skull and crossbones is a universally recognized symbol of warning. It has been used on bottles and other containers to signify poisons since at least the 1850s.

**CAUTION**

**460** ☠ **VOLTS**

**४ ६ ०** ✖ **होल्टस**

**सावधान**

**DANGER**

**33000** ☠ **VOLTS**

**धोका ३३०००वोल्टस**

**खतरा ३३०००वोल्टस**

**Death by alcohol**

In this early 20th-century image of German or Eastern European origin, Death hovers like a spectre over a family whose head has succumbed to alcohol. The father is drinking despondently while the mother pleads with him and one of the children entreats his father on his knees. With the popularity of gin – cheaper and stronger than wine or beer – from the 18th century, alcoholism became a major health and social issue. Many artworks and theatrical productions were inspired by alcohol and its ill effects on family and society. Alcohol was seen to lead to personal addiction, poverty and despair, and to social and moral ruin.

**Death by tobacco**
Two novelty postcards from the late 19th or early 20th century. In the late 19th century, the introduction of new machinery allowed for the cheap automated production of cigarettes, which led to widespread addiction. The first person to establish the link between smoking and cancer was Dr Isaac Adler in 1912.

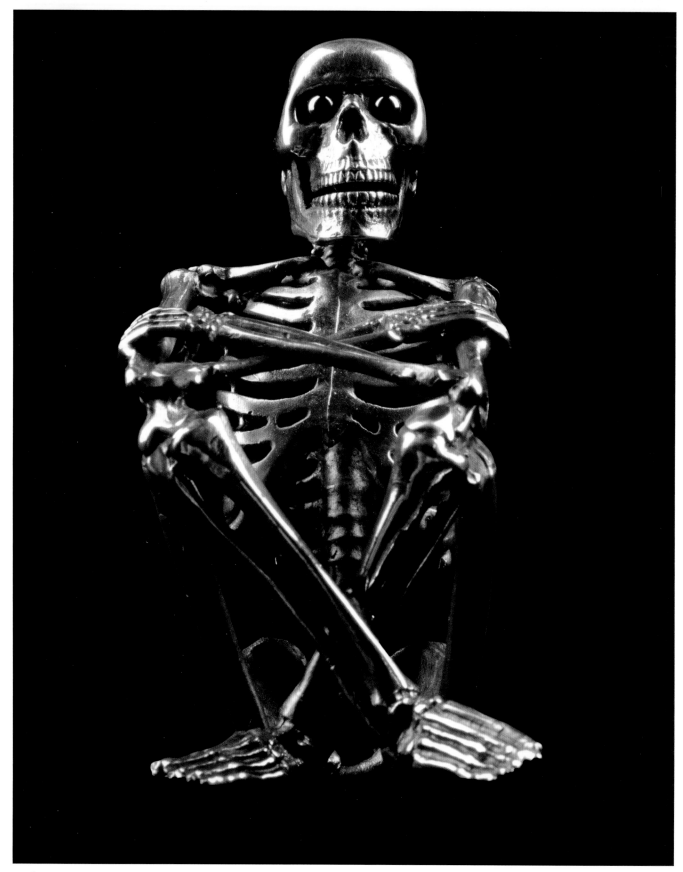

**Modern vanitas**
French sculptor Jean-Marc Laroche's watchful skeleton in silver-plated
bronze, 1990–2000, is a modern take on the skeleton as a symbol of mortality.
The popularity of Laroche's skeletons reflects a resurgence of interest in
artwork related to death and mortality.

**Death stamps**
Death-themed imagery is not uncommon on postage stamps, as seen in the
varied collection above. Some of the stamps relate to World War II, some
are cautionary or even threatening, and some are simply enigmatic, with
meanings lost to time.

**Aztec queen of the dead**
Mictlancihuatl was the queen of the dead in pre-Hispanic Mexico. With her
spouse Mictlantecuhtli (opposite), she ruled over Mictlán, the underworld
realm of the dead, and kept watch over the bones of the dead. In pre-Hispanic
belief, Mictlán was just one of several places for the dead. The colonizing
Spanish often translated it as Hell.

**Aztec lord of the dead**
A ceramic figure from pre-Hispanic Mexico, created between 600 and 900 CE, represents Mictlantecuhtli. Known as the lord of the dead and keeper of the bones of all those who have died, he is commonly depicted as a tall bleached skeleton spattered with blood and wearing a necklace of eyeballs and owl feathers.

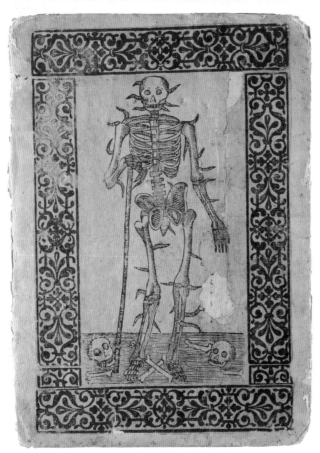

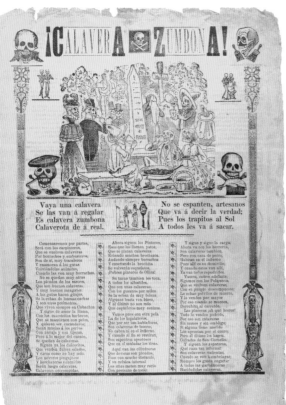

**The skeleton in print**
Above are examples of skulls and skeletons in printed works. Memento mori, woodcut, c. 1750 (top left); cover of a pamphlet for the theatrical production *La Almoned del Diablo* (The Devil's Auction), 1890–1920 (top right); *¡Calavera Zumbona!*, José Guadalupe Posada, 1900–10 (bottom left and right).

**José Guadalupe Posada**
Mexican political artist and engraver José Guadalupe Posada is well known for his use of human skeletons and skulls as social and political critique (opposite). Although his work went on to influence later artists and greatly impacted Mexican culture, he died penniless and was buried in an unmarked grave.

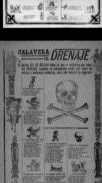

Posada and the *calavera*

The work of José Guadalupe Posada is typical of the Mexican approach to death, which draws from both Spanish Catholic and indigenous traditions. Posada's prints of animated skeletons include *La Calavera Oaxaqueña*, c. 1903 (top left), and *Gran baile de calaveras*, from the late 19th or early 20th century (top right).

The artist used the *calavera* (skull) to create social satires, employing skeletal figures to lampoon politicians and well-known figures as well as society's mores. His most famous work, *La Calavera Catrina* (The Dapper Skeleton, or Elegant Skull), 1910–13 (bottom), was intended as a critique of pre-revolution Mexican natives who adopted Spanish fashions and customs.

**Mexican icon**
Posada's *La Calavera Catrina* is reinterpreted in a hand-painted sign for a craft shop, photographed by Dana Salvo as part of his series *The Day, the Night and the Dead*, 1990–2004. Created by Posada as social satire, today the Catrina is the most recognizable icon of Mexico's distinctive death culture.

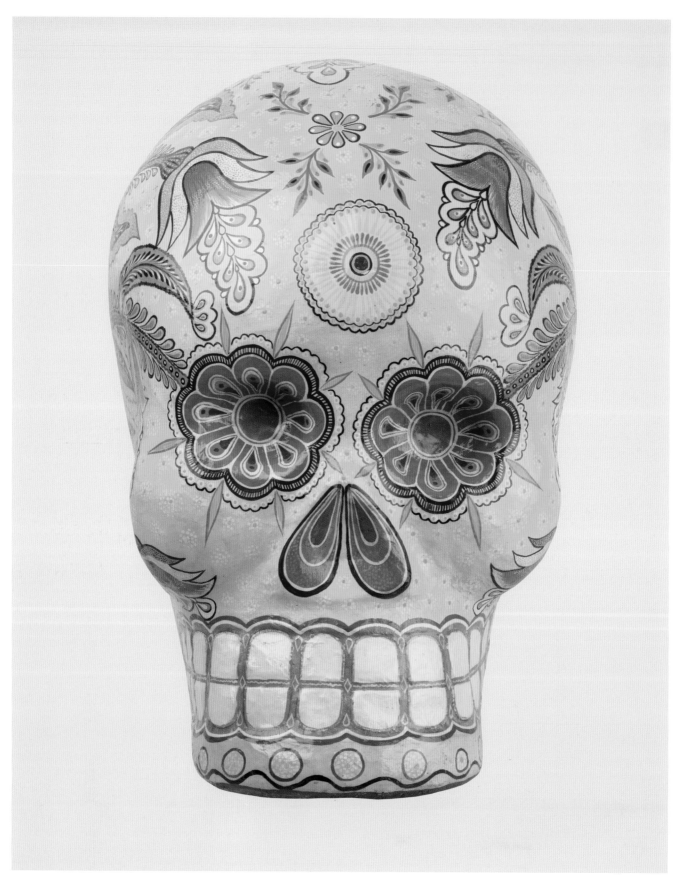

**Day of the Dead**
Mexico's Day of the Dead combines pre-Hispanic beliefs about death and
Catholic rituals relating to All Saints Day and All Souls Day, which were
imported by the Spanish colonists. On the Day of the Dead, families place
offerings, such as favourite food and drink, on altars prepared in honour
of the deceased. Above is a papier mâché Day of the Dead skull from 1978.

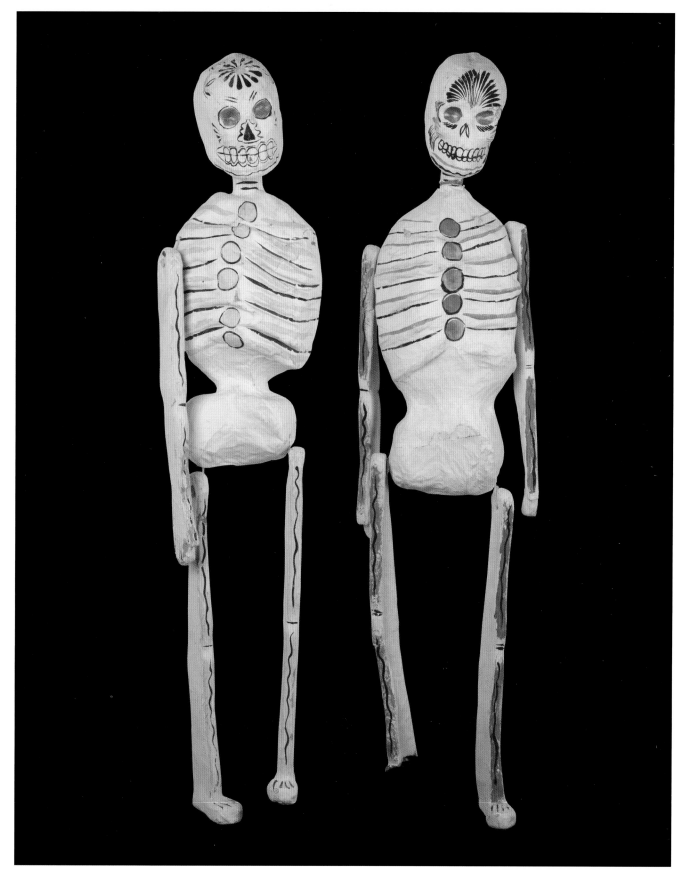

Day of the Dead skeletons
Skeletons and skulls made of papier mâché, sugar, chocolate or clay are a traditional part of Mexico's Day of the Dead festivities. Brightly painted, they symbolize the dead who will return to the land of the living on this day; such figures are also a lighthearted memento mori – a reminder that we, too, will die.

Revelling in death
The top photographs are by Graciela Iturbide; on the left is *Procession, Chalma, Mexico*, 1984, showing a typical Mexican masked procession; on the right is *Novia muerte* (Death Bride), 1990, in which a child poses in a skull mask and a wedding dress. Yolanda Andrade's *Como me Vez, te Veras* (As you see me, you will see you), 2001 (bottom), is a modern take on the vanitas genre.

**Death in costume**
Peruvian photographer Javier Silva-Meinel's *Qoyllur Rit'i – Cusco, Peru,*
*1993,* portrays two costumed participants at the Qoyllor Rit'i, an indigenous
religious festival that takes place annually near Cusco. Silva-Meinel's work
often revolves around the indigenous people of his home country, especially
the role of 'the sacred' in their lives.

**Death intrudes**
A contemporary vanitas, 2005, by Mexican-born artist Marcos Raya turns standard vintage portraits into comments on mortality. Aged sixteen, Raya moved to Chicago, where he became known for his street murals. Clockwise from top left: *Untitled* (family portrait: grandma); *Untitled* (family portrait: wedding); *Untitled* (family portrait: grandma); *Untitled* (family portrait).

Lady death
Artist Laurie Lipton's style of pencil drawing creates a rich sense of tone, depth and luminosity. Many of her images take death as a muse, evoking Mexican and early European precedents. Clockwise from top: *Family Reunion: Day of the Dead*, charcoal and pencil on paper, 2005; *La Catrina*, pencil, 2005; *Lady Death*, pencil, 2005.

# DEATH

## as amusement

*Macabre delights in 19th-century Paris*

PHANTASMAGORIA AND HORROR THEATRE

Le Grand Guignol

*Coney Island's death experience*

A MEDIC'S PERSPECTIVE

The last laugh

# Mervyn Heard

# playing dead — a gruesome form of amusement

*THE LATEST VOGUE IN PARIS:*
*From a Special Correspondent*
*The greatest attraction at the present time is*
*the 'Cabaret du Néant, Brasserie de la Mort' on*
*the Boulevard Rochechouart. The exterior is just*
*like an ordinary house with a doorway decked out*
*in black for a funeral. On pushing aside the pall,*
*you find yourself in a dimly lit room decorated*
*with funereal ornaments, pictures of dead bodies,*
*skeletons, skulls and the like. The tables are coffins,*
*and the garçons call for 'Biers' instead of 'Beer'.*
*Dressed as mutes, these garçons have tall hats,*
*black gloves and so on. When ten or fifteen persons*
*personas are there, you go down into a vault-like*
*passage, and knock at a door, which is opened by*
*a monk, who shows you into a chapel where all are*
*seated. In front of the congregation is a coffin standing*
*on end, and well back, with the drapery all round.*
*Anyone is invited to step into it, and is covered up*
*to the shoulders with a white clot, the harmonium*
*is played solemnly, the light gradually goes down,*
*and the person in the coffin seems to turn into a*
*skeleton.... On leaving you put your 'tip' into a hole*
*in a skull and look through a window which has an*
*arrangement of glasses and see yourself decked out in*
*your coffin. Happily for the nerves of the ladies, and*
*many of the men as well, there is plenty of laughing.*

PALL MALL GAZETTE, 1 OCTOBER 1894

Page 280
The English Dance of Death
The frontispiece of master caricaturist Thomas Rowlandson's *The English
Dance of Death*, 1816, depicts Death as a weary skeleton sighing as he sits atop
a globe. Rowlandson mined the comic potential of the genre (see page 291).

wo similarly themed immersive cabarets artistique, the Cabaret du Ciel and Cabaret de l'Enfer, stood just opposite the Cabaret du Néant at 64 Boulevard de Clichy. The first of these was staffed by angels dressed in white robes, with wings, ringlets and halos, under the direction of St Peter, who with a great key tucked under his arm sang ribald songs to an organ accompaniment. Next door, in the 'pit of hell', devils served strong German beer while musicians performed in a fiery cauldron. However, there can be no doubt that Cabaret du Néant was the more popular attraction. Its drinks menu listed cocktails named after various poisons, which were served under ghastly green lighting by grim-faced waiters who were forbidden to laugh. Subterranean ghost shows invited the audience to partake of an intimate, full-body brush with the inevitable. The name of the establishment, Néant (nothingness), was also fashionably irreligious, suggesting there was nothing but oblivion beyond the dark veil. The venue's memento mori, which appear on eBay today, give some measure of the popularity of this outwardly unimposing venue within the vast array of spectacular and colourful cafés and nightspots of Montmartre.

Conceived by the French magician Antonin Dorville, the Cabaret du Néant began life as the Cabaret de le Mort in Brussels in 1892 before transferring to Paris under the same name. However, it appears that the French authorities disapproved of its name and the notion of serving drinks in human skulls, so it changed its name and bought more conventional tableware. The success of the venue was instantaneous and widely copied. The nearby Cabaret des Refroidis was one of its main competitors. In June 1895, a correspondent for the *Glasgow Herald* admitted to being drawn to a tented version of the venue at Neuilly Fair, where the transformation of a member of the audience into a skeleton was conducted by three 'monks' chanting in Latin.

The Cabaret du Néant was not the first immersive theatrical event of its kind to entice and entomb Parisian audiences. A century earlier, in the 1790s, the fashionable elite of post-revolutionary Paris enjoyed even more elaborate and no less macabre delights in the *fantasmagorie* – seance-based entertainments that eventually captured the imagination of the whole of Europe. Initially the 'professors of natural magic' who conducted these lively shows described them as 'rational entertainments'. Their purported aim was to dispel the public's long-held belief in the existence of ghosts and other supernatural forces through the use of natural science. Despite these claims, wealthy sensation-seekers interested in the latest craze saw it for what it really was – a theatrical performance.

The most sensational *fantasmagorie* was put on by Belgian showman Étienne-Gaspard Robert (later Robertson) in Paris at the end of the 18th century. He invited his audience to assemble at night on a roadside in the centre of Paris. Here they encountered a mysterious cowled figure, who led them through a graveyard full of crumbling tombs and brambles to the derelict Convent of the Capucins. After an impressive display of galvanism (electricity produced by chemical action) by Robert, purportedly proving his abilities to restore life to the departed (frogs in this case), the witnesses were summoned to the inner sanctum – a large room draped in black velvet and decorated with symbols of death. After a while, the minimal light source was extinguished and the room was cast into darkness. As they sat on uncomfortable narrow pews, the audience could hear the doors behind them being bolted.

Eventually, the learned necromancer reappeared and began to conjure ghosts and other supernatural entities, chiefly, but not entirely, through the use of projection. Phantoms and shadows drawn from classical literature, history, the recent revolution and Robert's own imagination were made to appear around the room, rising from the floor, growing in size and suddenly vanishing into thin air, accompanied by storm effects, eerie music from the nerve-shredding glass harmonica and ventriloquial voices. Misdirection and other psychological tricks, not least the inclusion of humour to create an emotional roller coaster, were intrinsic to the impact of the experience. Other shows included delivering electric shocks through the soles of the audience's stockinged feet, the use of hallucinogenic incense and the passing around of alcoholic aperitifs.

The 'phantaz' arrived in Britain in 1801, courtesy of the German magician Paul de Philipsthal. It was adopted by large and small theatres, often as a short phantasmagorical lantern show prior to the main programme. The attractions of the phantasmagoria to the audience were many and varied. It appealed to the prevailing taste for Gothic horror in literature and art, and it was also a chance to experience public entertainment in an entirely new and exciting way – in a darkened auditorium with opportunities for mischief.

The Theatre Royal in Bath was one of the first provincial English venues to stage the phantasmagoria beyond London. In 1802, a regular attendee, Margaret Groves, reported in a letter to her niece:

*The House was crowded; the lights extinguished; & every Door fast locked; the noise of the galleries*

*very disagreeable; enveloped in darkness; they uttered abject fear & vulgar impatience; with shrill whistles; & loud screams; the first appearance was an imitation of forked lightning; too dull to be terrifying; then skeletons came forward; & one figure that seemed in pain; they receded & grew less as they left the stage.*

This account suggests that audience reactions were more like modern responses to the haunted mansion or the 'dark ride' than the stark terror often suggested by historians.

One offshoot of the popularity of the phantasmagoria was that it led to renewed interest in the magic lantern, which had been around since the middle of the 17th century. In the first decades of the 19th century, amateur showmen intent on becoming phantasmagoria professors could buy a wide range of lantern slide imagery. This enabled them to amaze, but better still to terrify children and nervous relatives, in particular at Christmas time.

In the 1860s, a new form of phantom-raising technology was introduced, which came to be known as 'Pepper's Ghost'. The technique was very simple. An angled sheet of plate glass was strategically placed on part of the stage. When a bright light was thrown on some ghostly figure either lying beneath the stage or in the wings, dependent upon which way the glass was angled, the figure would appear alongside the actor. Originally, this effect was devised in Britain by the civil engineer Henry Dircks, but it was modified from the cumbersome original by the director of the Royal Polytechnic in London, Professor Henry Pepper. It was this that became the basis for the Cabaret du Néant's subterranean sideshows.

By the middle of the 19th century, the concept of immersive theatre was out of fashion. Theatre owners of the Victorian era were far more interested in the proscenium arch and the separation of actors and audience. However, in the late 19th century, a new avant-garde movement re-examined, challenged and combined many forms of art, giving rise to confections such as the *cabaret artistique*. Meanwhile in the fairgrounds, exhibitions of Pepper's Ghost offered an element of continuity. These 'ghost shows' often included additional pandemonium with shrouded characters running around the audience in sheets to give punters their money's worth.

Since the 1960s, there has been greater interest shown in the concept of interactive, site-specific and submersive theatre, and to some extent its extrapolation in conceptual art. Now new technologies promise ever more extraordinary theatrical experiences. But will they ever succeed in outdoing the all-pervading visceral impact of the phantasmagoria?

Mel Gordon

# theatre, death and the grand guignol

During the first decades of the 20th century, Greek scholars and anthropologists at Oxford and Cambridge universities traced the origin of scripted theatre to seasonal rites and death cults in the preliterate world. Cambridge professor Sir William Ridgeway, in his influential *The Dramas and Dramatic Dances of Non-European Races* (1915),[1] wrote that the earliest recorded costumed performances took place near an imperial burial ground in northern Persia. There, celebrants pretended to resurrect the corpse of a warrior-king and re-enacted scenes from his heroic conquests and internecine struggles. Productions in classical Athens and Rome also dramatized episodes of murder, ritual slaughter and other end-of-life expositions, but these were normally choral descriptions of off-stage developments. In Western Europe, the first visual displays of death were presented in medieval mystery plays. Gory and bloody exhibitions of mutilation and saintly executions were created with animal parts substituted for the severed limbs and organs of the characters. Beginning in the Renaissance, butchery and homicide were presented as symbolic enactments or as obvious theatrical simulations.

After the French Revolution, a thirst for more credible stage violence developed. Graphic blood-and-guts spectacles, known as melodramas, captivated the Parisian public. White slavers, perverted plantation owners, captains of industry, sadistic military officers and other exploitative characters mistreated their innocent and defenceless charges until the oppressed protagonists had no choice but to strike back. This lopsided and superhuman battle between society's monsters and angels resulted in a scrapheap of corpses. (The scenic purpose of mass carnage was to further stimulate feelings of revenge.) Usually, these mad battles ended with a sunny-faced boy and girl raising their arms in victory as the curtain fell.

Paris's Theatre of Fear and Terror, the Grand Guignol (1897–1962), borrowed elements from the melodrama, such as surprising plot twists, unbearable moments of physical cruelty, vivid characterization, pitiful portrayals of madness and mental fragility, and intense spectator response. But the Grand Guignol evolved from the late 19th-century Naturalist Theatre movement, too. Its narrative inspiration and acting style came from the startling and grotesque underbelly of real life.

The queasy world of the Grand Guignol theatricals consisted of train wrecks, termite-infested cargo ships, abandoned country asylums, back-alley dens of sexual perversion and eerie suicide clubs. It was populated by scatterbrained hypnotists, psychologically impaired surgeons, vengeful lovers concealing beakers of acid, panic-stricken schoolchildren, evil magistrates and demented misfits barricaded in castle ruins.

In Grand Guignol plays – usually four or five plays comprised an evening – death was a constant theme and often inhabited human form. The most popular dramas in its repertoire were *Harakiri*, *The Man Who Killed Death*, *The Torture Garden*, *The Crucified*, *A Crime in the Madhouse*, *The Living Corpse*, *Child Murderer*, *Embrace of Death*, *The Slaughter*, *The Headhunter*, *The Floating Coffin* and *A Parody of Death*.

While the villains of melodrama normally conducted their nefarious activities with manic purpose and swift delivery, the evildoers on the Grand Guignol stage were often protracted and measured in their actions. In one early hit, *Him* (1897), a Parisian courtesan gradually realizes that her gentleman client is none other than the neighbourhood serial murderer just before he strangles and stabs her. In another disturbing sketch, *At the Telephone* (1902), a wealthy businessman calls his wife at their country house to assuage her dread of loneliness and isolation. In the midst of their mundane conservation, the husband hears the cottage door being battered down and her desperate struggle with a criminal band who are about to rape and murder her.

In the Grand Guignol, death by sword or knife, asphyxiation, mauling, battery and thrashing was slow and realistic. Blood not only flowed freely, it coagulated and gelled. Eyes, ears and bunches of hair dangled from hacked skulls; skin sizzled and blistered; severed limbs spurted rhythmic arcs of blood that pooled on the floorboards.

*A Crime in the Madhouse* (1925) casts a deathly light over France's religious and medical establishments. An innocent girl, an atheist, is placed in an asylum for observation over a Christmas weekend. In an adjoining cell, three insane female inmates conspire to savagely attack the girl. Despite the girl's pleas to the Mother Superior and head physician, she is kept in the infirmary. Finally, the trio of madwomen break into her room and poke out her eye with scissors. (They do this in the belief that it will release a cuckoo lodged inside her head.) When the girl dies, and no bird flies free, one of the mad inmates turns on one of her companions and fries her face on a tea stove.

One of the most talked about plays was *The Orgy in the Lighthouse* (1956). In this, a sailor takes two prostitutes to a remote lighthouse on the coast, where the sailor and his religious brother dance and make love with the girls. Because the lighthouse-keeper, an alcoholic, falls asleep and lets the reflecting lamp go out, a boat carrying the brothers' mother crashes against the treacherous shoals. The brothers blame the prostitutes, who have stolen religious relics from a church. They slit the throat of one of the girls and toss her into the water below. They burn the other girl alive in the lens chamber.

In *The Floating Coffin* (1960), a nutty husband and wife kidnap saucy Parisiennes and slice off their body parts – including feet and nipples – until they fit into wooden coffins that could be dumped in the Seine.

The Grand Guignol performers presented their audiences with more than simple scenes of execution; they enacted the horrid and savage details that mirrored the everyday atrocities of real life.

# death-themed amusements

oney Island in New York City was the world's first amusement park. Created in c. 1880, it took the idea of a World's Fair – with its education and spectacle, its focus on commerce, excitement and the exotic, and its variety of attractions all in one place – and made it a permanent concern in a permanent location. In 1909, while in America for a series of lectures at Clark University, Sigmund Freud and his protégé Carl Jung paid a visit. There is no known record of Jung's thoughts, but Freud – the founder of psychoanalysis and pioneer of ideas about the unconscious, dream analysis, the pleasure principle and the death drive – is reported to have said that of all the things he saw in the United States, Coney Island was the only one that interested him.

Although it is best remembered today for hot dogs and roller coasters, both of which originated there, Coney Island at the time of Freud and Jung's visit was a far more surprising place, filled with countless opportunities for titillation, spectacle and danger at a safe remove. On an average day, visitors might encounter Lilliputia or Midget City, where 300 little people lived in a half-scale reproduction of 15th-century Nuremberg; Dr Couney's Infant Incubators, where premature babies where kept alive by novel technology that had yet to be adopted by hospitals; an ersatz native village populated with genuine Bontoc tribesmen from the Philippines (America's newest and most exotic colony); the destruction of Pompeii by a firework Vesuvius, featuring a cast of costumed chorus girls; and a re-enactment of the Boer War starring 600 Boer War veterans. There was even a recreation of a tenement fire, complete with daring rescues performed by a cast of 2,000 men, women and children, at a time when such fires were a constant peril of overcrowded urban life, as tragically demonstrated by the Triangle Shirtwaist Factory fire of 1911, only a few years after Freud's visit.

Coney Island was also home to a dizzying array of immersive amusements that capitalized on recent natural disasters. These included the eruption of Mount Pelée, which killed more than 25,000 people on the Caribbean island of Martinique in 1902. With the help of 'electric appliance, water and pictorial effect', the attraction promised to recreate the thrill of horror that ran through the entire civilized world when news of the great disaster was received with 'not a single detail lacking'. Another attraction, the San Francisco Earthquake, was unveiled in 1906, the same year the earthquake and subsequent fire had decimated the city. It featured a cast of 350 actors, fire, smoke and 'a quaking machine'.

Similar attractions included the Galveston Flood of 1902, which used water, model buildings, sets and lighting effects, as well as a narrator, to relate the thrilling account of a flood that killed 6,000 people in 1900, and the Johnstown Flood, which re-enacted the dramatic story of a dam that burst in Cambria County, Pennsylvania, destroying the local town and killing thousands of inhabitants because an alert was not received in time. A review of the Johnstown Flood in a guidebook of 1904 gushed: 'Words are powerless to express the horror of the situation as this town was crumbling away and the people by the thousands were sinking to their doom.... Hundreds of the most thrilling scenes were being enacted everywhere.... Where the morning before had stood a noble town full of prosperous and happy people, now all was desolation and death.... And the dead were everywhere.... The Johnstown Flood appeals to all, young and old, and should be seen by every visitor to the Island.'

There were also death and disaster spectacles drawn from the Bible, which promised edification and moral improvement as well as titillating horror. The Deluge, introduced in 1906, presented the story of Noah in three acts – from Noah warning the licentious sinners of their fate, to the mighty flood – with the help of a cast of fifty and a narrator. Another immersive amusement, the End of the World, recreated the apocalypse as described in the Book of Revelation. Archangel Gabriel heralded the action with a trumpet blast, upon which fire and brimstone rained down and the skeletal deceased could be seen rising from their coffins. Viewers saw the good ascending to heaven and the wicked, with attendant devils, descending into hell, a red lake of fire. This was followed by a trip to purgatory and then, finally, heaven.

But of all the Coney Island attractions, the most fascinating and surprising – and the one that most clearly illuminates the relationship between primal fear and compelling amusement, which characterized many of the park's most memorable offerings – was Night and Morning: or, A Journey Through Heaven and Hell. In this attraction, which opened in 1907, visitors could, incredibly, experience their own premature burial in the form of an immersive recreation. The fear of being buried alive – taphophobia – was quite common at the time, and not as far fetched as it seems today. In his book *Premature Burial, and How it May Be Prevented: With Special Reference to Trance Catalepsy, and Other Forms of Suspended Animation* (1896), British social reformer William Tebb – who co-founded the London Association for the Prevention of Premature Burial – reported on hundreds of live or near-live burials, as well as dissections and the embalming of living bodies. Edgar Allan Poe famously dramatized these fears in several short stories, including 'The Premature Burial' (1844), in which Poe's narrator asserts that 'to be buried while alive is, beyond question, the most terrific of these extremes [of agony] which has ever fallen to the lot of mere mortality.' This fear even led to a fad for safety coffins, complete with bells, flags and other ways to alert the living if you found yourself trapped beneath the ground.

In Night and Morning, visitors entered a room shaped like a coffin. Through the glass lid, as reported by an article in *The New York Times* in 1907, they saw dirt being thrown atop the coffin, after which they were lowered into the ground with 'shivers and shakes' and 'a voice above [giving] a warning to be careful'. Then, after the summoning of a spirit guide, they encountered a skeleton who delivered 'a solemn lecture in which he tells the people that they must "leave all hope on the outside" – a gentle perversion of the old "abandon hope all ye who enter here"'.

The attraction also included a visit to the River Styx to see the torments of those condemned to hell, including 'monopolists frying in pans and janitors fastened to hot radiators', and then a chamber in which skeletons would sing, shake one's hand and 'smoke cigarettes most unconcernedly all the time just like live men'. This was followed by a panorama of hell, 'a vision of all the condemned spirits being washed down by the River of Death', and by a rebirth in a large room 'with cathedral-like windows through which you can look outside and see the graveyard which looms up with a weird effect'. The newspaper reporter described how he saw, 'like great mist', the spirits rising from the graves and ascending to heaven: 'There is thunder and lightning and the music of an organ. The flashes of lightning form a cross.... The whole graveyard floats off into space with the single exception of an immense cross, where the form of a young girl is seen clinging to the Rock of Ages. Fountains foam with all their prismatic colour, and the air is filled with troops of circling angels. The room itself vanishes and you find yourself in a bower of flowers under a blue sky. At the climax, an angel comes down with a halo which she places on the head of the girl who is still clinging to the cross. Then all that vanishes and you are within four blank walls once more.'

Although such amusements, which were commonplace a century or so ago, might seem odd today, it is clear that death and darkness have long thrilled humans. The reason such attractions died out was not that humankind outgrew this vicarious pleasure; rather, it was a shift of mediums: the actored, ephemeral spectacle endlessly repeated was supplanted by cinema. Film could create immersive amusement far more cheaply, for it need be created only once before being distributed with ease around the world.

In 1911, one of the great parks of Coney Island – Dreamland – was destroyed in a incident uncannily like its disaster-themed attractions. The fire began in a ride aptly titled Hell Gate, in which little boats transported passengers though a whirlpool to a vision of hell in the caverns of Earth's interior. (Russian writer Maxim Gorky remarked that 'Hell [was] very badly done.') Workers were fixing up the old ride for the season opening, scheduled for the following day, when a spark from a burst light bulb set fire to a bucket of tar. This led to a conflagration that engulfed not only the attraction but the entire park.

Dreamland was never rebuilt. If it had been, I am certain that someone would have crafted a lavish spectacle in which visitors could experience the thrill of the great park's destruction, complete with daring but futile heroics by Lilliputia's fire brigade, a black-maned Nubian lion called Black Prince ascending ersatz mountains with its mane aflame before being shot by policemen, and the cries of Little Hip the elephant, who would not leave his concrete block without his trusted handler Captain Andre, who arrived from Manhattan just in time to hear the animal's final cries. The irony that this epicentre of disaster spectacles – many revolving around fire – had come to experience a conflagration of the very highest order would not have been lost on the makers. They would have recognized the irony in the timing of the fiery destruction of Dreamland, just as the amusements for which it was famous were becoming obsolete.

Designed & done on Stone by E. Hull.          Printed by C. Hullmandel.

  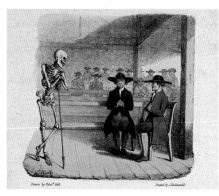

**Hull's Dance of Death**

In these Dance of Death lithographs, 1827, by Edward Hull, Death is a skeleton armed with a spear, who springs on the unsuspecting as they go about their business. The text for the image bottom row, centre explains that 'Death found an author writing his life, but he let him write no further; for Death who strikes whenever he likes, is jealous of all self-murther.' The scenarios, left to right, top to bottom: 'Death saw two players playing cards'; 'The dreary old king of death'; 'Death sees a dustman ringing his bell'; 'Death meets a coachman'; 'Death sees a patient'; 'Death finds an author writing his life'; 'Death sees two Quakers'.

WINES!

BILLIARDS!

DISSIPATION!

GAMING!

VICE!

SEDUCTION!

FINISH

ASHES TO ASHES

DUST TO DUST!

POVERTY!    FOLLY!    IDLENESS!

Fair play . Rob: Cruikshank Inv: et Fecil: Original Suggester & Artist of the 2. Vol. Adieu.

ONE, NEGRO SAY ONE TING, YOU NO TAKE OFFENCE!
BLACK AND WHITE BE SAME COLOUR ONE HUNDRED YEARS HENCE:
AND WHEN MASSA DEATH POPS YOU INTO DE GRAVE!
HE SPARES NEITHER TOM, LOGIC, KATE, OR ONE SLAVE.

**Satire and death**
Sinners face the consequences of their actions in Isaac Robert Cruikshank's *Fair Play*, c. 1830–40 (opposite). In the centre of the print, Death upsets a drunken banquet with his arrows, demonstrating the biblical adage 'the wages of sin is death'. An illustrator and caricaturist, Cruikshank belonged to a circle of notable social satirists that included his brother George Cruikshank.

**Death stalks Regency London**
In *The English Dance of Death*, 1814–16 (above), British caricaturist Thomas Rowlandson uses the Dance of Death theme not as a moralizing reflection on mortality, but as a device for poking fun at the pretensions of a range of social types in Regency London. Rowlandson's prints were issued monthly, three at a time, with accompanying texts.

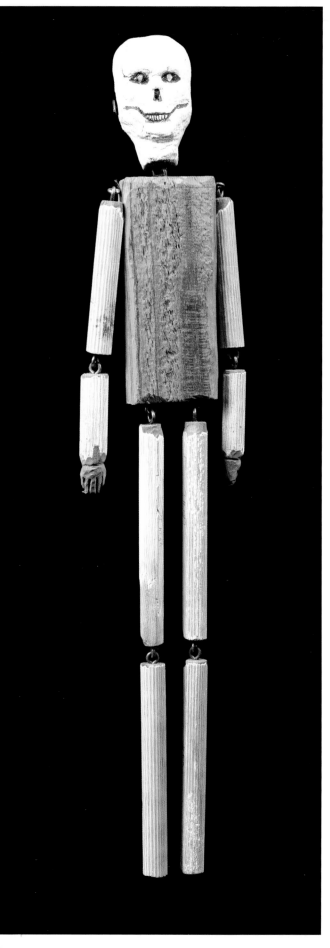

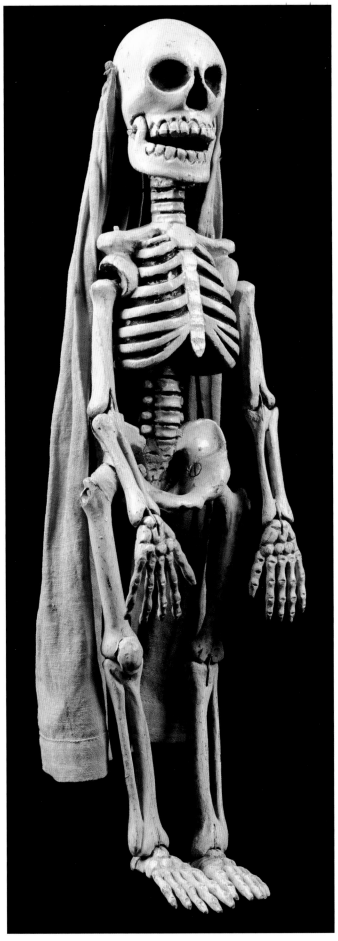

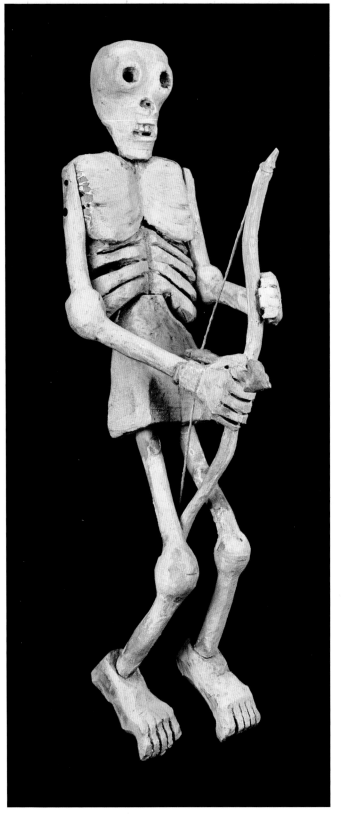

**Skeletal puppets**
Often part of a religious or magical tradition, puppets feature in nearly all civilizations. Top to bottom, left to right: late 19th-century, plaster and cloth puppet; wooden skeleton puppet with cape, unknown date and maker; wooden puppet, unknown date and maker; skeleton puppet with cape, unknown date and maker; *New Mexican Carved Skeleton with Bow*, Nicholas Herrera, c. 1950.

## Death in advertising

Antikamnia Chemical Company of St Louis, Missouri, issued skeleton-themed calendars as promotional materials from 1897 to 1901. The artworks on the calendar were created by Louis Crusius, a pharmacist, doctor and anatomy professor. Antikamnia Chemical Company derived its name from the Greek for 'opposed to pain' and their product was a tincture they described as a coal-tar derivative. It was advertised as a pain killer, and also as a mood enhancer and solution for nervousness and insomnia. The compound contained acetanilide augmented by codeine and quinine for added pain reduction. In 1907, acetanilide was found to be toxic and addictive, and in 1914 the American government prosecuted the company.

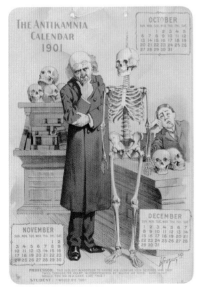

**Death in miniature**

These early 20th-century coin-operated automatons are attributed to British model maker John Dennison. The top row above and the image opposite show 'St Dennistoun Mortuary'. When a coin is inserted, the doors open, a light comes on and a miniature mortician starts working on one of the bodies lying on the embalming slabs. One body is labelled 'Found stabbed', the other 'Believed murdered', and two policemen examine evidence. Outside the building, two women express their grief, dabbing their eyes with handkerchiefs. In 'The Undertaker' (above, bottom row, courtesy of James D. Julia Auctioneers, Fairfield, Maine, USA), a skeleton turns its head to peer out of the coffin (left) and a corpse sits up as the devil pops up behind his coffin in the funeral parlour (right).

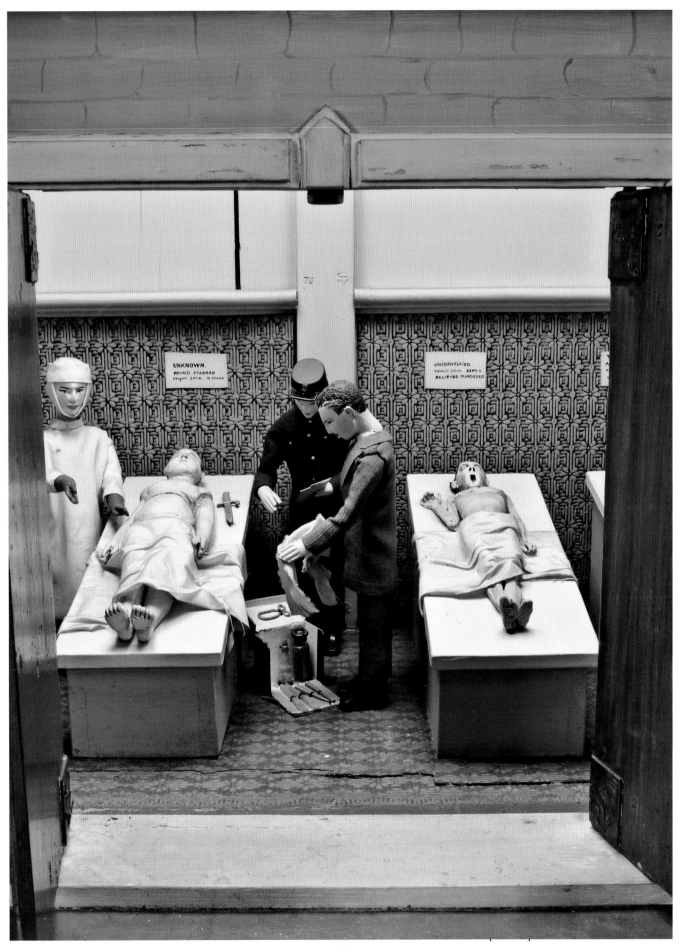

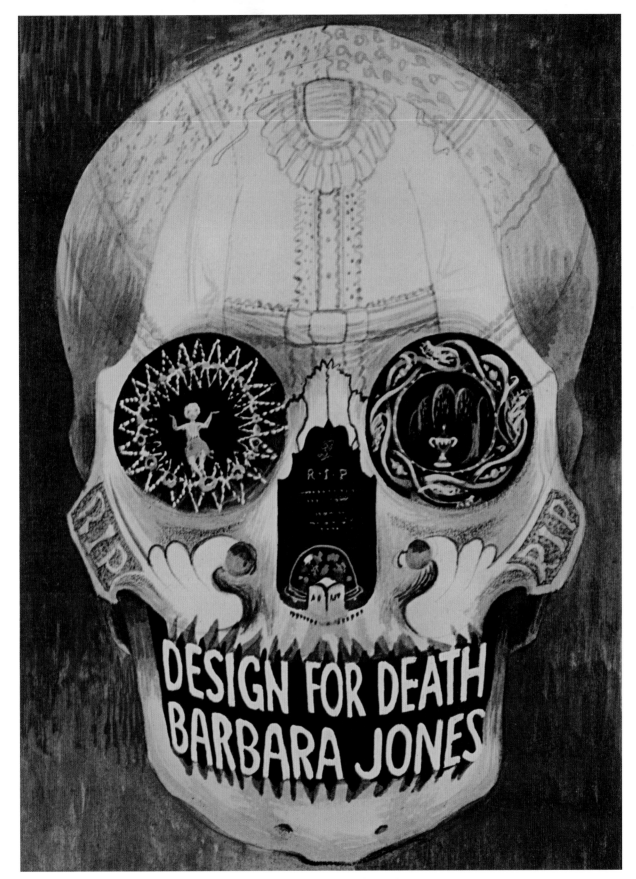

**Tête de Mort**
In the early 20th century, optical illusion postcards such as 'Tête de Mort' (opposite) became a hugely popular novelty. As a vanitas of the era, they imply that death is everywhere – whether in the courtship of a young couple, the face of a beautiful woman, children playing with a puppy or two friends enjoying a drink together.

*Design for Death*
British artist and writer Barbara Jones created this artwork (above) for the cover of her classic cult book, *Design for Death*, published in 1967. Filled with her own stylish – sometimes fanciful – illustrations and wry text, the book explores the customs, rituals and memorials associated with death.

N.C.R.

with the dead

...graphs of people posing with skeletons and cadavers were common in
...e 19th and early 20th centuries, especially among medical students and
...s, whose business was life and death. Some group portraits convey the
...urpose of the profession (above, bottom right), echoing the paintings of

the Surgeons Guild in 17th-century Amsterdam; others
humour, often anthropomorphizing the skeleton. In their
were shared freely and even sent as postcards. In the imag...
the text written above the students reads: 'When shall w...
corpse's head is held up as if it, too, is posing for the ph...

## Death scenes

Sarah Bernhardt, one of the most celebrated actresses of the 19th century, was especially well known for her performances in death scenes in such works as *La Dame aux Camélias*, *Cleopatra* and *Hamlet*, in which she played the title role. Above she is depicted as Medea in an 1898 poster by Art Nouveau artist Alphonse Mucha, who created most of her promotional materials. The other images are postcards of Bernhardt performing the 'Alas, poor Yorick, I knew him' scene in an 1899 French adaptation of *Hamlet* that was later brought to London. When Bernhardt herself died in 1923, her funeral procession brought the streets of Paris to a standstill.

MELANDRI.              PARIS.

Sleeping in a coffin
In this 19th-century photograph, Sarah Bernhardt poses as a 'sleeping beauty', the contemporary term for beautifully laid-out corpses, usually of women or children, immortalized in post-mortem photographs. The satin-lined coffin belonged to Bernhardt, who claimed to have slept in it from time to time since her sickly childhood.

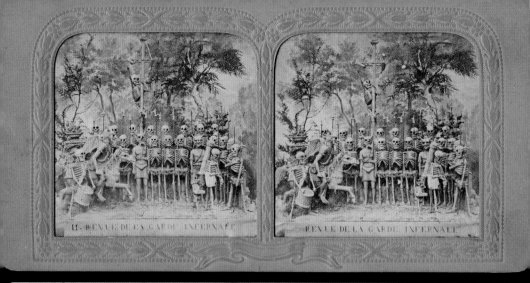

...nce from c. 1860 until 1900, Les Diableries (above, opposite [....07] were a series of stereoscopic views of the devil's daily [....er], intended in part as a critique of the decadence of Paris [....nd Empire of Napoleon III. The images were created by photographing clay dioramas with stereo cameras that simu... vision; when viewed through a home stereo viewer, the pictur... three-dimensional. Although the images normally appear ... white, when backlit the eyes of the devils and other diabolica... illuminated in red. Other colour was added by hand.

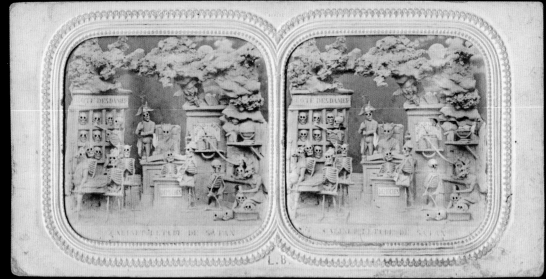

ORPHÉE À LA COUR DE PLUTON.     ORPHÉE À LA COUR DE PLUTON.

57 LA TORTURE EN ENFER.     LA TORTURE EN ENFER.

DIABLERIES

OU VOYAGE DANS L'AUTRE MONDE

48    VISITE DU SOLEIL A SATAN.

VISITE DU SOLEIL A SATAN.

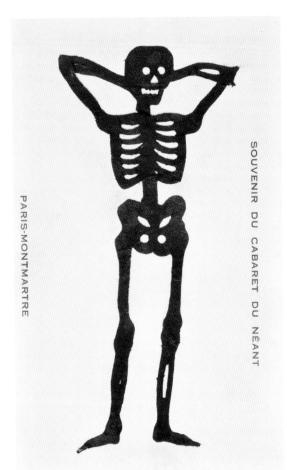

SOUVENIR DU CABARET DU NÉANT

CABARET DU NÉANT - Paris-Montmartre
n° 2, Lampadaire funéraire

## Ghost shows
Phantasmagoria, or projected magic lantern ghost shows (above, bottom), originated in 18th-century Paris, in the wake of the atrocities of the French Revolution and the Reign of Terror. They were made famous by Étienne-Gaspard Robert (later Robertson), who staged them in the ruins of an abandoned convent.

## Cabaret du Néant

At the end of the 19th century, Paris was gripped by a new entertainment – the Cabaret du Néant (Tavern of the Dead), an immersive, death-themed nightclub in Montmartre. Customers sat at tables made of coffins, drank cocktails served by waiters dressed in funeral garb (bottom left and right) below a candelabra in the form of a skeleton (opposite, top right), and watched deathly entertainments, such as a woman dissolve into a skeleton (middle left and right). Similar clubs, also in Montmartre, included L'Enfer (Hell) (top left) and Cabaret des Truands (Cabaret of the Truants) (top right). In London, Soho's Cafe Le Macabre was attracting customers as late as the 1950s.

**Death and the Lady Vaudeville**
In the early 20th century, the centuries-old Death and the Maiden theme was adapted for the vaudeville stage in America, in this case to deliver a moralizing message about the dangers of alcohol, promiscuity and gambling. These photographs of the touring production were taken by Joseph Hall in 1906.

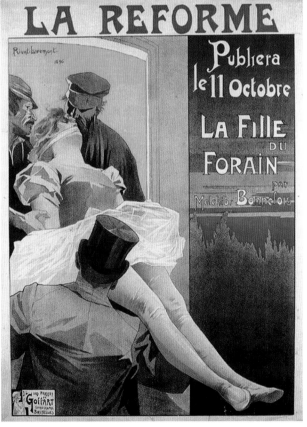

**Tales of murder**
These late 19th-century posters were created to advertise the crime and mystery serials that appeared each week in the Belgian newspaper *La Reforme*. The sensational and shocking tales – filled with scandal and murder and published in cliff-hanging instalments – were hugely popular. The artist who created these images, Henri Privat-Livemont, was a well-known Art Nouveau poster artist of the time, most renowned for his iconic poster for Absinthe Robette. Clockwise from top left: *The Anarchist Mask* (1897), *The Daughter of the Fairground* (1895) and *The Mother's Pride* (1896).

**Death and the magic lantern**
Slides such as these 19th-century examples (opposite) were used in phantasmagoria and other magic lantern shows. The originator of the phantasmagoria, Étienne-Gaspard Robert, created particularly spooky effects by projecting the images through drifting smoke.

**Conjuring the dead**
'Phantasmagoria in the Capuchin Convent 1797' (top) served as the frontispiece for the memoirs of Étienne-Gaspard Robert, published in 1831. The dramatic portrayal of Robert's showmanship, 'Fantasmagorie' (bottom), is from Fulgence Marion's book *L'Optique*, 1867.

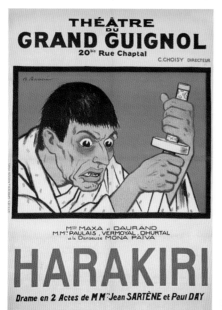

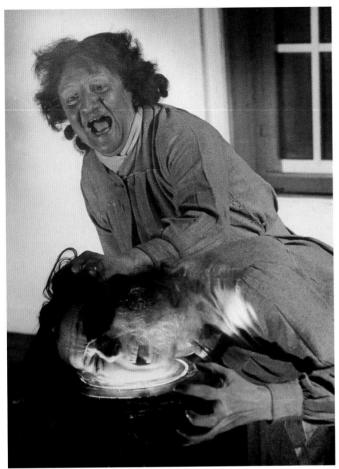

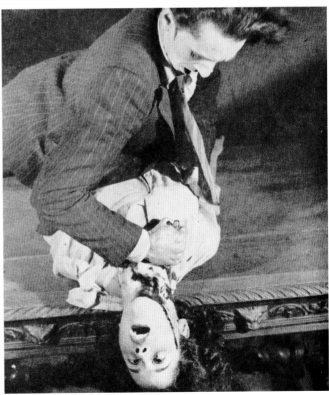

**Paris's theatre of horror**
In addition to the Cabaret du Néant and L'Enfer, Paris was home to the Théâtre du Grand Guignol (opposite and above), which operated from a former chapel between 1897 and 1962. A forerunner of the slasher movie genre, the Théâtre du Grand Guignol presented a challenging and heady mix of plays, often featuring violence, horror, gore, insanity and the supernatural. Fainting was rife amongst the audience; within a year of opening, proprietor Max Maurey capitalized on this by hiring a house doctor, thereby attracting more publicity for his theatre. By the 1920s, improvements in lighting and sound facilitated long drawn-out torture scenes – scalpings, disembowelments, strangulations and burnings. Author Anaïs Nin fondly remembered the Grand Guignol as a place where 'all our nightmares of sadism and perversion were played out'.

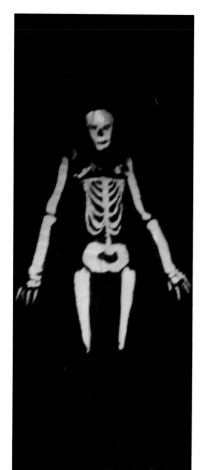

Celebrating Hallowe'en
The widespread love of the ghoulish is expressed at Hallowe'en, when the boundaries between the worlds of the living and the dead are deemed to be especially permeable. Some scholars believe the donning of masks and costumes was originally a way to ward off unwanted attention from the dead.

**Found photographs**
In these enigmatic found photographs from the 20th century, people pose merrily with human remains. The stories behind the images are unknown, yet the impact of the pictures is immediate. They draw on our age-old fascination with death and the dead, made all the more powerful by the everyday context.

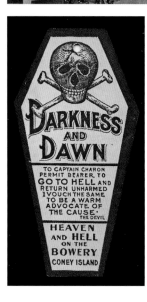

**Death at Coney Island**

In the late 19th and early 20th centuries, Brooklyn's Coney Island, the world's first amusement park, was like a year-round World's Fair. Its three great parks – Luna, Steeplechase and Dreamland – were home to a variety of lavish spectacles with huge casts of actors. Many of the attractions revolved around themes of death or disaster, and drew their inspiration from recent calamities, contemporary fears or well-known biblical tales. The San Francisco Earthquake attraction (top) opened in 1906, the year the earthquake and subsequent fire destroyed most of the city. Other attractions included Fighting the Flames (above, second row, right), which dramatized a tenement fire, complete with

daring rescues at intervals throughout the day, and Darkness and Dawn (opposite, bottom row, left), the precursor to the later attraction Night and Morning, in which visitors would experience their own premature burial followed by a trip to heaven and hell. Coney Island was also home to girly shows and freak shows of various kinds. The best known of these was Lilliputia, a town populated by small people who lived in a half-scale reproduction of 15th-century Nuremberg. The Lilliputians had their own opera house (above, top) and a fire department from which fire engines rushed out hourly in response to false alarms. Hellgate (opposite, second row, centre) was the epicentre of a fire that destroyed one of Coney Island's three great parks, Dreamland, in 1911.

# the dead after LIFE

*Books of the dead*

GHOSTLY PLEAS IN ROME'S PURGATORY MUSEUM

The ethereal work of spirit artists

*Investigating the seance*

THE PARADOX OF ECTOPLASM

Victorian spirit photographers

# art and afterlife: ethel le rossignol and georgiana houghton

**S**piritualism – the belief that the souls of the dead can communicate with the living – was all the rage in late 19th-century London. A number of artists were drawn to the seance room, including Dante Gabriel Rossetti, James Abbott McNeill Whistler and William Holman Hunt. Most of them (Rossetti was an exception) soon tired of table tipping and slate scraping, and lived on – celebrated and immortal – through their work. Meanwhile, some mediums, often moving in the same Bohemian social circles as the artists, were inspired to illustrate their experiences, or the teachings of their spirits.

At the forefront of the spiritualist movement is the College of Psychic Studies in Kensington, London. Founded in 1884 as the London Spiritualist Alliance, it has hosted many celebrated mediums, including founder William Stainton Moses, and had notable supporters, such as Arthur Conan Doyle and Alfred Russel Wallace. Between 1926 and 1930, psychic investigator Harry Price's National Laboratory of Psychical Research occupied its top floor. Today, the college contains a library, runs courses in mediumship training and counselling, and occasionally displays interesting items from its prodigious archives. Among these are artworks by two extraordinary woman artists who worked, seemingly under spirit guidance, to depict their own unique visions of the incorporeal world.

Paintings from Ethel Le Rossignol's series *A Goodly Company* (1920–33) have hung on the walls of the college since 1968. Le Rossignol donated them two years before her death, with the proviso that they would be displayed there permanently. The only time they have left the college was in early 2014 when they were exhibited at London's Horse Hospital gallery for a month; this was probably the first time the paintings had been hung in one room.

Constance Ethel Le Rossignol was born in Argentina in 1873, to a colonial family who returned to their home in the Channel Islands when Ethel was

*Page 320*
**Gillray's ghost**
British caricaturist James Gillray's *A Phantasmagoria: Scene Conjuring Up an Armed Skeleton*, 1803, uses the phantasmagoria as a political critique of a peace treaty with France; the witches from *Macbeth* represent the politicians Addington, Hawkesbury and Fox, and the skeleton in the smoke is Britannia.

in her teens. During World War I, Ethel trained as a nurse and ambulance driver, eventually ending up in France. In 1917, like many others exposed to the horrors and losses of the Great War, she attempted to make contact with the spirit world through the well-established spiritualist technique of automatic drawing, in which the hand is guided by unconscious forces or, as spiritualists believe, by spirits. It is assumed that she had some artistic training as a young woman, and this approach would have been natural to her.

In her book *A Goodly Company*, published in 1933,[1] Le Rossignol relates how, in February 1920, her automata took on the appearance of a dead friend, known only as J. P. F. He began to communicate with her at some length, although 'as he had been an agnostic, his surprise at this was great'. For the next twelve years, Ethel was in regular contact with J. P. F., who described life in the spirit world, both in text and in a series of forty-four remarkably executed drawings and paintings.

J. P. F. insisted to Ethel that he was merely an instrument of 'a circle of wise spirits who are in touch with the sphere of Holiness and have learned the secret of the soul on earth, and of the soul in its spirit form'. Ethel, meanwhile, insisted that she was merely a tool employed by J. P. F. to get the message of these wise spirits across the great gulf of death. Working through Ethel, J. P. F. demonstrated how, in his world of spirit, the power of thought could create spirit homes and temples; how the spirits fed on ideas and flew through their world, their bodies shimmering with flames of rainbow light; how they healed lost and damaged souls; how human and animal souls were born into the astral plane and travelled between material and spirit domains; and how everything was as one, entwined with the 'Perfect Master' and the 'Omnipresent God', through the wisdom, harmony and unity of souls.

J. P. F's written communications, channelled through Ethel, do not correspond to any specific teachings, but reflect the spiritual ideas and practices circulating at the time, such as spiritualism, theosophy and yoga. Similarly, the paintings, also credited to J. P. F., display a range of styles in their depiction of J. P. F.'s world of light, colour and energy. Radiant and ecstatic, their elegant, if occasionally gaudy, vision of 'spirit' is consistent and coherent, portraying a luminous realm of kaleidoscopic colour, inhabited by sylphs and demons, apes and tigers, all of which have symbolic meanings explained by J. P. F. In a combination of watercolour, gouache, gesso and thick swirls of gold leaf, they appear to have emerged fully formed from the visual consciousness of the time, incorporating aspects of Art Nouveau and Art Deco, popular playbills, Eastern mysticism, mandalas and miniatures, while also being prescient of the psychedelic art that would emerge decades later.

Ethel's paintings have been viewed by visitors to the College of Psychic Studies for decades. However, those by the 19th-century medium Georgiana Houghton could, until recently, only be found inside a privately bound book held in the college archives or at the headquarters of the Victorian Spiritualists Union in Melbourne, Australia. Yet, a full half-century before Ethel began her spirit quest, Georgiana Houghton was exhibiting her automatic channelled artworks in Mayfair, London.

Like Ethel, Georgiana spent her early years abroad. She was born on the island of Gran Canaria in 1814, and then moved with her family to London. It was a modest Victorian existence. She had eight siblings, and outlived all but one of them; she was particularly devastated by the loss of her sister Zilla in 1851. A few years after Zilla's death she approached a spiritualist medium, and from 1859 onwards began to immerse herself in London's burgeoning spiritualist scene. At the time, this was a rather unusual bohemian environment, in which women held much of the power, and attitudes towards death and religion were shifting away from Victorian norms. Here, Georgiana befriended leading spiritualists, including the levitating psychic celebrity Daniel Dunglas Home; Mrs Agnes Guppy, famed for teleporting across London to appear at a seance in her nightgown; and the American John Murray Spear, who would later start a heretical sect and hail an electrical device as the new Messiah.

Again like Ethel, Georgiana found automatic drawing, painting and writing to be the most effective means to contact the spirits. Her early automatic paintings feature identifiable forms, particularly flowers, but they soon became intensely abstract, comprising great curved trajectories of colour densely layered. These ceaseless swirls create a sense of spiritual energy, arcing across the page as if powered by a celestial Spirograph. Yet each painting is tied to a clear message, usually written on the back of the canvas, along with the name of the spirit who channelled it through Georgiana. The note on the back of *The Sheltering Wing of the Most High*, dated 2 October 1862, begins: 'Through the hand of Georgiana, I, Thomas Laurence, have attempted to symbolize the marvellous love of God....' Strongly Christian, the contents of Georgiana's spiritual messages were less radical than her art.

In 1871, Georgiana decided that it was time to share her decade-long vision with the public, and booked the New British Gallery on London's Old Bond Street for four months over the summer. She oversaw almost every aspect of the exhibition: pricing, hanging and framing the 155 works on display, and compiling a comprehensive catalogue. On arrival, visitors were handed a magnifying glass by Georgiana, who would lecture them at length on the message contained in each painting. Among those in attendance was the medium Leah Fox Underhill who, through a series of raps and bangings had, along with her sisters Margaret and Kate, instigated the first wave of spiritualist fervour in upstate New York in 1848.

Georgiana drummed up public interest through the spiritualist and mainstream newspapers. Reviews were mixed. *The Pall Mall Gazette* described a 'gallery of painful absurdities', while the critic from the *News of the World* was charmed, writing: 'The idea presents itself to the imagination of a canvas of Turner's, over which troops of fairies have been meandering, dropping jewels as they went.' Financially, the exhibition was a failure, with only one painting sold, but the artist's work was done: her message had reached a wide, if not necessarily receptive, new audience.

Georgiana never exhibited again, but she published two books: one on her spirit collaborations with photographer Frederick Hudson and the other a memoir, *Evenings at Home in Spiritual Seance* (1881).[2] After her death in 1884, seven of her pictures disappeared into the archives of the College of Psychic Studies, while thirty-five travelled to the Victorian Spritualists Union in Melbourne, Australia, where they remained until they were transported to London for an exhibition at the Courtauld Institute in 2016.

The paintings of Houghton and Le Rossignol were created under similar automatic conditions, but stylistically they could not be more different. They do, however, share a message of a vibrant colourful life in death, the paintings blurring the lines between the representational and the gnostic modes of visionary spiritual art. Le Rossignol's works are as fantastical as they are figurative, and she clearly believed that the vision belonged not to her but to J. P. F. Houghton's works, on the other hand, appear abstract and unfiltered but represent specific themes, ideas and entities, giving them a representational basis. As always, when it comes to matters of spirit, there are no clear borders.

We have to wonder whether Ethel Le Rossignol might have seen Georgiana Houghton's paintings in the archive of the College of Psychic Studies. She certainly visited the organization on multiple occasions. They do not appear to have had any stylistic or spiritual influence on her work, yet they share a mission, in the words of J. P. F., to 'open the eyes of all men to the glorious world of spiritual power which lies about them'.

Elizabeth Harper

# holy spiritualism

The Church of the Sacred Heart of Suffrage in Rome is not haunted, but it is full of ghosts. You can see them if you ask the sacristan to unlock the back hall for you. This is where the church keeps its museum – a collection of items that allegedly prove that the souls of the dead sometimes contact the living. Nearly 4,000 visitors find their way to the museum every year even though the church does not advertise this unusual attraction.

The collection itself is small; it fits inside a lone pegboard case, a place where you might expect to find notices of meetings or the church flower rota. Here it contains missives from another world, the objects used by ghosts to communicate with the living. Most are mundane things such as clothing, money and books. However, everything bears the same proof that it was touched by the souls of the dead: everything is marred by charred fingerprints left by burning hands.

There is only one type of proof here because only one type of ghost is approved by the Catholic Church – the soul in purgatory. According to Church dogma, when Catholics die, their souls do not normally ascend to heaven immediately. First, most have to atone for their sins in purgatory, a kind of temporary hell where traces of sin left on the soul are burned away metaphysically. The amount of time spent in purgatory corresponds to the amount of sin a person committed in life. The only things that can speed up this purification by fire are prayers said by the living for the dead. The message from burning Catholic souls is therefore always the same: help me.

Consider the case of Joseph Leleux from Belgium. The purgatory museum features his nightshirt with a hand-shaped hole burned through it. According to the museum, the ghost of Joseph's mother woke him for eleven nights and then addressed him on the twelfth. Joseph had strayed from the Church since her death and, more importantly, he had neglected a crucial condition of his inheritance, a clause that stipulated he must pay to have masses said for his parents' souls to speed their way through purgatory. Joseph had been spending the money less piously. 'Leave the cabarets and the dances,' the spectre of Joseph's mother begged him. She then scorched his nightshirt by touching him, a reminder that she would only burn longer without his help.

Joseph found himself changed by this encounter. The singed handprint reminded him that his mother, like Shakespeare's King of Denmark, was

*Doom'd for a certain term to walk the night,*
*And for the day confin'd to fast in fires,*
*Till the foul crimes done in my days of nature*
*Are burnt and purg'd away.*

But Joseph was no Hamlet – his underlying Catholic faith gave him no cause to doubt or question what he saw that night. Instead, he returned to the Church, had masses said for his parents and founded a congregation of pious laymen. He lived the rest of his life like a monk.

The purgatory museum is full of such stories, all told through the artefacts collected by Father Victor Jouet, a priest at the church in the 19th century. Jouet began his collection in 1897 after a portrait of Our Lady of the Rosary caught fire and left a face singed in the wall behind the painting. For him, the face was proof that a burning soul in purgatory could make its presence known to the living.

Father Jouet's urge to communicate with the dead and to back up these encounters with evidence was shared by many others in the late 19th century. During the years he was building his collection, spiritualism reached its peak in Europe and America; more than eight million people believed they could communicate with the dead. Spirit mediums who appeared to convince souls to reveal themselves through knocking, moving furniture or congealing into ectoplasm became celebrities. Father Jouet's collection added a Church-sanctioned alternative to these heretical seances.

However, as with spiritualism (whose ectoplasm looks far more like cheesecloth when studied in the light), the items in the museum at the Church of the Sacred Heart of Suffrage become less remarkable upon closer inspection. Although hard to spot initially, there is a surprising number of photographs and reproductions in Father Jouet's collection. Joseph Leleux's nightshirt, for example, is actually a framed photograph, and it is only the clarity of the image that makes it seem real. In the language of ghost stories, the photographs here swear that these events really happened, albeit to a friend of a friend. In fact, they mimic one specific kind of ghost story – the urban legend. The burnt handprint on Joseph's nightshirt is like the serial killer's hook dangling from the car door on Lover's Lane. It is a warning – not only to the protagonist in the story but to anyone who encounters the tale: 'Repent,' it says, 'or suffer these consequences.'

Modern Catholic mediums such as George Anderson peddle a different message. Anderson holds seances, albeit in hotel conference rooms instead of Victorian parlours, but the ghosts with which he claims to communicate are almost perfect inversions of the tortured souls sought by Father Jouet. Anderson's dead do not haunt; they are sought out by the living. It is the tortured living who ask the dead to help them, usually by providing some kind of closure or answers. However, this type of seance is considered beneficial to both the living and the dead. After providing this final service, the soul is described as 'released' or 'at rest,' so both the living and dead find peace. Anderson describes his seances as a form of therapy.

Although mediums such as Anderson often use the language of psychology to describe what they do, and assuage fears of impropriety by alluding to Catholic precedence, the experience they provide has far more in common with a folk tradition found in Naples and southern Italy. There, the living have sought the help of the dead for centuries, perhaps because their history of calamities – plagues, battles, earthquakes, volcanic eruptions – make the boundary between life and death seem more porous. Like modern Catholic mediums, those who engage with the dead in this way see contact with the afterlife as an extension of their faith. The Church, however, condemns the practice, which is often referred to as the Cult of the Dead.

The participants in the Cult of the Dead share the Catholic belief that the recently deceased go to purgatory. It is common to see street shrines featuring dioramas of people engulfed in flames and photographs of dead loved ones. The hope is that passersby will see these shrines, say a quick prayer for the dead and move their soul into heaven as quickly as possible.

In this regard, the souls of the people represented in the street shrines are similar to those represented in Rome's purgatory museum. However, the Cult of the Dead includes a second class of souls in purgatory who tend not to haunt. As in spiritualism, it is the living who contact them. These are souls whose names have been forgotten or who have died a bad death, usually by violence, disaster or even execution. Cult adherents believe such souls are doomed to an eternity in purgatory.

Although the fate of these souls sounds grim, the living contact them, hoping to forge relationships that become reciprocal. The prayers of the living bring the dead *refrisco*, or temporary relief, from the flames of purgatory. In return, the souls stranded in purgatory help the living by delivering warnings and assistance.

Comfort for the living is never far from the desire to contact the dead. For many, the image of a soul in heaven is too abstract to soothe grief. Survivors want something immediate and tangible. Even the burning souls in the purgatory museum offer evidence that the people we loved can still participate in the world of the living, and therefore still exist in some form.

The Catholic Church warns that contacting the dead constitutes heresy, no matter how therapeutic these practices may be. But the concept of souls – the spectral thing that makes us unique – existing after death is too enticing for priests, scientists and sceptics to banish from the collective imagination. The living want to believe we can live on in hauntings, ghostly knockings or, best of all, soothing visits to the people we loved. We want to believe in spirits, if only to prove we have them.

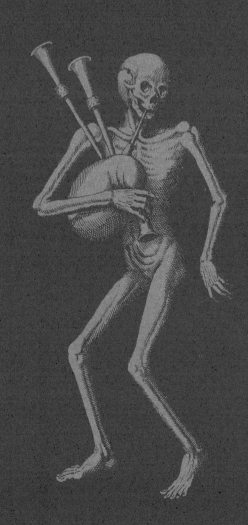

Shannon Taggart

# spritualism
# and
# photography

Spiritualism and photography are death-defying practices. Spiritualism – the American-born religion that believes we can communicate with the dead – attempts to demonstrate through the intercession of a medium that death is not the end, but a transition. Like spiritualism, photography also blurs the line between life and death, trapping time, freezing the reflection and preserving a person's disembodied presence. Both use representation to insert the past into the present. However, these are not their only similarities: ideological, material, geographical, historical and metaphysical correspondences abound.

Spiritualism and photography were popularized in the same city in the mid-19th century: Rochester, New York. There, in 1849, teenagers Kate and Margaret Fox, the accidental founders of spiritualism, premiered their method of communicating with the dead using coded rapping – called the 'spiritual telegraph'. This first public display of spirits speaking through female mediums took place at Corinthian Hall, less than half a mile from where Kodak would establish its headquarters in 1888 and introduce photography to the masses. Spiritualism quickly spread across the Western world. At its height, millions of people regularly gathered in dark rooms to make contact with the dead. In order to legitimize their activities, they attempted to capture the spirits with cameras.

Spiritualism developed at a time when photography and other scientific developments were exposing many forces operating beyond human perception. Disease-causing bacteria could be photographed through microscopes; the vastness of the universe was glimpsed through astrophotography; electricity was made visible when placed in contact with photographic materials; X-rays revealed the body's interior. What else, people wondered, could photography uncover? In addition, disembodied forms of communication were introduced via the telegraph, the telephone and the radio, and discarnate voices spoke and sang on phonographic recordings. Spiritualism and photography were brought together in an attempt to create scientific proof of the spiritual dimension, an endeavour that ultimately revealed the complicated relationship that spiritualism and photography had with truth

Initially thought of as an objective tool, the photographic method turned out to be full of subjective complications. Temperature variations, light leaks, motion blur, lens distortion, double exposures and other types of mechanical or chemical artifice could – accidentally or purposefully – prevent the camera from operating reliably. In the 1860s, William Mumler, the first 'spirit photographer', produced pictures that appeared to show the living and the dead together, in parlour settings. This photographic technique came about by accident when Mumler, an amateur photographer who reused glass plate negatives, unwittingly created a self-portrait that seemed to include the ghosted apparition of his deceased cousin. He soon launched a lucrative business producing similar post-death portraits. This controversial practice called photographic reality itself into question. To the sceptic, the images looked like manipulated exposures. To the believer, they were spiritual revelations.

When French experimenter Dr Hippolyte Baraduc photographed wafts of white floating above his wife's body at the time of her death, he interpreted the image as a document of her soul in flight. Baraduc's critics challenged this assertion and surmised that tiny holes in the camera bellows had simply fogged his picture plane. Baraduc and others experimented with the photographic process in attempts to record prayers, dreams, feelings, thoughts and the efficacy of the spirits. Their experimentation included placing photographic plates in contact with religious spaces, human body parts, nature at night and active seance rooms. The patterns that appeared after processing could be given physical or metaphysical explanations, illuminating the fact that individual interpretation played a primary role in photographic communication.

Spiritualism's photographic past contains some of the most bizarre and uniquely unsettling images in the history of photography. Among the most dramatic are the photographs of mediums during seances. Bodies (mainly female) are seen contorted in states of undress, flailing naked or literally sewn into body bags to keep them from cheating. Before a seance, investigators (usually male) sometimes subjected mediums to cavity searches, including a vaginal probe, as another precaution against fraud. Once entranced, the mediums often produced manifestations they claimed were physical evidence of spirits. Many are depicted excreting phantom forms – phenomena known as ectoplasm – from their orifices. The term 'mediumistic labour' was used to describe the production of ectoplasm, and the sights, sounds and smells that accompanied it were often compared with those of semen, menstruation, orgasm and birth. The intensity of such seances defied the etiquette of the era. Some of the male photographers found the sight of ectoplasm so absorbing that they would forget to fire the flash.

The dubious quality of the ectoplasmic photographs stand in stark contrast to the testimony of many eyewitnesses. The cold artificial flashes of light that blasted into shadowy seance rooms rendered the ethereal creations flat, grotesque and two-dimensional. Entities that to witnesses had been infused with life appeared like papier mâché dolls, cut-up faces from magazines or constructions made of cotton, cord or cheesecloth. One of the primary documentarians of Victorian seances, the German physician and hypnotist Albert von Schrenck-Notzing, concluded that 'a photograph reproduces only an instant, abstracted from the flow of the living.... For this reason, the effect it produced could only be crude and deceptive.' Photography applied to the spiritualist seance seemed to act as a negating lens that cleansed the events of their mystery. It reported a reality that stood in blunt opposition to the experience of those present. Like other photographic representations introduced in the second half of the 19th century – microphotography, astrophotography, high-speed motion studies, electrographs and X-rays – ectoplasmic photographs confused the relationship between seeing and knowing.

Spiritualism became the first religion to create an original iconography through the medium of photography. Spirit photographs can be read as parables of mourning, aching records of love and loss that connect to the eternal question: what comes after death? Ectoplasm – spiritualism's iconic symbol – visually signifies the belief that life and death remain connected. For spiritualists, ectoplasm is a paradoxical substance that is both spiritual *and* material. It is described as a fluid that emanates from the medium's body, comes to life and then morphs into shape. The term, taken from the Greek words *ektos* and *plasma* – meaning 'outside formed' – was coined in 1894 by French physiologist and winner of the Nobel Prize in Physiology or Medicine Charles Richet. He observed ectoplasm as 'a whitish steam, perhaps luminous, taking the shape of gauze or muslin, in which there develops a hand or an arm that gradually gains consistency. This ectoplasm makes personal movements. It creeps, rises from the ground and puts forth tentacles like an amoeba.'

Since the dissemination of early spirit photographs, ectoplasm has taken a place in culture's visual vocabulary. It appears within the work of artists Mike Kelley, Tony Oursler and Paul Laffoley, is referenced in the cartoon *South Park* and in the television series *The X-Files*, and, most famously, appears in the movie *Ghostbusters* (1984), co-written by Dan Aykroyd – a fourth-generation spiritualist.

Today, a small number of spiritualist mediums (mostly male, from Europe) continue to present ectoplasm. The experience of witnessing these seances is like watching the Victorian spirit photographs jump to life before your eyes. The German medium Kai Muegge even blogs the photographic documentation of his ectoplasmic manifestations alongside vintage images that resemble his acts. Many of these mediums offer their seance participants the opportunity to commune with dead celebrities. Louis Armstrong, Freddie Mercury and Michael Jackson are among the most sought after post-death performers.

Despite its evidential shortcomings, spirit photography has enjoyed cycles of rebirth. It has evolved into the digital age through DIY orb photography, popularized by grieving mothers seeking to communicate with their deceased children. Practitioners use digital cameras to capture photographic phenomena known as 'orbs'. Although there is a large amount of literature analysing the cause of these glowing circles of light – are they reflected off dust or water particles? – the point of photographing an orb is to interact with it. Experimenters ask their loved ones or spirit guides to manifest in photographs as orbs through a technique known as 'orb calling'. They command the orbs to appear in certain areas of the frame, or read meaning into the patterns they create. Computer software is often used to zoom into orbs and search for recognizable faces. These modern spirit photographers are embracing the medium of photography for the exact reason Schrenck-Notzing abandoned it: its ambiguity.

Spiritualists and the photographic process share many traits. Both use the term 'medium' to describe their function as an intermediary instrument for communication. Ectoplasm – spiritualism's sacred substance – is said to be soft, soggy and light sensitive, as are the activated surfaces of photographic materials. Mediumistic trance states develop under red lights, like latent images that materialize in the warm fluid of chemical darkrooms. The seance room and the camera are dark womb-like chambers used to capture disembodied presence and transmit its emanation. The mechanism of both mediums – the click of a shutter or the blink of an unconscious mind – delivers dead doubles through an act of automation. Spiritualism and photography simulate what was once present, but is now gone. Both give life to the dead.

**Death and the ancient Egyptians**
This ancient Egyptian funerary stela, c. 1184–1153 BCE, created for a man called Anhorkhawi, shows the deceased kneeling beneath the falcon-headed Re-Harakhty (Horus of the Horizon), a god of sun and creation who was believed to ride his boat through the sky by day and the underworld by night. The stone was probably set into a small pyramid above Anhorkhawi's tomb.

Et dyabolus qui seducebat illos, missus est in stagnu ignis et sulphuris ubi et
bestia et pseudo phete cruciabuntur die ac nocte in secula seculozum.

Et vidi thronu magnu candidum et sedente sup eum a cui[us]
Aspectu fugit terra et celum. et locus non est inuentus ab
eis. et vidi mortuos magnos et pusillos stan-
tes in conspectu throni. et libri aperti sunt. et
alius liber apertus est qui est uite. et iudicati
sunt mortui er hijs que scripta erant in libris
secundu opa ipsozum.

Et dedit mare mortuos suos qui in eo erant. et mors et ibernus dederunt mortuos
qui in ipsis erant. et iudicatum est singlis secundu opa ipozum. et ibern[us] et mors
missi st in stagnu ignis. et h[ec] mors secda est stagnu ignis. Et qui no inuentus est in
libro vite scriptus missus est in stagnum ignis.

## Mouth of hell

An illuminated parchment codex, c. 1400, illustrating scenes from the life of John the Evangelist (opposite), shows a 'hell mouth' – a pit that swallowed the damned. The hell mouth was based on ideas of the devil as a lion or dragon who feasts on souls, and the Old Testament monster Leviathan as a metaphor for Satan.

## Impending doom

These visions of the end of time portray how the bodies of the dead will rise and be reunited with their souls for the Final Judgment. Clockwise from top left: *Four Horsemen of the Apocalypse* (detail), 1511, Albrecht Dürer; *The Last Judgment: The Barque of Hell*, Pieter de Jode I; and *Resurrection of the Dead*, 1554, Giorgio Ghisi.

**The Last Judgment**
In the central panel for Hieronymus Bosch's triptych *The Last Judgment*, c. 1482 (above), Christ – flanked by the Virgin Mary, John the Evangelist and the apostles – judges the dead from on high. Below, demons torture people in a variety of imaginative ways. From the 12th century, fear of the Final Judgment came to dominate ideas of the afterlife.

**Tormented by demons**
Details from the central and right panels of Hans Memling's triptych *The Last Judgment*, c. late 1460s, depict the fate of sinners. Having had their souls weighed by the Archangel Michael, they are driven towards hell (opposite) and then tormented by demons as they descend into the fiery flames (opposite, far right).

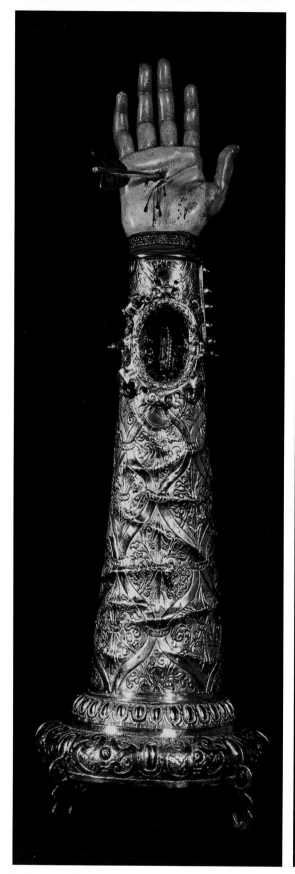

Body and soul

Pages 334–35: In the tumultuous central panel of *The Last Judgment* by Jehan Bellegambe the Elder, c. 1520–25, the dead climb from their graves, a reminder of the reunion of the soul and the resurrected body on Judgment Day: 'The trumpet shall sound, and the dead shall be raised incorruptible' (Corinthians 15:12).

Holy body parts

The arm reliquary of St Benedict and foot reliquary of St Maur (above) were created in Brazil in the 17th century. In the Catholic tradition, the physical remains of saints and martyrs are believed to have miraculous properties, especially in matters of healing. Known as relics, they are kept in reliquaries, fashioned in the shape of the body part they contain.

Holy cards
These mid-19th century *Épinal* prints depict four Catholic saints in bright, naive illustration style, typical of this folk printing press, which was founded by Jean-Charles Pellerin in 1796 in the French town of Épinal. Each saint is depicted with his or her accoutrements and every card features a prayer or oration.

River Styx
In Greek mythology, the dead must cross the River Styx in Charon's boat in order to reach Hades, the land of the dead. Top to bottom: *Charon Crossing the Styx*, c. 1520–24, by Joachim Patinir; *Orpheus and Eurydice on the Banks of the Styx*, 1878, by John Roddam Spencer Stanhope; *La Barca de Caronte* (The Barque of Charon), late 19th or early 20th century, by José Benlliure y Gil.

相馬の古内裏に
將門の姫君瀧夜叉
妖術を以て味方を集
むる太宰太郎光國
輕き試みと思へしも
竟に是を亡ぼし給ふ

瀧夜叉姫

**The Island of the Dead**
Swiss symbolist painter Arnold Böcklin is said to have painted *The Island of the Dead* (preceding page) for a widow who wanted 'something to dream by'. Böcklin made several versions, and copies were owned by Hitler, Lenin and Freud. It even inspired a symphonic poem by Rachmaninoff. The above versions were painted in (top to bottom) 1880, 1883 and 1886.

**Skeleton spectre**
Utagawa Kuniyoshi's *ukiyo-e* (pictures of the floating world) *Mitsukuni Defying the Skeleton Spectre Invoked by Princess Takiyasha*, c. 1844, was inspired by a popular novel titled *Story of Utō Yasutaka* by Santō Kyōden, published in 1807. Using a spell in her scroll (left panel), the princess summons a giant skeleton to scare off Ōya no Mitsukuni, the man who killed her father. The beautiful

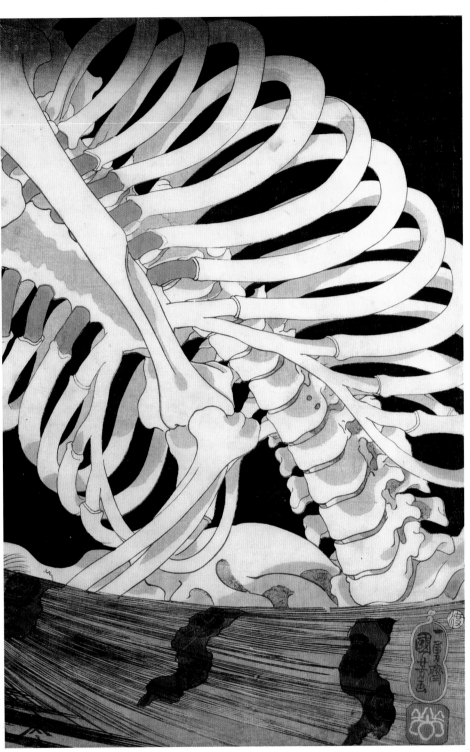

rendering of the skeleton was probably the result of the artist's study of human anatomy; Utagawa Kuniyoshi is said to have owned a copy of *Kaitai Shinsho*, published in 1774, the first Western anatomical book to be translated into Japanese. Visually dynamic, and often populated by monsters, demons and other supernatural entities, Kuniyoshi's works anticipate the 20th-century phenomenon of manga.

**Book of demons**
A border of skulls and skeletons frames the watercolour title page of the
*Compendium of Demonology and Magic*, c. 1775. Below the title is the ominous
warning *'Noli me tangere'* (Do not touch me). The date '1057' was probably
added to make the book appear older, more venerable and more valuable
than it really was.

Merecd. Nabhi. Tirama. Nüdaton. Eihanim.
Zagrion. Alogiel. Kilik.
Eloson. Zagal.
Iglion. Ioloma
Lapador.

**Summoning the dead**
The *Compendium of Demonology and Magic* was written in German and Latin
in c. 1775 by an unknown author. It contains more than thirty watercolour
illustrations, many quite graphic, of demonic creatures, witches, necromancy
and cabbalistic signs. The image above probably represents figures of the dead
raised through necromancy.

**William Blake and the soul**
*The Death of the Good Old Man* (top) and *The Soul Hovering Over the Body* (bottom) are hand-painted etchings by British artist, poet and printmaker William Blake for Robert Blair's poem 'The Grave,' 1793, about death. Blake's illustrations accompanied an 1808 edition of the poem.

**Chopin and the ghost**
In these mid-20th-century postcards (opposite), Death comes for Polish composer Frédéric Chopin at his piano. The images are probably intended to evoke the tragedy of the musician's early death at only thirty-nine years of age. The artwork at the foot of the page is *Chopin's Last Chords*, 20th century, by Józef Męcina-Krzesz.

# SPECTROPIA
## OR
## SURPRISING
## SPECTRAL ILLUSIONS.

### SHOWING

## GHOSTS
### EVERYWHERE
### AND OF ANY COLOUR.

#### BY J. H. BROWN.

LONDON:
GRIFFITH & FARRAN, CORNER OF ST. PAUL'S CHURCHYARD.
H & C. TREACHER, BRIGHTON.

Spectral illusions
The coloured engravings (opposite) from *Spectropia*, 1864, by J. H. Brown
were created as part of an anti-spiritualist crusade. The author's aim was to
show how persistent vision can create the optical illusion of ghosts. To try
this yourself, simply stare at any of the figures on the page opposite for twenty
seconds, then direct your eyes to a neutral surface.

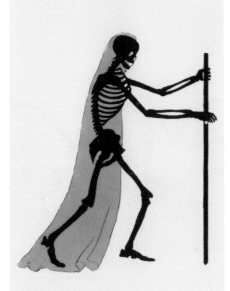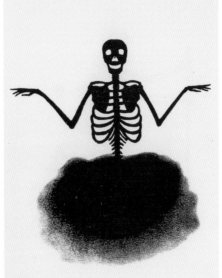

...phing ghosts
... Jacoby-Harms was a German magician. His 1886 book *Eine
...irée: illustrirtes prachtwerk von Jacoby Harms* (A Spirit Soiree:
...ed Memorabilia of Jacoby-Harms) includes photographs by
...nlstrom, who utilized the relatively recent technology of double
... to create the impression of ghosts.

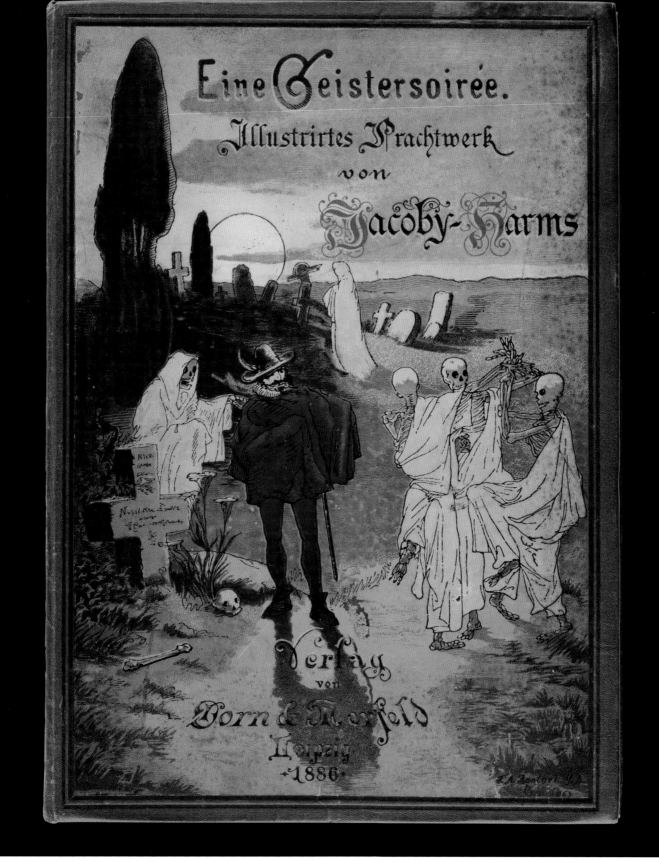

**Magicians and spiritualism**
The book cover of Professor Jacoby-Harms's *Eine Geistersoiree: illustrirtes prachtwerk von Jacoby-Harms*. Magicians of the time – including Jacoby-Harms himself – performed a variety of acts that revolved around the contemporary religion of spiritualism, in which the spirits of the dead were thought to return and communicate with the living.

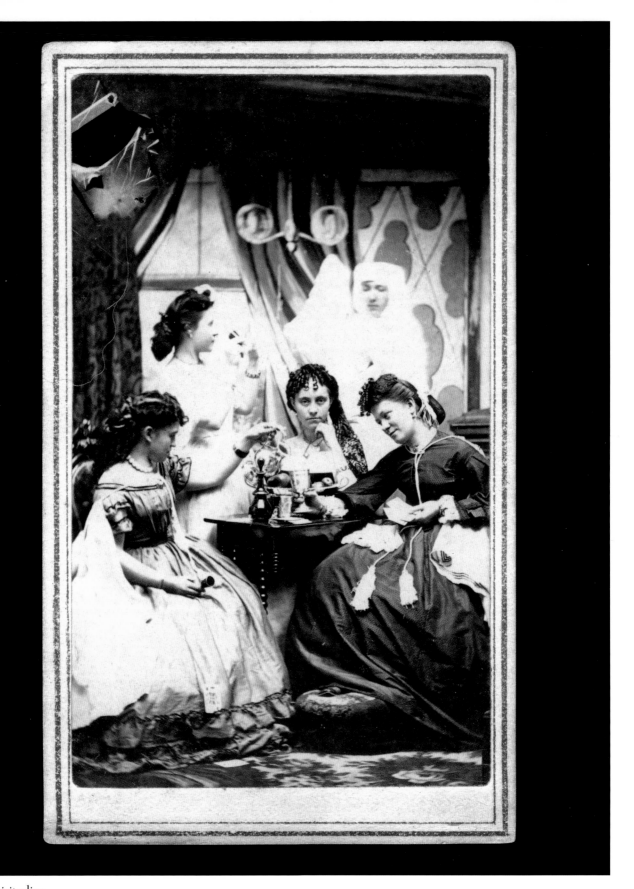

**Sisters of spiritualism**
This photographic carte-de-visite depicts a seance that took place in Northport,
New York, in c. 1865. In 1848, the Fox sisters inadvertently started the religion
that became known as spiritualism when they claimed to communicate with
ghosts through a series of rappings. Spiritualism sought to make contact
with ghosts and prove their existence through photography and other means.

**Death cards**
A card of the tarot, often included in other decks used for divination, the death card connotes endings, change, transition and rebirth. Top, left to right: sorrows/mourning/mortality card, from *Jeu du Petit Oracle* (The Little Oracle), 1795–99; death card from the Visconti Tarot, 1428–47; mortality/death card from the 'Grand Etteilla' or Egyptian tarot, 1890.

**Talking to the spirits**
Spiritualists used spirit boards or talking boards to communicate with spirits before the commercial release of the ouija board in 1890. The board is related to automatic writing, in which the writer acts as a channel for communications that derive, depending on one's point of view, from the spirit world or the unconscious.

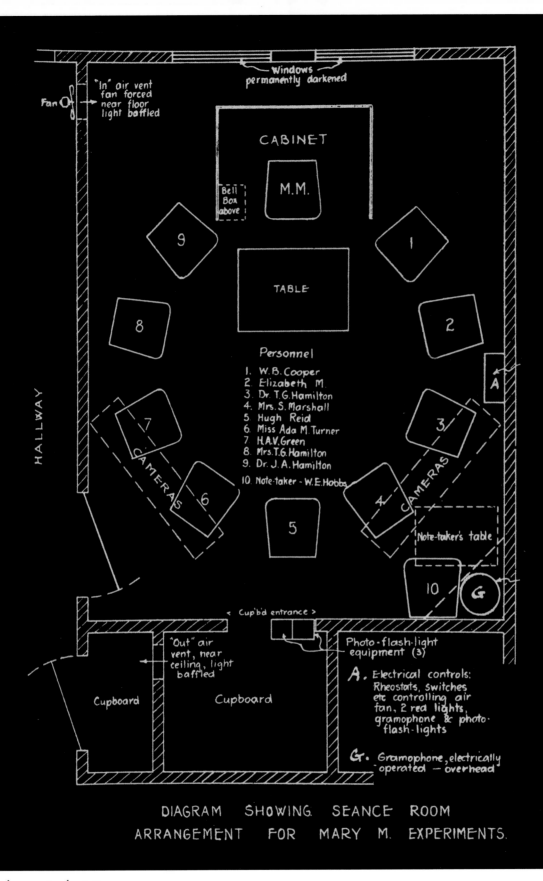

**DIAGRAM SHOWING SEANCE ROOM ARRANGEMENT FOR MARY M. EXPERIMENTS.**

Diagram of supernatural activity
This diagram was created to accompany the photographic evidence (see pages 356–57) of phenomena witnessed by Thomas Glendenning Hamilton. A medical doctor and surgeon, Hamilton hosted investigations of psychic phenomena at his home in Manitoba, Winnipeg, between 1918 and 1945. His group's activities were intended as controlled scientific experiments.

**Experiments in levitation**
These photographs document levitation seances held at the home of Danish photographer Sven Türck in the 1940s. The experiments took place in the dark and the images were captured with a flash. In 1945, Türck published his findings in a book titled *Jeg var dus med Aanderne* (I Was on Familiar Terms with the Spirits).

### Spirit orbs and ectoplasm

These images document the practices of spiritualism, an American-born religion built on the belief that the living can communicate with the dead. Central to spiritualist practice is the medium: a person, often a woman, who purports to act as a channel for the spirits of the dead. The medium's activities, which include seances invoking the spirit world for guidance or healing, are performative displays intended to demonstrate that death is not the end, but a transition. Spiritualists used the new technology of photography in attempts to prove scientifically that during the seance the spirits of the dead can manifest physically as ghostly forms, orbs and ectoplasm with which the living can communicate. The photographs can be read as parables of mourning, records of love and loss that connect to the eternal question – what comes after death?

The infamous Stanisława P
Taken at a seance by German physician and hypnotist Albert von Schrenck-Notzing, this photograph depicts Polish medium Stanisława Popielska, with a tendril of ectoplasm emerging from her mouth. Stanisława P, as she was known, was proclaimed a fraud in 1930 after she was caught repositioning objects that she claimed had moved of their own volition.

Medium Mary Marshall
Pages 356–57: A photograph album documents psychic investigations hosted by Thomas Glendenning Hamilton at his home in Manitoba, Canada. Taken in the 1920s and 1930s, they purport to show medium Mary Marshall producing ectoplasm in the form of the face of Victorian evangelist Charles Haddon Spurgeon (page 356, top left) and a spirit named Lucy (page 357, top left).

Dec. 23, 1928
2nd Mass, 7min
after Spurgeon

This H face said by
many m... and her
relatives, to be an
excellent likeness of
her father, who lived &
died in this old Country
and who had never
been photographed in
life.

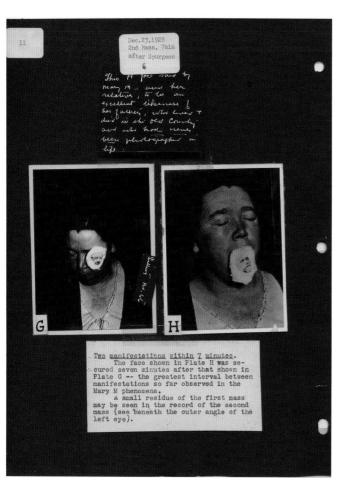

G    H

Two manifestations within 7 minutes.
    The face shown in Plate H was se-
cured seven minutes after that shown in
Plate G -- the greatest interval between
manifestations so far observed in the
Mary M phenomena.
    A small residue of the first mass
may be seen in the record of the second
mass (see beneath the outer angle of the
left eye).

BELOW
Double Exposure of Mass, Aug. 18/29
and
Mass Oct. 27/29

The above mass a preparatory
extrusion, prior to mass &
face-forms of Oct 27.
    (see full reports in
"Intention to Survive")

No 25.   Oct. 20, 1929.

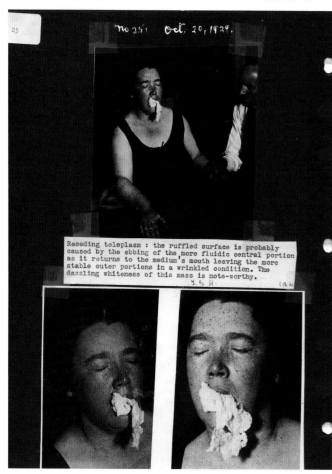

Receding teleplasm : the ruffled surface is probably
caused by the ebbing of the more fluidic central portion
as it returns to the medium's mouth leaving the more
stable outer portions in a wrinkled condition. The
dazzling whiteness of this mass is note-worthy.
                        T. G. H.

No 26.  Oct. 27, 1929.
The "Raymond Lodge" likeness in teleplasm

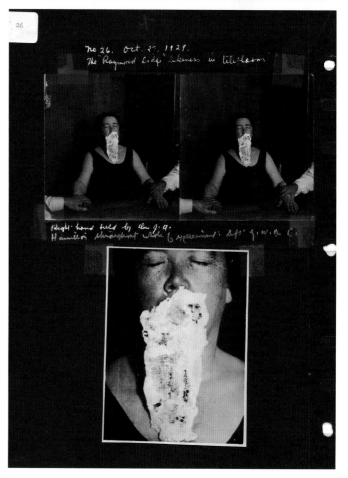

Right hand held by the G. G.
Hamilton throughout whole experiment: Left by W. B. G.

March 10/30. This view recorded by H.A.
Reed, using his own camera & plates and did his own
developing.

B

B

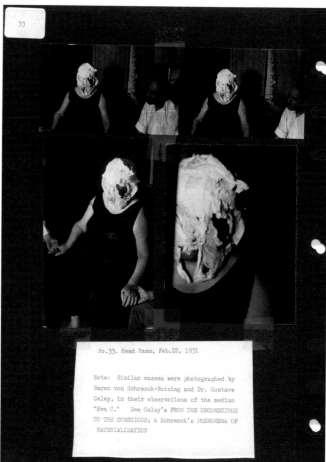

No.33. Head Mass, Feb.22, 1931

Note: Similar masses were photographed by
Baron von Schrenck-Notzing and Dr. Gustave
Geley, in their observations of the medium
"Eva C." See Geley's FROM THE UNCONSCIOUS
TO THE CONSCIOUS; & Schrenck's PHENOMENA OF
MATERIALISATION

No 48. JUNE 27/32. 2nd Day. SITTING 333

Sitters & mediums clockwise:
L.H.; Ewan (enhanced); Mary M (enhanced);
Mercedes (enhanced); W.B.C.; Elizabeth (enhanced).

The teleplasm (63) of March 30, 1939.
The first to appear in three years.
Note fine thread over left ear.

Clockwise; Mr W.A. Luther; Dawes; Mrs Archer (enhanced)
L.H.; Mrs Reed who had charge of the
photographic end of the experiment.

357

**Spirit art**
*Glory Be To God*, c. 1868 (top), and *The Eye of God*, c. 1862 (bottom), are among several hundred works produced by spirit artist Georgiana Houghton. A trained artist and medium, Houghton was a founding member of London's College of Psychic Studies and pioneered the use of drawing as a means of channelling communications with the dead.

Art from the other side
*Consummation*, c. 1933, by British spirit artist and medium Ethel Le Rossignol
is crafted from watercolour, gold leaf and gesso. Le Rossignol took no credit
for her work, which she claimed was the product of a spirit called J. P. F.,
who used her as a channel to share the secrets of the soul with the living.
Le Rossignol produced a series of forty-four paintings between 1920 and 1933.

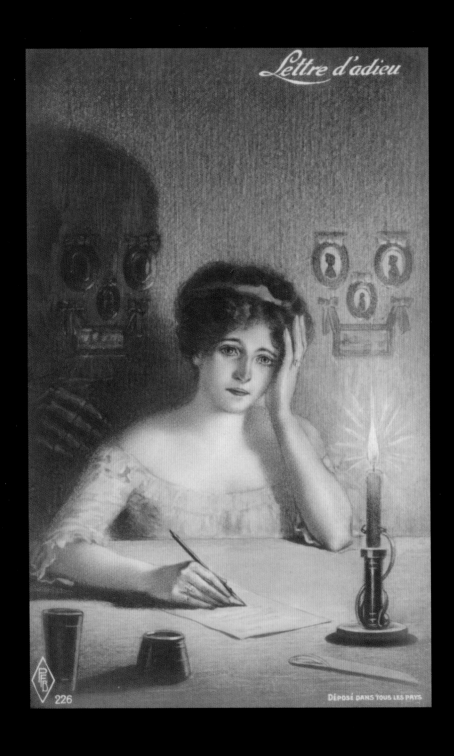

**Lettre d'adieu**
The text on this late 19th- or early 20th-century postcard reads: *Lettre d'adieu*, or 'Goodbye Letter'. A figure of Death as a skeleton looms behind a young woman who seems to be writing a difficult letter, perhaps one of suicide. In the foreground, a candle burns, perhaps lighting her way to the next life.

# CONTRIBUTORS

## general editor

JOANNA EBENSTEIN is a Brooklyn-based writer, curator, photographer and graphic designer. She is the creator of the Morbid Anatomy blog and was co-founder and creative director of the recently closed Morbid Anatomy Museum in Brooklyn. Her books include *The Anatomical Venus* (2016) and *The Morbid Anatomy Anthology* (2014). Ebenstein's writing and photography have been published and exhibited internationally, and she speaks regularly around the world on topics at the intersection of art and medicine, death and culture.

## the richard harris art collection

THE RICHARD HARRIS ART COLLECTION is an unparalleled accumulation of more than 1,500 objects exploring themes of death and mortality, ranging from incidental pieces of ephemera and vernacular art to rare and beautiful masterpieces. Representing every medium and gathered from around the world, Richard Harris's peerless collection has been exhibited at the Wellcome Collection, London, UK, and the Chicago Cultural Center, Chicago, Illinois.

## essayists

EVA ARIDJIS is a Mexican filmmaker. She is the director of *The Favor* and *The Blue Eyes* and of the documentary features *Children of the Street*, *Chuy*, *The Wolf Man* and *La Santa Muerte*. She also lectures on death in pre-Hispanic and modern Mexican culture at institutions all over the world.

KAREN BACHMANN is an adjunct professor at Pratt Institute's Fine Arts and History of Art departments. A collector and maker of hairwork jewelry for more than two decades, she has lectured on mourning culture and hairwork at various museums.

LAETITIA BARBIER is a French independent scholar and art historian who lives in Brooklyn, New York. She was the head librarian of the recently shuttered Morbid Anatomy Museum.

ELEANOR CROOK is a European sculptor and effigy maker who has made a special study of human anatomy and pathology in relation to wax modelling and life-like media. She is artist-in-residence at the Gordon Museum of Pathology, King's College London, and exhibits internationally in both gallery and medical museum contexts.

MARK DERY is a cultural critic whose writings often touch on 'dark matter' such as the Pathological Sublime. His latest book is *I Must Not Think Bad Thoughts: Drive-By Essays on American Dread, American Dreams* (University of Minnesota Press, 2014).

LISA DOWNING is professor of French Discourses of Sexuality at the University of Birmingham. Her books include *Desiring the Dead: Necrophilia and Nineteenth-Century French Literature* (2003) and *The Subject of Murder: Gender, Exceptionality and the Modern Killer* (2013).

BRUCE GOLDFARB has been writing about Frances Glessner Lee and the Nutshell Studies of Unexplained Death for more than twenty-five years. He is executive assistant to the Chief Medical Examiner for the State of Maryland and public information officer for the Office of the Chief Medical Examiner.

MEL GORDON is professor emeritus at the University of California, Berkeley, and the author of *Voluptuous Panic: The Erotic World of Weimar Berlin* (2000) and *The Theatre of Fear and Horror: The Grisly Spectacle of the Grand Guignol of Paris* (2016).

ELIZABETH HARPER writes about Catholic relics and oddities on her blog All the Saints You Should Know. She has lectured on incorrupt saints at the Mütter Museum and on the Neapolitan Cult of the Dead at Virginia Commonwealth University.

MERVYN HEARD is a showman and historian of magic lantern entertainment. He has created installations in the UK for Tate Britain and the Royal Opera House as well as for theatres, festivals and film companies worldwide. He is the author of *Phantasmagoria: The Secret Life of the Magic Lantern* (2006).

LISELOTTE HERMES DA FONSECA, a lecturer at Leuphana University Lüneburg, specializes in scientific representations of man and the notions of life and death that accompany them. She has written about La Specola, Body Worlds, Ötzi the Iceman, crucifixions in science and anatomical representations of man.

EVAN MICHELSON is an antiques dealer and collector specializing in objects of curiosity and mourning. She is co-owner of New York City's Obscura Antiques and Oddities, where she has been buying, selling and displaying wondrous and melancholy objects for many years.

MARK PILKINGTON founded and runs Strange Attractor Press. He has written for publications such as *Frieze* magazine, the *Guardian* and *Fortean Times* and in 2014 curated the first exhibition of Ethel Le Rossignol's paintings at London's Horse Hospital gallery.

KEVIN PYLE is the author of several graphic novels including *Blindspot* (2007) and *Lab USA: Illuminated Documents* (2001). He recently co-taught a Princeton Atelier on the subject of art and death, resulting in the immersive theatre piece *The Last Boat*.

MICHAEL SAPPOL is a senior fellow at the Swedish Collegium for Advanced Study, Uppsala. He is the author of *A Traffic of Dead Bodies* (2002) and *Dream Anatomy* (2006). His recent book is *Body Modern: Fritz Kahn, Scientific Illustration and the Homuncular Subject* (2017).

SHANNON TAGGART is a photographer based in New York. Her work has been featured in *TIME*, *The New York Times Magazine* and *Newsweek*. From 2014 to 2016, she was scholar and artist-in-residence at the Morbid Anatomy Museum. Her sixteen-year-long project on spiritualism – 'Séance: Spiritualist Ritual and the Search for Ectoplasm' – will be published in 2018.

JOHN TROYER is the director of the Centre for Death and Society at the University of Bath, UK. He is a co-founder of the Death Reference Desk website (www.deathreferencedesk.org) and the Future Cemetery Project (www.futurecemetery.org) as well as a frequent commentator for the BBC.

BERT VAN DE ROEMER is assistant professor in the Cultural Studies Department of the University of Amsterdam. His fields of interest are the history of collecting and the relationship between the arts and the natural sciences. He has published works on Dutch collectors including Simon Schijnvoet, Frederik Ruysch and Levinus Vincent.

# ENDNOTES

### poe and the pathological sublime (Ch. I, p.28)

1 Edgar Allan Poe, 'The Philosophy of Composition' [Text-02], *Graham's Magazine*, vol. XXVIII, no. 4, April 1846, 28:163, archived on the website of The Edgar Aleen Poe Society of Baltimore, www.eapoe.org/works/essays/philcomp.htm

2 Elisabeth Bronfen, *Over Her Dead Body: Death, Femininity, and the Aesthetic* (Manchester, UK: Manchester University Press, 1992), 59.

3 Sylvia Plath, *Ariel: The Restored Edition: A Facsimile of Plath's Manuscript, Reinstating Her Original Selection and Arrangement* (New York: HarperPerennial/Modern Classics, 2005 reprint), 17.

4 Edgar Allan Poe, 'Morella' (reprint), *The Works of the Late Edgar Allan Poe* (1850), 1:460, archived on the website of The Edgar Allan Poe Society of Baltimore www.eapoe.org/works/tales/mrllah.htm.

5 Edgar Allan Poe, 'Ligeia' in *Selected Tales* (New York: Vintage Books/Library of America, 1991), 42.

6 Camille Paglia, *Sexual Personae: Art and Decadence From Nefertiti to Emily Dickinson* (New York: Vintage Books, 1990), 572.

7 Ibid., 573.

8 Poe, 'Ligeia', in *Selected Tales*, 53. The italics are Poe's.

9 Quoted in Paul Collins, *Edgar Allan Poe: The Fever Called Living* (Boston/New York: New Harvest/Houghton Mifflin Harcourt, 2014), 80.

10 Edgar Allan Poe, 'The Raven' [Text-16], *Richmond Semi-Weekly Examiner* (Richmond, VA), vol. II, no. 93, September 25, 1849, 2, archived on the website of The Edgar Allan Poe Society of Baltimore, www.eapoe.org/works/poems/ravent.htm.

11 James M. Hutchisson, *Poe* (Jackson, MS: University Press of Mississippi, 2005), 28.

12 Edgar Allan Poe, 'Preface', *Tales of the Grotesque and Arabesque* (1840), 6, electronic version archived on the website of The Edgar Allan Poe Society of Baltimore www.eapoe.org/works/misc/tgap.htm.

13 'Ghoul-haunted woodland of Weir': Thomas Ollive Mabbott (and E. A. Poe), 'Ulalume', *The Collected Works of Edgar Allan Poe – Vol. I: Poems* (1969), 416, archived on the website of The Edgar Allan Poe Society of Baltimore www.eapoe.org/works/mabbott/tom1p099.htm. 'Mansion of gloom': Poe, 'The Fall of the House of Usher' in *Selected Tales*, 55.

14 Poe, 'Ligeia' in *Selected Tales*, 39, 46.

15 C. G. Jung, 'The Theory of Psychoanalysis' in *Freud and Psychoanalysis* (Princeton, NJ: Princeton University Press, 1961), 134.

16 Collins, *Edgar Allan Poe*, 8.

17 Diane Johnson, 'Introduction,' Edgar Allan Poe, *Selected Tales*, xvi.

18 Ibid., xvii.

19 Mabbott (and Poe), 'Introduction', *The Collected Works of Edgar Allan Poe – Vol. I: Poems*, 157, archived on the website of The Edgar Allan Poe Society of Baltimore www.eapoe.org/works/mabbott/tom1p043.htm.

20 Poe, 'The Philosophy of Composition', *Graham's Magazine*.

21 Poe, *Selected Tales*, 29, 139.

### the power of hair as human relic in mourning jewelry (Ch. III, p.84)

1 Caroline Walker Bynum and Paula Gerson, 'Body-Part Reliquaries and Body Parts in the Middle Ages', *Gesta*, vol. 36, No. 1 (1997)

2 Ibid.

3 Christiane Holm, 'Sentimental Cuts: Eighteenth-Century Mourning Jewelry with Hair', in *Eighteenth-Century Studies*, vol. 38, No. 1 (Fall, 2004), 140.

4 Kathleen M. Oliver, 'With my Hair in Crystal: Mourning Clarissa', *Eighteenth-Century Fiction*, vol. 23, No. 1 (Fall 2010), 41.

5 Ibid.

### the anatomy of holy transformation (Ch. III, p.86)

1 Emanuele Insinna, *Cera, ceroplasti e cirari*, (Terme Vigliatore 2014), 19–36.

2 Farida Simonetti (ed.): *Sortilegi di cera. La ceroplastica tra arte e scienza* (Genova, 2012).

3 Regina Deckers, 'La Scandalosa in Naples: A Veristic Waxwork as Memento Mori and Ethical Challenge', *Oxford Art Journal* (2013) 36 (1): 75–91.

4 For further information: Joanna Ebenstein: *The Anatomical Venus* (London, 2016).

5 Piero Camporesi, 'The Consecrated Host: A Wondrous Excess', in Michel Feher (ed.): *Fragments for a History of the Human Body, Part One* (New York, 1989), 221–237.

6 Julia Kristeva, 'Holbein's Dead Christ', in Michel Feher (ed.), *Fragments for a History of the Human Body, Part One* (New York, 1989), 238–269.

7 As described in texts by Martin von Cochem, 1634–1712.

8 Ibid.

9 Caroline Walker Bynum, 'The Female Body and Religious Practice in the Later Middle Ages', in Michel Feher (ed.), *Fragments for a History of the Human Body, Part One* (New York, 1989), 160–219, here 161.

10 Ibid.

### eros and thanatos (Ch. IV, p.134)

1 Anaïs Nin, 'The Woman on the Dunes', in *Little Birds* (1979) (Harmondsworth: Penguin, 2002).

2 Georges Bataille, *The Accursed Share* (1946–49), trans. Robert Hurley (1988), 3 vols (New York: Zone Books, 1991).

3 Sigmund Freud, 'Our Attitude Towards Death' [1915], *Beyond the Pleasure Principle* [1920], 'The Ego and the Id' [1923], in *The Standard Edition of the Complete Psychological Works*, translated from the German under the general editorship of James Strachey, 24 vols (London: The Hogarth Press and The Institute of Psycho-Analysis, 1956–74).

4 Lisa Downing, *Desiring the Dead: Necrophilia and Nineteenth-Century French Literature* (Oxford: Legenda, 2003).

5 Lisa Downing, Iain Morland and Nikki Sullivan, *Fuckology: Critical Essays on John Money's Diagnostic Concepts* (Chicago: University of Chicago Press, 2015).

6 Elisabeth Bronfen, *Over Her Dead Body: Death, Femininity, and the Aesthetic* (Manchester, UK: Manchester University Press, 1992).

7 Phillippe Ariès, *Western Attitudes Towards Death: From the Middle Ages to the Present*, trans. Patricia M. Ranum (Baltimore and London: Johns Hopkins University Press, 1974).

### theatre, death and the grand guignol (Ch. VI, p.284)

1 William Ridgeway, *The Dramas and Dramatic Dances of Non-European Races in Special Reference to the Origin of Greek Tragedy* (Cambridge: University of Cambridge Press, 1915).

### art and afterlife: ethel le rossignol and georgiana houghton (Ch. VII, p.322)

1 Ethel Le Rossignol, *A Goodly Company: A Series of Psychic Drawings Given through the Hand of Ethel le Rossignol: As an Assurance of Survival After Death This Sequence of Designs is Shown to Open the Eyes of All Men to the Glorious World of Spiritual Power Which Lies About Them* (London, The Chiswick Press, 1933).

2 Georgiana Houghton, *Evenings at Home in Spiritual Séance* (London: Trübner & Co., 1881)

# SELECTED BIBLIOGRAPHY

Ariès, P. & Lloyd, J. *Images of Man and Death* (Cambridge, MA: Harvard University Press, 1985)

Ariès, P. (Translated by H. Weaver) *The Hour of Our Death: The Classic History of Western Attitudes Toward Death Over the Last One Thousand Years* (Oxford: Oxford University Press, 1991)

Becker, E. *The Denial of Death* (New York [u.a.]: Simon & Schuster, 1997)

Becker, E. *The Birth and Death of Meaning: A Perspective in Psychiatry and Anthropology* (New York: Free Press of Glencoe, 1962)

Burke, E. *A Philosophical Enquiry into the Origin of Our Ideas of the Sublime and Beautiful* (London: Printed for J. Dodsley, 1767)

Burns, S. B. *Sleeping Beauty: Memorial Photography in America* (Altadena: Twelvetrees Press, 1990)

Caveney, M., Steinmeyer, J., Daniel, N. & Jay, R. *Magic: 1400–1950s* (Cologne: Taschen, 2009)

Cheroux, C. *The Perfect Medium: Photography and the Occult* (New Haven: Yale University Press, 2005)

Cosentino, D. J. *Sacred Arts of Haitian Vodou* (Los Angeles: UCLA Fowler Museum of Cultural History, 1995)

De Pascale, E. & Shugaar, A. *Death and Resurrection in Art* (Los Angeles: J. Paul Getty Museum, 2009)

Ebenstein, J. *The Anatomical Venus* (London: Thames & Hudson 2016)

Ebenstein, J. & Dickey, C. *The Morbid Anatomy Anthology* (New York: Morbid Anatomy Press, 2014)

Fabre, C. et al. *L'Ange du Bizarre: Le Romantisme Noir de Goya à Max Ernst* (Ostfildern: Hatje Cantz, 2013)

Gillon, E. V. *Early New England Gravestone Rubbings* (New York: Dover Publications, 1981)

Glass, A. 'A Cannibal in the Archive: Performance, Materiality, and (In)Visibility in Unpublished Edward Curtis Photographs of the Kwakwaka'wakw Hamat'sa'. *Visual Anthropology* 25, no. 2 (2009): 128–49

Gordon, M. *The Grand Guignol: Theatre of Fear and Terror* (Cambridge, MA: Da Capo Press, 1997)

Gorer, G. 'The Pornography of Death'. *Encounter* (October 1955): 49–52

Guthke, K. S. *The Gender of Death: A Cultural History in Art and Literature* (Cambridge: Cambridge University Press, 1999)

Heard, M. *Phantasmagoria: The Secret Life of the Magic Lantern: A Full-Blooded Account of an Extraordinary Theatrical Ghost-Raising Entertainment of the Early Nineteenth-Century and the True Exploits of its Mysterious Inventor, Paul De Philipsthal, in Britain and Abroad* (Hastings: Projection Box, 2006)

Hell, M., Los, E., Middelkoop, N., Molen, T. V. D. & Spies, P. *Portrait Gallery of the Golden Age* (Amsterdam: Hermitage Amsterdam, 2014)

Herlihy, D. & Cohn, S. K. *The Black Death and the Transformation of the West* (Cambridge, MA: Harvard University Press, 1997)

Hollander, S. C., Laderman, G. & Radice, A.-I. 'Securing the Shadow: Posthumous Portraiture in America' (2016)

Jung, C. G., Henderson, J. L., Franz, M.-L. V., Jaffé, A. & Jacobi, J. *Man and His Symbols* (Garden City, NY: Doubleday, 1964)

Kemp, M. & Wallace, M. *Spectacular Bodies: The Art and Science of the Human Body from Leonardo to Now* (Berkeley: University of California Press, 2000)

Klein, N. M. *The Vatican to Vegas: A History of Special Effects* (New York: New Press, 2014)

Lomnitz-Adler, C. *Death and the Idea of Mexico* (New York: Zone, 2008)

May, B., Pellerin, D. & Fleming, P. R. *Diableries: Stereoscopic Adventures in Hell* (London: Stereoscopic Company, 2013)

Miller, M. E. & Taube, K. *The Gods and Symbols of Ancient Mexico and the Maya: An Illustrated Dictionary of Mesoamerican Religion* (London: Thames & Hudson, 1997)

Ronnberg, A. & Martin, K. *The Book of Symbols* (Cologne: Taschen, 2011)

Sappol, M. *A Traffic of Dead Bodies: Anatomy and Embodied Social Identity in Nineteenth-Century America* (Princeton, NJ [u.a.]: Princeton University Press, 2004)

Taylor, R. P. *The Death and Resurrection Show: From Shaman to Superstar* (London: A. Blond, 1985)

Townsend, E. *Death and Art: Europe 1200–1530* (London: V&A Publishing, 2009)

Whitenight, J. *Under Glass: A Victorian Obsession* (Atglen, PA: Schiffer Publishing, 2013)

## web resources

archive.org

bibliodyssey.blogspot.com

www.bl.uk

britishmuseum.org

www.metmuseum.org/art/collection/search/334871Morbid Anatomy

themorgan.org

publicdomainreview.org

rijksmuseum.nl/en

wellcomeimages.org

# PICTURE CREDITS

All illustration materials from the Richard Harris Art Collection, courtesy of Richard Harris, unless otherwise indicated below. All photographs of the Richard Harris Art Collection by Dan Gottesman © Dan Gottesman.

t = top | b = bottom | c = centre | l = left | r = right | fl = far left | fr = far right

6 Courtesy Morbid Anatomy | 8l Archeological Museum, University of Tarapacá, Arica 8c Wellcome Library, London | 8r National Archaeological Museum, Athens | 9fl Private Collection | 9l Parco Archeologico di Pompei | 9cl, 9cr Wellcome Library, London | 9r From *The Somonynge of Every Man*, published by John Sklot, c. 1530 | 9fr © Chris O'Donnell Tattoo 10fl Wellcome Library, London | 10l From *Une des dix-sept gravures sur bois de la Danse macabre du cloitre des Saints Innocents à Paris*, published by Guyot Marchant et Verard, 1485 10cl Achenbach Foundation for Graphic Arts, Fine Arts Museums of San Francisco 10cr *Codex Laud*, MS. Laud Misc. 678, Folio 8, Bodleian Library, Oxford | 10r Kunstmuseum Basel | 10fr, 11fl Wellcome Library, London | 11l Uffizi, Florence | 11cl, 11cr Wellcome Library, London | 11r Yale Center for British Art, Paul Mellon Collection (B1992.8.11.54) 11fr Wellcome Library, London | 12fl Musée Fragonard d'Alfort, Paris | 12l Museo Cappella Sansevero, Naples | 12cl Wellcome Library, London | 12cr From *La Guillotine en 1793*, H. Fleischmann, 1908 | 11r From *Mémoires récréatifs, scientifiques et anecdotiques du physicien-aéronaute*, E.G. Robertson, 1831, Vol. 1 | 11fr Wellcome Library, London | 13fl The J. Paul Getty Museum, Los Angeles | 13l Missouri History Museum, St. Louis | 13cl Tate, London 13cr Wellcome Library, London | 13r The J. Paul Getty Museum, Los Angeles | 13fr The Royal Collection, London (RCIN 2906527) | 14fl The Victorian Spiritualists' Union, Melbourne 14l, 14cl Private Collections | 14cr Wellcome Library, London; | 14r Museo delle anime del Purgatorio, Rome | 14fr Collection Mel Gordon | 15fl *Dr. Mabuse the Gambler*, Fritz Lang, 1922 15l Private Collection | 15cl Library of Congress, Prints and Photographs Division, Washington, D.C. | 15cr, 15r Wellcome Library, London | 15fl National Archives, Washington, D.C. (127-N-123170) | 16fl *Reefer Madness*, Louis J. Gasnier, 1936 | 16l Photo Gerard Fouet/AFP/Getty Images | 16cl Private Collection | 16cr Rune Hellestad/Corbis Entertainment | 16r Collection of the College of Psychic Studies, London | 16fr Courtesy Capsula Mundi | 17tl, 17tr Rijksmuseum, Amsterdam | 17bl Wellcome Library, London | 18 Royal Museum of Fine Arts of Belgium, Brussels (7618)/Photo J. Geleyns – Ro scan | 19 Royal Museum of Fine Arts of Belgium, Brussels (7619)/Photo J. Geleyns – Ro scan | 22 Metropolitan Museum of Art, New York. Fletcher Fund, 1933 (33.92ab)/Art Resource/Scala, Florence | 23 Collage, courtesy the artist. Photo Chad Gerth | 24 Wellcome Library, London | 33tl Musée Antoine Lecuyer, Saint-Quentin, France/Bridgeman Images | 33tr Segovia Cathedral. Capilla de la Concepción de la Catedral de Segovia. Photo Art Collection/Alamy Stock Photo | 33bl Private Collection 33br Museo del Pueblo de Guanajuato | 34 Wellcome Library, London | 36–37 Hermitage Museum, St Petersburg. Photo Prisma Archivo/Alamy Stock Photo | 38t Galleria Nazionale d'Arte Antica, Palazzo Barberini, Rome | 38c Uffizi, Florence | 38bl Musée du Louvre, Paris 38br Museum of Fine Arts, Budapest | 39tl Private Collection | 39tr Photo STF/AFP/Getty Images | 39cl, 39cr Mary Evans Picture Library/Alamy Stock Photo | 39c Photo Alan Kole from the collection of John Whitenight and Fred LaValley | 39bl, 39br Private Collection 40 From 'A Portfolio of Aubrey Beardsley's drawings illustrating *Salome* by Oscar Wilde', published by John Lane, London, 1907, pl. XV | 41 From 'A Portfolio of Aubrey Beardsley's drawings illustrating *Salome* by Oscar Wilde', published by John Lane, London, 1907, pl. XIV 42t Tate, London | 42b Musée du Château, Rueil-Malmaison (MM. 40.47.2095). Photo akg-images Laurent Lecat | 43t Yale Center for British Art, New Haven. Paul Mellon Collection (B1981.25.648) | 43b Yale Center for British Art, New Haven. Bequest of Pamela Askew (B1998.26.2) | 44t Wellcome Library, London | 44b Royal Museum of Fine Arts of Belgium, Brussels (1968). Photo akg-images/Fototeca Gilardi | 45 Metropolitan Museum of Art, New York. The Whitney Collection, Promised Gift of Wheelock Whitney III, and Purchase, Gift of Mr. and Mrs. Charles S. McVeigh, by exchange, 2003 (2003.42.53). Photo 2017 Metropolitan Museum of Art/Art Resource/Scala, Florence | 46 Courtesy US National Library of Medicine, Bethesda, MD | 47 top row: l, second row: l, third row: r, bottom row: l Ralph Smith for The Wellcome Collection | 47 second row: c, bottom row: r Joanna Ebenstein | 47 (all remaining images) Office of the Chief Medical Examiner, Baltimore, MD | 57 Photo © 2010 Nigel Cummings/fotoLibra. All Rights Reserved | 59 Photo akg-images/Erich Lessing | 62 Private Collection | 64t Rijksmuseum, Amsterdam | 64b Wellcome Library, London | 65t, 65bl, 65br Amsterdam Museum, Amsterdam | 65c Amsterdam Museum, Amsterdam. Photo Peter Horree/Alamy Stock Photo | 66tr The Wroblewski Library of the Lithuanian Academy of Sciences, Vilnius | 66bl Universiteitsbibliotheek Gent (BIB.BL.003536) | 66br, 68–69 (all images) Wellcome Library, London | 70–71 Museo di Palazzo Poggi, Università di Bologna. Photo Joanna Ebenstein | 72t UCLA Library, Los Angeles. QL61.R985TA 1710 | 73t Michel de Spiegelaere | 73b Le musée de l'Ecole nationale vétérinaire d'Alfort. Photo Patrick Forget/sagaphoto.com | 74 Alinari/Topfoto | 75tl Nationalmuseum, Stockholm | 75tr Private collection 75b Musée du Louvre, Paris (4884) | 76t, 76b Museo di Storia Naturale Università di Firenze, sez. Zoologica. 'La Specola', Italy. Museo di Storia Naturale/Florence | 77 Université de Montpellier, collections anatomiques. Photos © Marc Dantan | 79 Royal Academy of Arts, London | 80 Profimedia.CZ a.s./Alamy Stock Photo | 89b The Print Collector/Getty Images 91tl *Skull* by Ryan Matthew Cohn; photo Sergio Royzen | 91tr © Igor Siwanowicz | 91bl Photo The Bone Room | 91br David Howard Tribal Art www.tribalartasia.com | 100 Edward S. Curtis Gallery | 102l, 102r Found in western side chamber (Jb), Tomb of Amenhotep II – XVIIIth Dynasty from Valley of the Kings – KV35 | 104, 107 (all images) © Linda Connor 108 (all images) © Carlo Vannini | 110–11 (all images) Museo di Storia Naturale Università di Firenze, sez. Zoologica, 'La Specola', Italy. Photo Saulo Bambi – Museo di Storia Naturale/Florence | 112 (all iamges) akg-images/Paul Koudounaris | 115 Museo dell'Agricoltura e del Mondo Rurale, San Martino in Rio (Reggio Emilia, Italy). Photo Costantino Ferlauto, IBC Emilia-Romagna | 116t George Grantham Bain Collection, Library of Congress, Prints and Photographs Division, Washington, D.C. | 116b Photo Hulton Archive/Getty Images | 117c Photo Joanna Ebenstein | 117 (all remaining images) Wellcome Library, London | 118 Photo Joanna Ebenstein | 119 Andy Macdonald/Alamy Stock Photo | 120–21 (all images) © Dana Salvo | 122br Museo de Arte del Banco de la Republica, Bogotá, Colombia | 123t Jeffrey Kraus 123bl Collection of Jack and Beverly Wilgus 123bc, 123br Courtesy of Jack Mord/The Thanatos Archive | 125 top row: lt, lc, lb Private Collections | 125 top row: c Science Museum, London, Wellcome Images | 125 top row: r Private Collection | 125 middle row: l, cl Victoria & Albert Museum, London | 125 middle row: cr Private Collection | 125 middle row: r Victoria & Albert Museum, London | 125bl, 125br Private Collections | 126 From *Early New England Gravestone Rubbings*, Edmund Vincent Gillon, Jr., Dover Publications, 1966 | 127t akg-images | 127b akg-images/arkivi | 128 Century Guild Museum of Art, Los Angeles | 137t Charenton-le-Pont, Médiathèque de l'Architecture et du Patrimoine (PM010266). Photo Ministère de la Culture – Médiathèque du Patrimoine, Dist. RMN-Grand Palais/image Médiathèque du Patrimoine 137b Charenton-le-Pont, Médiathèque de l'Architecture et du Patrimoine (PM6135). Photo Ministère de la Culture – Médiathèque du Patrimoine, Dist. RMN-Grand Palais/image RMN-GP | 150 Wellcome Library, London | 162lt, 162lc, 162tr Wellcome Library, London 162b Kunsthistorisches Museum Vienna, Ecclesiastical Treasury (Treasury Chamber, GS Chapter 244). KHM-Museumsverband | 163t, 163b Bibliothèque nationale de France, département Estampes et photographie | 165 Sepp Frank | 166t Museo del Prado, Madrid | 166b Galleria Regionale, Palazzo Abatellis, Palermo. Photo Scala, Florence – courtesy of the Ministero Beni e Att. Culturali | 167 (all images), 169–171 (all images) Wellcome Library, London 177b British Museum, London (1852,0612.603) | 178 The Morgan Library & Museum, New York | 179rc Rijksmuseum, Amsterdam. Purchased with the support of the F.G. Waller-Fonds 179bl Wellcome Library, London | 181 Photo DeAgostini/Getty Images | 182br Rijksmuseum, Amsterdam | 184–85 (all images) Church of Santa Grata Inter Vites, in Borgo Canale, Bergamo, Italy. Photo akg-images/De Agostini Picture Library | 188 Ensor © DACS 2017 | 189 © Association Edmond-Bille | 190tl Maurice Berdon | 190tr, 190bl Kubin © Eberhard Spangenberg, München/DACS 2017 | 190br Dix © DACS 2017 | 193 © Denenberg Fine Arts, Inc., Los Angeles | 194 Daniel Robert Fitzpatrick (1891–1969), Editorial Cartoons, The State Historical Society of Missouri | 195 Hans Erni | 196 Öffentliche Kunstsammlung, Basel. Photo Art Collection/Alamy Stock Photo | 197 (all images) Rijksmuseum, Amsterdam 199 Royal Museums of Fine Art, Brussels (1935). Photo akg-images | 200t Neue Pinakothek, Munich | 200b Museo del Prado, Madrid | 201 Wellcome Library, London | 202 World History Archive/Alamy Stock Photo | 203 Ergy Landau | 204 Franz Fieldler | 205t, bl © František Drtikol | 206t, 206c 20th Century Fox Film. Photo Everett Collection Inc/Alamy Stock Photo | 206b 20th Century Fox Film. Photo Topfoto | 207 © Dr. Lakra/kurimanzutto, Mexico City | 208 Alte Nationalgalerie, Berlin | 218 Birmingham Museum of Art 219t Denver Art Museum | 219bl National Gallery of Art, Washington, D.C. Gift of Maida and George Abrams (1995.74.2) | 219br Musée des Beaux-Arts, Pau, France/Bridgeman Images | 220t Wellcome Library, London | 220bl Rijksmuseum, Amsterdam | 220br Kunsthistorisches Museum, Vienna | 221tl Metropolitan Museum of Art, New York. Rogers Fund, 1949 (49.107) | 221tr Kunsthistorisches Museum, Vienna | 221b Rijksmuseum, Amsterdam 223t, 223br Wellcome Library, London | 225t Musée du Louvre, Paris (inv. 1442-1443). Photo RMN-Grand Palais (musée du Louvre)/Jean Schormans | 225bl, 225br Wellcome Library, London | 226–27 Manchester Art Gallery, UK/Bridgeman Images | 228 National Gallery, London | 229 Metropolitan Museum of Art, New York. Bequest of Mary L. Harrison, 1921 (21.105) | 232tr Private Collection | 236 British Museum, London (1845,0809.232) 237b Bibliothèque nationale de France, département Estampes et photographie, Paris 240 British Museum, London (1893,1020.4) | 241, 244bl, 244br, 245l, 245r Wellcome Library, London | 245c Museum für Kunst und Gewerbe, Hamburg (1962.58,a,b) | 246tl Pinacoteca del Templo de San Felipe Neri La Profesa, Mexico City | 246c, 246bl, 246br, 247 Wellcome Library, London | 248 Museo Nacional del Virreinato, Tepotzotlán | 250 Rijksmuseum, Amsterdam | 252 History of Medicine Collections, David M. Rubenstein Rare Book & Manuscript Library, Duke University, Durham, NC | 253tr Rijksmuseum, Amsterdam 257 Wellcome Library, London | 259 Photo SSPL/Getty Images | 260 Photo Joanna Ebenstein 261tl British Museum, London (1874,0718.41) | 261tc Science Museum, London, Wellcome Images | 261c Private Collection | 261bl, 261br Science Museum, London, Wellcome Images 266 © Jean-Marc Laroche | 268 Museo Nacional de Antropologia, Mexico City | 269 Granger Historical Picture Archive/Alamy Stock Photo | 270tr, 271 (all images), 272tl, 272tr, 272b Library of Congress, Prints and Photographs Division, Washington, D.C. | 273 © Dana Salvo 274 © Miguel Linares | 276tl, 276tr © Graciela Iturbide | 276b © Yolanda Andrade | 277 Javier Silva Meinel | 278 (all images) © Marcos Raya | 279 (all images) © Laurie Lipton | 280, 289 (all images), 291 (all images) Wellcome Library, London | 296tl, 296tr Courtesy Skinner, Inc. www.skinnerinc.com | 296bl, 296br Courtesy James D. Julia Auctioneers, Fairfield, Maine, USA, www.jamesdjulia.com | 297 Courtesy Skinner, Inc. www.skinnerinc.com | 299 The Estate of Barbara Jones | 302l Les Arts Décoratifs, Paris, Gift Georges Pochet, 1901 (11148.1)/Jean Tholance/akg-images | 303 Musée Carnavalet, Paris | 304–05 (all images) Courtesy Ronni Thomas | 306–07 Courtesy Corey Schjoth | 308b Chronicle/Alamy Stock Photo | 309tl, 309tr Private collections | 309cl Collection Mervyn Heard | 309cr Private Collection | 309bl Collection Mervyn Heard | 309br, 310 Private Collections | 311t Library of Congress, Prints and Photographs Division, Washington, D.C. | 311bl Stedelijk Museum, Amsterdam | 311br Private Collection | 312 1st row l,c,r and 4th row c: Collection Martin Gilbert, 312 2nd row l, 3rd row l and 4th row l: Helsinki University Museum, 312c Collection Thomas Weynants, 312 2nd row r and 3rd row r: Hauchs Physiske Cabinet, Sorø, Denmark, 312 4th row: r Collection Mervyn Heard | 313t Mary Evans Picture Library/Alamy Stock Photo | 313b Chronicle/Alamy Stock Photo | 314 Collection Mel Gordon | 315tl, 315tr Photo Hans Wild/The LIFE Picture Collection/Getty Images | 315bl, 315br Collection Mel Gordon | 318t Coney Island History Project | 318cl, 318c Private collections | 318cr The Paul and Nancy Brigandi Museum Collection | 318bl Private Collection | 318br Library of Congress Prints and Photographs Division, Washington, D.C. | 319t, 319c Private Collection | 319bl, 319br Museum of the City of New York | 329 Brooklyn Museum, New York | 330 British Library (add.38121 f.042v)/Bridgeman Images | 331 (all images) Wellcome Library, London 332 Photo DEA/G. Nimatallah/De Agostini/Getty Images | 333l, 333r Photo Scala, Florence 334–35 Gemaldegalerie, Berlin. Photo Prisma/UIG via Getty Images | 336 Mosteiro de São Bento da Bahia, Salvador | 338t Museo del Prado, Madrid | 338c Private Collection/Photo Christie's Images/Bridgeman Images | 338b Museo de San Pio V, Valencia, Spain/Photo AISA/Bridgeman Images 330t Kunstmuseum, Basel | 339c Alte Nationalgalerie, Berlin | 339b Museum der bildenden Künste, Leipzig | 340–41 British Museum, London (1915, 0823.0.915-916) | 342, 343 Wellcome Library, London | 344t, 344b Private Collections | 345c Tadeusz Korpal | 350 Photo Transcendental Graphics/Getty Images | 351tl, 351tc, 351tr, 351b Private Collections 352 University of Manitoba Archives & Special Collections, Hamilton Family fonds, Winnipeg, Canada | 353 Sven Türck | 354tl The Barlow Collection, British Library, London | 354tc, 354tr Institut für Grenzgebiete der Psychologie und Psychohygiene, Freiburg im Breisgau, Germany 354cl The Barlow Collection, British Library, London | 354c, 354cr Private Collections | 354bl The Barlow Collection, British Library, London | 354bc Private Collection 354br, 355 Institut für Grenzgebiete der Psychologie und Psychohygiene, Freiburg im Breisgau, Germany | 356–57 (all images) University of Manitoba Archives & Special Collections, Hamilton Family fonds, PC 12 (A.79-41), Winnipeg, Canada | 358t, 358b The Victorian Spiritualists' Union, Melbourne | 359 Collection of the College of Psychic Studies, London.

# INDEX

Here lyes Buried

JOANNA EBENSTEIN: I would like to thank Heather Chaplin, Charlie Mounter, Shannon Taggart and especially Rebecca Purcell for their invaluable assistance in shaping the introduction. Special thanks are also due to my family: Robert, Sandy, Donna, Laura and Judy Ebenstein. For inspiration and encouragement, I would like to thank Patricia Llosa and Ami Ronnberg and the Archive for Research in Archetypal Symbolism (ARAS). Also, for their support, assistance and suggestions, I would like to thank Laetitia Barbier, Catherine Crawford and the Montandons (Maccabee, Oona and Daphne), Mark Dion, Megan Fitzpatrick, Aaron Glass, Mel Gordon, George Hansen, Eric Huang, Barbara Mathe, Evan Michelson, Matt Murphy, Cristina Preda, Mark Pilkington, Josh Powe, William Rauscher, Amy Slonaker, John Swenson and Daisy Tainton. My essay on death-themed amusements has its roots in an exhibition I co-curated with Aaron Beebe as artist-in-residence at The Coney Island Museum in 2011. Thanks are due to my collaborators, and also to Dick Zigun, founder of the museum. In addition, I would like to thank all those who contributed essays and donated images, most especially Richard Harris and the Richard Harris Art Collection as well as Ryan Matthew Cohn, Mervyn Heard, Jeffrey Kraus, Jack Mord of The Thanatos Archive, Sergio Royzen, Corey Schjoth, Ronni Thomas, John Whitenight and Fred LaValley, and Jack and Beverly Wilgus. Thanks also to Crestina Forcina and the brilliant staff at the Wellcome Collection. Finally, I would like to thank the amazing team at Thames & Hudson – Tristan de Lancey, Jane Laing, Dorothy Stannard, Maria Ranauro and Kate Cooper – for their passion, vision and perseverance; this book would not be what it is without them.

First published in 2017 in the United States of America by Thames & Hudson Inc., 500 Fifth Avenue, New York, New York 10110

www.thamesandhudsonusa.com

Library of Congress Control Number 2017931788

ISBN 978-0-500-51971-4

Printed and bound in China by Toppan Leefung Printing Limited

Front cover illustration: *Ein Totentanz* (frontispiece), 1918, by Alfred Kubin; © Eberhard Spangenberg, München/DACS 2017

Back cover illustration: *Dancing Skeletons*, 1799, by F. Turner; courtesy of the Richard Harris Art Collection